End of a Rainbow

DESMOND DENTON

Contents

Act 1 5

Mozambique 7

The Diamond Rush - Kimberley 11

Nightime 20

Cellblock 23

A Tall Story 26

Flashback: Bethlehem, August 28

Back at the Cell 77

A Holiday Home 100

Arts Festival 117

A Country for Cowboys 127

Back at Cell 133

Stubborn Donkey 147

Town in the Middle of Nowhere 174

The Vet 209

Swim in the Dam 226

Date Night 232

Next Day at Work 269

Early the Next Morning – Small Town Hospital 281

A Walk in the Moonlight 287

The Betrayal 292

The Departure 298

Chapter: Burn the Trail 303

Smoke and Silver 307

The Road Splits 314

The Next Morning 330

In Greef's Headquarters 333

The Man in the Shadows.. 335
The Meeting.. 337
Aftermath... 344

Have you ever chased after a rainbow? Probably not. Only a fool would believe in such things. Chances are, you've probably read about the concept in a storybook once upon a time. Promises of discovering a pot of gold at the end of the rainbow.

Riches have a way of blinding a person and removing one's sense of reality. But what if you could have more than you ever imagined? Would you take it?

The cautious ones whisper that those who pursue the rainbow might never return, that they meet a destructive fate. Others claim it's all in vain, or worse, a myth. But I've stood at the rainbow's end, and let me tell you that it's no myth.

Be warned, though—at some point, you will face the question above and the consequences of your decisions. Only those who catch the heart of it will truly understand.

This might seem like the beginning of a tragedy, but don't be fooled quite so easily...

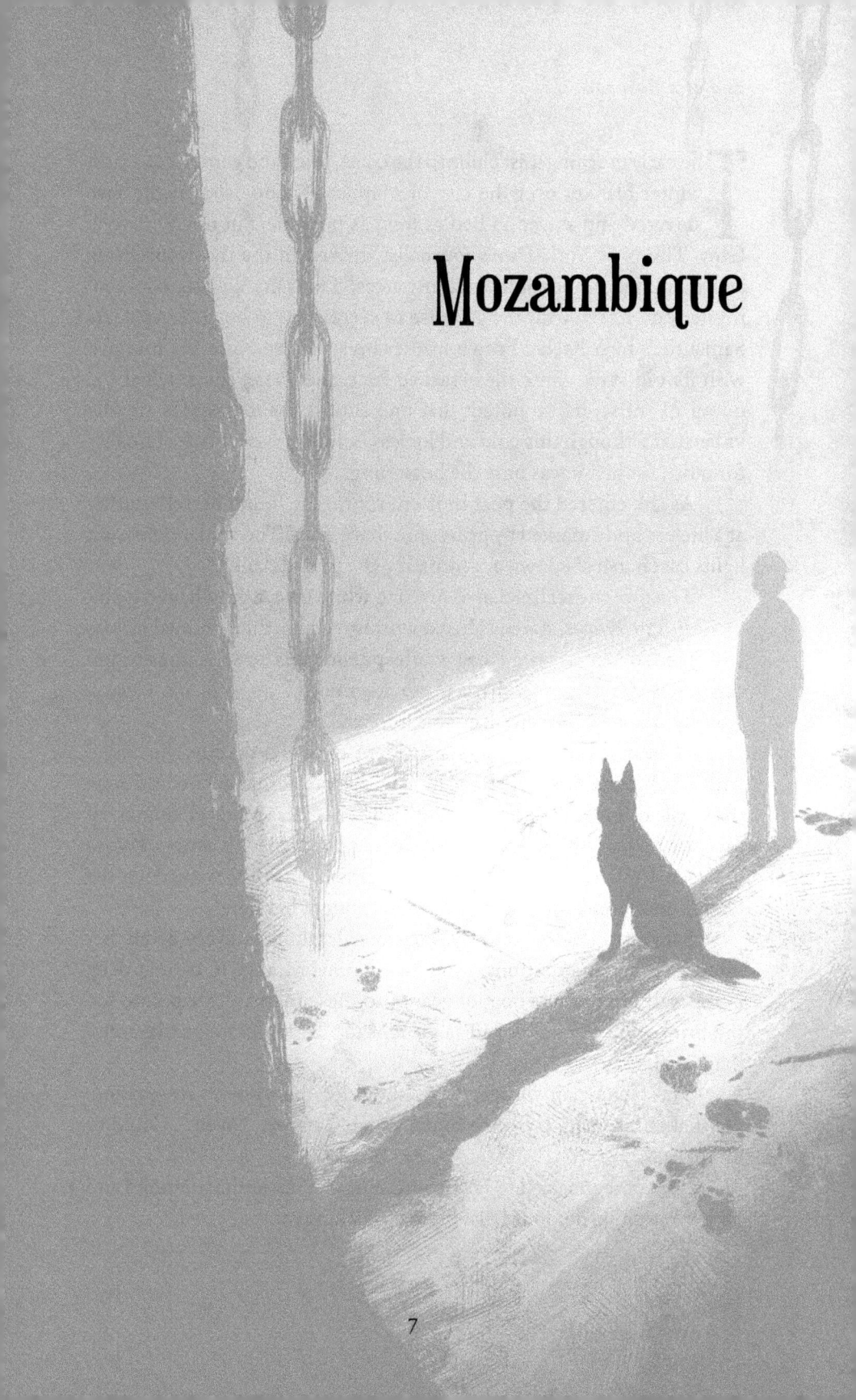

Mozambique

The early morning mist clung to the coast, thick and eerie, like a warm winter blanket over the city of Maputo. Anyone else might have shivered and stayed in bed as long as possible, but not Samantha Grey. The New York Times journalist thrived in the most unsettling and seemingly impossible circumstances. The salty air was cool and mysterious, heavy with the promise of secrets yet to be uncovered. As Samantha's high-heeled brown leather boots walked into the morgue, with its old stark white tiles cracked here and there, she smelled the odour of antiseptic, so potent that one almost has to gasp for air. She knew that although this cold and lifeless building was a place of finality for most, for her, it was only the beginning.

As she entered the post-mortem room, she found herself, staring at a lifeless body marked by gruesome shark bites. The cold, fluorescent lights cast harsh shadows, accentuating the gory details.

The morgue technician in his long white coat, a grey-haired gaunt man with tired eyes, stared at her solemnly over his thick-framed glasses and handed her a sealed bag while pursing his lips. "Carcharodon carcharias. Great white shark tooth fragments," he said, his voice a gravelly whisper. "Haven't seen this in years."

"There hasn't been a shark incident in over a decade," he added with a raised eyebrow, opening a file with a creak that echoed through the sterile room. "Fingerprints identified her as Elisa Matavel, runner-up for Miss Mozambique and ambassador for children with cancer. Found between the shark nets by local fishermen. Tourists were deep-sea fishing and found her body. Fishermen brought her here."

Samantha's hazel green eyes narrowed, taking in every detail, her mind racing with questions. "Any diving gear? Strange to be that deep in the waters without a boat or gear. And these marks?," she pointed to the bruises on the side of Elisa's forehead, "certainly looks like more than a fall."

The technician shrugged, his shoulders heavy with resignation. He shakes his head, trying to find a suitable answer. "Well…Could've hit rocks…"

"Or someone tried to hide something…" Samantha muttered and bit her lower lip, her journalist instincts kicking in.

A voice suddenly interrupted from behind, deep and authoritative. "That's enough 'Murder, She Wrote' for today." Captain Nhassengo, a tall, imposing figure with a presence that commanded attention, entered, flashing his badge. "Thought they'd send their finest."

"Samantha Grey," she introduced herself, extending a pale little hand with neatly trimmed nails, her eyes never leaving his for a moment. "I see you do your research."

Nhassengo shook her hand, his grip firm. "You write and sensationalize, even the death of a young girl, to get numbers. Makes me sick, eh"

"People have the right to know," Samantha countered, her voice steady and assertive.

"Right and wrong blur in this field," Nhassengo interrupted, muttering underneath a thick moustache with a voice carrying the weight of years in law enforcement. "The police report said death by shark, but the post-mortem suggests otherwise."

"There are always two sides to a story, Ms. Grey. The simple side and… well… the complicated side. We're stretched thin. We can't chase ghosts without solid evidence. Her body showed significant blood loss before the sharks got to her. We scouted the waters, interviewed the coast guards. Found nothing, except…" He placed an old heavy rifted silver suitcase on the steel table, packed with stacks of money, the sight of it incongruous in the clinical setting.

"A bribe?" Samantha asked, eyebrows raised, smirking through a voice edged with disbelief.

"Consider it a welcome gift to Mozambique, Ms. Grey. I'd leave it at a shark incident, but some important people want more information. You won't be left empty-handed." He stood there smugly with arms folded, demanding a reply.

"My job is to report the truth. I don't take bribes," Samantha said, with a stern voice while avoiding the eye-contact which he demanded this time.

"Truth is exactly what they want." Nhassengo leaned closer, his eyes dark and unreadable. "Any suspects? Obsessed boyfriend, old lover, family feud?"

"Nothing out of the ordinary. She was secretive, late nights, early mornings. A cold case, except for this." Nhassengo lifted a large diamond and held it up with large wrinkled hands, the room's light refracting into a rainbow of colors, casting dancing lights on the cream walls. "Barend Visagie. Legendary bank robber and cop killer. Kept the police on a wild chase for sure. This diamond's one of the missing stones."

"So what's the link? Visagie's locked up, isn't he?" Samantha's curiosity was piqued, the pieces of the puzzle slowly coming together.

"That's the question. Barend's in isolation in South Africa, sitting in Kimberley prison. We believe he might help us find the murderer as well as the missing diamonds."

"That's a long shot. Why would he get visitation rights?" Samantha asked, skepticism creeping into her voice, as she stood there leaning and supporting herself with one hand on the vacant steel table.

"Money opens many doors. I know someone who can arrange it." Nhassengo's confidence was unsettling, yet his words heavy with opportunity.

Samantha considered, weighing the risks and the rewards. The prospect of going to see Barend sounded illogical, a wild goose chase to make all that effort. Why would one go and speak to a man locked up for unrelated crimes? But Elisa's possession of the diamond was an intriguing story, one that other reporters would soon follow. It might not be much, but it could make headlines for a day.

She picked up the heavy suitcase, its weight a tangible reminder of the moral quandary she faced. "I hope this is clean. I have this on record," she said solemnly, showing her recording device, her eyes locked on Nhassengo.

He smiled, a cold, calculating smile that didn't reach his eyes, as she had already strutted out the door. "Sterile clean, welcome to Mozambique, Ms. Grey." he muttered to himself as his salt and pepper moustache moved once more with an almost unrecognizable smirk.

The Diamond Rush
- Kimberley

The small white airplane touched down on a barren airstrip, while the dry heat shimmered off the melting tar. Samantha, feeling slightly nauseous from the turbulent flight, peered through the window at the desolate scene. No welcoming party, no children running to greet loved ones—just a few idle taxis and a peculiar-looking Indian man holding a sign with her name. The plane came to a halt, and Samantha, weary but determined, gathered her bags and made her way out of the airplane to meet the Indian man. His grey hair and beard nearly blended with his dull, traditional attire. Samantha looked at what he was wearing. For a moment she thought he was a character that reappeared from the stone ages.

Then, for fear of looking rude, she quickly glanced away, tugging and pulling at her bag's strap over her shoulder.

"You been Samantha Grey?" The man blurted through a crooked smile as peculiar as ever. His accent was thick, his voice filled with enthusiasm.

"That would be me," Samantha replied, exhaustion evident in her voice. "And you must be..."

"Yes, yes," he interrupted, his smile broadening. "I am Ajatashatru Mohatmar Azharuddin, named after my great-great-grandfather. But you can call me Aja. At your service."

Samantha looked confused for a moment, but managed a polite, albeit awkward, smile. "Shall we?"

Aja took her suitcases, his awkward posture betraying their weight, yet he moved with surprising agility. "No need to help," he puffed, clearly out of breath but determined to maintain his composure. Samantha felt responsible for his heavy burden, but decided to let him have the satisfaction of helping her carry the luggage. Eventually, they made it through the busy crowds and reached his taxi, an old yellow vehicle with more rust than paint, and Aja loaded the luggage into the trunk. With a slam of the trunk's door, he stood there smugly, with his hands on his hips. "Here we are, my trusty transport. She has served me well for over 25 years, except for the time when... well, never mind."

Samantha raised her eyebrows, trying not to reveal her amusement, got in as he held the door open for her, and settled into the car. She noticed the interior. What a riot of rich Indian colors—cloths, beads, and small statues of Hindu gods. It was almost too much for the mind to take in at once.

Aja climbed in and started the engine. "Shall we go to the prison, then?" he muttered through his moustache, looking back at Samantha with the same enthusiasm as before.

Samantha nodded through her tired eyes once more, the fatigue from the journey catching up with her.

As they drove through the streets of Kimberley, the town's history was palpable. Old grey stone buildings, relics of the diamond rush, stood as silent witnesses to a bygone era. "Is this your first time in the historical town of diamonds, ma'am?" Aja asked with a smile, his eyes twinkling with pride.

Samantha nodded, managing to return a tired smile. Aja's father had come to Kimberley in 1890 and had even shaken hands with Gandhi, he told her. "In India, we believe that when you shake hands with a great man, some of his greatness rubs off on you."

Samantha chuckled, attempting to lighten the mood."Is that why you shook my hands?"

Aja looked at her blankly, not catching the joke. "I'm sorry, I don't understand."

Samantha sighed. "Never mind. Do you have some music? I've had a long, nauseating flight, and the heat…"

Aja's face lit up as he interrupted her with a resounding "But ofcourse!…" He quickly placed a CD in the front-loader. After a few seconds of anticipation, a typical Bollywood song blared through the speakers, and Aja began to sing along, his head bobbing to the rhythm. Samantha sighed and shook her head, thinking to herself that nothing beat a good cultural induction as such, especially if it has the potential to make one smile.

The car eventually arrived at the security entrance to the jail. As they slowly moved into a suitable parking space, Samantha could feel the knot in her stomach, a rising tension. Suddenly a guard with a dog approached, inspecting the car with a mirror-tipped stick. Samantha watched as Aja swiftly got out of the car and conversed with the police. The seasoned alsatian sniffed the suitcases, and Samantha climbed out of the car very cautiously.

"This is all just my personal possessions, clothing, paperwork. Nothing important," she insisted, her discomfort noticeable.

The stocky guard raised a hand, his expression serious. "*Maak asseblief die slot oop,*(Open the lock please)" he commanded.

Aja looked at her and translated, "He wants you to open the suitcase."

Samantha rolled her eyes. "You can't be serious. You think I'm carrying a bomb?"

The guard's unflinching gaze was her answer. Sighing, she complied, opening the suitcase. Another dog, a German shepherd approached, sniffing her belongings. Samantha patted the dog, trying to appear unbothered as her clothing, including her underwear, was being examined.

"Oh come on now... Is that really necessary?" she muttered.

Aja intervened to reassure the guard, "That can all stay with me in the car, Mr. Police. I will wait."

The dog growled at Aja, who quickly retreated to the car. The guard found a bag of herbs. "Herbal tea—it's prescribed by my doctor. It helps me sleep."

The guard sniffed the bag and handed it back, closing the trunk. Samantha re-entered the car, fuming. "A warm welcome indeed."

Aja chuckled, "They are more bark than bite, Miss Grey. Don't let them bother you, eh?"

The guard waved them through. "Welcome to Kimberley's Hoogs gevangenis aanhouding (High level prison)," he said, "or, as they call it in English, the Big Hole of Kimberley."

Another guard added a friendly warning, "Stay away from the bars. Men here... they don't see a lot of your kind."

The prison had an atmosphere of intimidation, being surrounded by multiple layers of gates. Samantha noticed the strong, gigantic guards in dull attire patrolling with rifles. The lifeless, grey buildings stood in stark contrast to the vibrant past Samantha had learned about. As she cautiously walked past the courtyard, the sound of her boots echoed in an eery rhythm while sly prisoners' eyes followed her every move. One inmate, sporting a faded white vest showcasing bulky arms covered in crude tattoos, licked his fingers the moment he saw Samantha's pathetic appearance. He called out lewdly in a thundering voice. Samantha quickened her pace, escaping the madness of the prison's hallways and entering the office of Mr. De Wet at once.

The prison warden, a man in his late fifties with greying black hair dressed in old-fashioned khaki pants and a grey shirt, rolled up his sleeves, stood up assertively from his meal of curried fish and shoved the chair aside with a scraping sound that made Samantha cringe. He wiped his hands and mouth flippantly and threw the crumpled serviette into the little bin next to the door. His eyes, set wide apart and dark brown, scrutinized her while his one hand wiped the last remainder of curry bits from the corners of his mouth. "Mr. De Wet?" Samantha extended her hand, appearing bold while being uncomfortably aware of her own nerves.

He inspected his hands to ensure cleanliness one last time before shaking hers. "Samantha Grey, New York Times."

"De Wet. So we have ourselves a Yankee." He smiled wryly. "Born and raised."

"Welcome to the Big Hole in Africa, Miss Grey. Here, the only thing that shines is the past and the pockets of those controlling the mines. The rest of us... well, we wait for the hereafter." He stood still facing the other side of the wall for a moment with his hands on his hips, before attempting to pace the room.

Samantha first mistook his strange gesture for indifference, but soon noticed the limp in his walk and the prosthetic leg. "How can I be of service to you?" he blurted so suddenly that Samantha got a little fright, but quickly calmed herself down as he looked her in the eyes with a piercing stare. The last thing she wanted was to be perceived as timid.

Clearing her throat she uttered, "I'm doing an article about prisoners and their sense of regret for their wrongdoings."

De Wet paused while maintaining his piercing stare. Then he chuckled, shaking his head "I can show you hundreds of them, but don't expect much real regret. Many join the church group here out of sheer boredom."

"I understand…" she started, thinking carefully about her next sentence, and continued speaking swiftly before De Wet could interject. "I'm interested in a specific prisoner—Barend Visagie, number 713."

De Wet's frown deepened as he thought of a direct, yet compassionate response. "7134831. I can't help you there, Miss Grey. Even as pretty as you are… chasing after dead man's gold, are you?" he asked, staring at her once more with thick raised eyebrows

Samantha folded her arms, expressing her dissatisfaction and shook her head. "It's a story of great interest to our readers. This is a man who escaped the death penalty, and what's more… the mystery of the missing gold."

"This is a state prison, and only direct family is allowed to see him."

Samantha took off her uncomfortable fitted navy jacket and plonked it on the table before reaching for her briefcase. De Wet stared at her suspiciously as she placed a package on the table. "Maybe this will show that I am family, then. All I want is to talk with him."

De Wet's eyes widened at the sight of the stacks of money. "I can clearly see the resemblance. My apologies for the delay." he muttered through a pretentious half-grin.

As they proceeded to walk through the hallways together, De Wet signed them in, while the thick steelgates locked firmly behind them. He thought to give her a word of warning before they could reach Barend. "They are all animals, Miss Grey. It's my job to keep them here. I never dreamed of ending up here, but with my leg… well, let's just say I was given the honor of remaining in active duty." He grinned. "*Ons sal lewe ons sal sterwe… vir jou Suid-Afrika.*" (We will live and we will die for you, South Africa.)

Samantha swept her red shoulder-length fringe behind her ears and carefully considered how she could obtain more information without offending the man, "If I may ask, what happened to your leg? Was it in war?"

De Wet sighed deeply, almost telling the disheartening story by the expression on his face before he could utter one word. "I was lucky to have lost only the leg. Many others were not so lucky. Most of them were as young as 17, fighting for *volk en vaderland*. In the end, we were all but forgotten."

"Do you regret being in the army?" she asked after an awkward pause

"Regret?" He laughed bitterly through his raspy voice. "By no means, Miss Grey. Things were simpler then. You served, even the law. Now we have all these human rights... human wrongs, if you ask me. If I had my way, I would hang the whole lot of them." To this, Samantha had no response. She quietly kept following him, the sound of her footsteps still audible.

They reached another zone, and De Wet signed them in. "Justice doesn't pay, Miss Grey. We keep them here, helping them with their 'salvation.' Actually, we just do damage control. We simply keep the zoo away from the rest of society."

With pursed lips and arms folded, Samantha followed him into a dimly lit room with a table in the center. "I can't promise you anything, Miss Grey." De Wet remarked in a serious tone. "The man has a way with words... or rather, the lack of them. After all these years, he's never had any visitors, you know."

Samantha sat down cautiously, then got a sudden fright when she heard the slow, dragging footsteps of a man approaching. A tall figure with broad shoulders emerged from the darkness but stopped just short of the light. Samantha paused, then nervously and obsessively set her notebook and recorder straight in front of her on the table. She cleared her throat assertively, uttering a strong "Good morning!", to break the silence. Although nervous, she kept her gaze fixed on him without flinching. Samantha displayed a slightly forced smile as Barend eventually looked her straight in the eyes. She could sense the intimidation emanating from his entire being, but pulled herself together, sat up straight with arms folded and proceeded. "Samantha Grey, writer from the Times. I've come to tell your side of the story. I would like to find out more about the man who spent 26 years here, in isolation."

Barend's piercing blue eyes locked onto hers from the shadows. He turned, as if to leave.

"So... is it true?", she bravely asked, her question echoing through the room and hitting the walls. "You're the legend... the man who disappeared with all the diamonds and gold, leaving nothing but corpses behind?" she questioned hastily to capture his attention.

Barend remained silent, staring into the distance with a deeply etched frown.

Samantha was determined to get under his skin. "Mr. Visagie, after all these years, do you have any sense of regret for what you did?" she asked with a brazen expression, eagerly awaiting his response.

Barend's eyes darkened as he looked down at his forlorn shoes. Regrets don't help me much, he thought.

"You were quite busy, weren't you? Armed robbery, assault, murder... The list is endless", she continued, her taunting questions hanging in the air.

Barend remained silent, apparently immovable. Although the frown on his forehead deepended, his gaze left unyielding, like steel.

After a long awkward silence, Samantha leaned forward, resting her lean arms on the table in front of them. With her chin resting on her hands, she calculated her next question very carefully. "One of your diamonds was found off the coast of Mozambique—with the body of a young girl. Dead, believed to be murdered."

Barend's attention sharpened as he looked her straight in the eyes.

"The police believe it's a murder someone tried to cover up. You've been inside, so it couldn't have been you.

Samantha leaned in closely, her voice steady yet urgent. "But my suspicion is that you still know the whereabouts of the missing diamonds. Therefore, you can be crucial in helping us…the police… find the murderer."

Barend's sudden, loud outburst echoed through the room as he rapidly threw the plastic chair aside. "You want diamonds... gold!?... then you'd better start digging elsewhere, I suggest!" The atmosphere went from slight tension to tangible fear, while Samantha sat there staring at him with widened eyes.

He turned sharply, his chain clanging against the cold, concrete floor as he walked toward the door. With every footstep he took, Samantha shuddered, but she sheepishly swallowed her nervousness and dared to break the ice.

"I… I can tell your story to these people if you give me a chance. I'm willing to… shed new light on it," Samantha called after him, her voice resolute. "If you help with this case, one can even appeal for a reduced sentence. You can gain your life back again. Doesn't that sound good to you?."

Barend's sudden laughter rang through the room, cold and mirthless. Samantha remained silent, staring into the dark space where he stood.

"Have you ever chased a rainbow?" Barend's deep voice resonated through the small room as he sat down once more.

Samantha thought carefully about her response.

"Figuratively, or what do you mean by that?" Samantha asked, her brow furrowing.

Barend stared straight into her eyes, then stood up from his chair again and turned around. His retreating figure was that of a man determined to guard his secrets. Samantha watched him carefully, vexed but with a hint of a smile on her lips.

As the cold steel door clanged shut, the guard escorted Miss Grey back outside. She pursed her lips and whispered to herself, "He will talk, sooner or later. I just need to find a way to break him. Even the toughest can be broken."

The oppressive air of the dark, cold prison seemed to lift slightly as she exited the building and stepped into the sunlight. Barend quietly watched from the window of his cell, his narrowing eyes following her every step to the car. Who would believe the stories of an old man, even worse, a convicted criminal?

ACT 2: THE DIAMOND RUSH - KIMBERLEY

Nightime

A s Samantha went up the stairs of the old Kimberley Hotel hasty to get to her room, she kept thinking about her encounter with Barend. As she came through the frontdoor, she took off her chic black coat and threw it over the edge of the couch. She sat down and froze for a moment, trying to gather her thoughts. After pouring a last cup of filter coffee for the day, she sat at the wooden round table and pulled her files closer. As she scanned through a file of yellowed newspaper clippings, the dark room reeked of smoke and dust, mingling with the oppressive heat. The ceiling fan spun noisily, offering no respite but she couldn't bear the thought of switching it off. After wiping the sweat from her forehead and sighing deeply with exhaustion, her eyes flitted across the headline: "Legend Finally Caught, the Loot Still Missing."

A sudden loud thump interrupted her concentration. Startled, she looked out of her window to see a drunken man sprawled on the sidewalk. Another man with a dark, angry countenance stood nearby, gripping a large wooden plank. Samantha's heart pounded as she anticipated his next move. The man cursed loudly as he struck the drunk over the head with the plank.

"Stop it!" Samantha shouted frantically while leaning out of her hotel window. The assailant looked up, swearing even more, and raised the plank again.

"Hey, you! STOP THAT! You're going to kill him!" she yelled in a high pitch as a last attempt to bring an end to the chaos. The man hit the drunk over the back once more and the abused candidate groaned desperately.

The hotel manager burst out of the building's front entrance, angrily cursing at the attacker and grabbing him by the throat. The young man dropped the plank as the manager furiously shoved him to the ground.

"*Skoert hier voor ek die polisie bel jou vullis,*" the manager growled. (Go away or I will call the cops, you rubbish.)

The young man laughed defiantly in a hoarse voice. "*Die varke kan aan my niks maakie… Ek soek my geld, die man skuld my.*" (I ain't scared of no cop, this man owes me money.)

The manager pushed the assailant down the road, shaking his fist. A young woman emerged around the corner with a bucket of water and anxiously splashed it over the unconscious man, who began to stir and groan painstakingly.

Samantha nervously watched as they attempted to help the drunken man to his feet. Mr. De Wet's words echoed in her mind: "All animals... we just keep them in the zoo." The zoo seemed to be all around her, she thought and shook her head.

Could there be more to Barend and his story? Samantha mused as she sat deeply contemplating while eating the Thai noodles she'd bought earlier. This case was more mysterious than any she'd encountered. How did it connect to the incident in Mozambique? Why only one diamond after all these years? She couldn't wait to finish her food, instead taking small bites while continuing to sift through the piles of news reports. She discovered that Barend had been found guilty of murdering nine policemen involved in the case.

"This murderous man, after all these years, responds with a symbolic question? It makes no sense," Samantha muttered to herself. "I need to find a way to interest him." As she peered at the clock, she realised that she had better get some rest. However, her mind was on autopilot throughout the night, sifting through thoughts and questions even as her head rested on the soft clean pillow.

Cellblock

arly morning sunlight began to seep through the clouds and bake the dry land. Samantha waited in the interview room once more, her thoughts racing anxiously. As Barend approached, he looked through the window and saw an Indian man (South Asian) chasing seagulls from his car, a futile attempt to keep it clean. Barend shook his head slightly before pulling the chair out to sit solemnly in front of Samantha.

"Good morning, Mr. Visagie," Samantha greeted him.

Barend nodded curtly, his folded hands revealing his guardedness.

"We seem to be very talkative again today..." Samantha ventured, trying to break the ice.

Barend remained silent, one corner of his mouth pulling to the side while staring down at the table.

"Mr. Visagie, I think we got off on the wrong foot. I apologize. Cigarette?" Samantha offered, cheerfully holding out a pack of Chesterfield Lights.

Barend looked at it with an expression of disdain and swiftly pushed it away.

"I am confident that I can help you," Samantha persisted. "There must be something I can interest you in... good wine, books, your story told. Tell me what you need in exchange for the interviews."

Barend burst out in loud laughter, almost maniacally.

"I'm sure it has been difficult for you to have no communication with anyone you care for outside," Samantha pressed on. "To be cut off like this... But there must be somebody you want to see again. I might be able to help you with that, you know..."

Barend remained silent, his cold, steel-like eyes fixed on her. At this point, the atmosphere was extremely tense, the air heavy with unresolved emotions. Samantha looked around nervously, knowing that visitation time was limited and she couldn't afford to waste it.

Samantha thought to herself, I knew I can't ask him directly about the diamonds or the woman in Mozambique. If she is somehow entrusted with the diamonds and gold...

"Come back tomorrow," Barend said suddenly. "I need some time to think..."

"Why not today, Mr. Visagie?" Samantha pressed. "I don't have time…"

Barend interrupted her. "You are not the first one to come sniffing for gold here.

I'm not going anywhere soon, you know. My story is a long one. Come back when you have time…" Barend is escorted back by the guard to the cell, for a return interview the next day. Barend knew this was a risky move for her and himself, but he need to test her and see how far she will go for this story.

Barend sat there deeply engulfed in his thoughts. She is young, beautiful, and seems to be driven by a need to uncover the truth. But if I am truly honest with myself, I realize she is not ready for it. How can I blame her, though? The truth is sometimes ugly, difficult to face, like an infected open wound. What if she could give a message to Katelyn? When you have been alone with your thoughts for so long, time becomes your only trusted companion.

Barend holds onto an old faded photograph as he peers out through his cell window, deep in thought. The photograph is of a younger Barend and Katelyn, their smiles bright and full of joy and maybe even hope. He traces her face with his finger, a deep, sorrowful sigh escaping his lips. He remembers that day and his plans to start a new life far away from the chaos. But those dreams had been painfully shattered by betrayal and greed.

His cell was a cold, cramped space, dimly lit by a single bulb flickering overhead. He started his day with the same routine—a splash of icy water from a small sink to wash his face and a meager breakfast served on a tin tray. Time crawled painfully slowly, punctuated only by the occasional shuffle of footsteps in the corridor. Being away from any other inmates the only voice that keeps him company is the one inside his head, except for the occasional directions from the guards. Day goes to night and another day starts with little change.

The cell door clanks open, and Barend is brought back to the reality of his confinement. The guard flippantly informs him of Samantha's return visit. Sighing heavily once more, he tucks the photograph back into his pocket and prepares himself for another round of questions.

A Tall Story

Barend in thought: *So this woman came searching for a story, a sensational headliner. Now I am indeed ready to tell her one.*

INTERVIEW ROOM

S amantha leans forward, her position at the table as poised as her notepad. "They say if any man managed to catch the end of a rainbow... they will find an unlimited amount of gold, diamonds, and riches... more than a hundred men can carry."

Barend's eyes light up and Samantha notices the twinkle with a hint of amusement. "It's a simple matter of calculation and some luck."

"TO YOU, I MAY BE NOTHING more than a thief, a criminal, even a murderer," Barend says in his beguiling Afrikaans accent. "Nonetheless, I'll tell you my story..."

Barend leans back and settles into his chair, his gaze distant as he begins to weave his tale.

Flashback:
Bethlehem, August

66 I t was all just supposed to be a simple bank robbery," Barend begins, frowning deeply. "I can assure you, I was a drifter, a nobody if you may, conning people out of money, making enough to keep myself afloat for a few months at a time, but good enough to keep out of reach of any authorities for a while. But you can't start a fire and stare at it too long before you get burned, they say… so I kept moving, running away from my fate."

It was a late night in the middle of August, in the town of Bethlehem. A drunken old man was sitting at the bar, sharing his stories of riches, of all the things he would do if he could lay his hands on the money. Whether it was his attempt to lure young girls or purchase expensive furniture, I was hanging on his lips, listening to every one of his stories. Now, the sum he was talking about was not close to what one might find at the end of a rainbow, but I'm sure it was enough to keep a few men happy for this lifetime at least.

The old man with his white hair and beard resembling a scrawny type of Santa Claus, had surely had more than one round of drinks, and for the flamboyant ladies strutting around, this meant that he would become an easy target. A flirty young blonde leaned over the old man, grabbing his glass with petite bronzed hands sporting long purple painted nails. She swiftly took a gulp from his glass, and responded brazenly, "Well, maybe a theft is too much of a job for a brute old man… but for a lady…" she hinted with a raspy smoker's voice while moving her legs over his and forward with her upper body. The old man was all eyes, but before he could reach out with a wrinkly hand to touch her, she swatted his hand away and shook her finger, signalling her disapproval. "For a lady, it's a mere matter of keeping their eyes busy."

She moved back and humorously waved her skinny arm, showcasing the man's wallet in the other hand. As he furiously attempted to grab back his wallet yet with no success, the girl gave a sly smirk while turning around. Barend, a handsome, strongly built man, quick on his feet, swiftly grabbed her hand in a strained position.

"Let go of me, you filthy—" she started squirming.

"Now that's no way to treat an elderly man, who happened to buy you your drink now… is it?" Barend asked in a calm tone, staring the girl in the eyes while nonchalantly recovering the wallet from her.

"Now, you go over there to the other side of the bar and buy for yourself and your beautiful butterfly friend another round of drinks... and we let the old man be. What do you say?" Barend touched the girl's hair gently, giving her no other option. She smiled half sweetly, her raised eyebrow revealing her disgust. Barend took out 20 rand from the wallet and gave it to her. "Now say thanks to the gentleman and go buy yourself a beer."

She remained standing there with her arms folded, looking at Barend with attitude. "Come now, before the man changes his mind," he said. The girl walked away, looking over her shoulder with disapproval, squinting and locking eyes with Barend. He pursed his lips with amusement and quickly put away the diamond necklace he had taken from the girl.

Barend gave the leather wallet back to the old man. "You owe me 20," the old man claimed thanklessly.

"What are you talking about, old man? I'd say you owe me a beer... I just saved you from losing the entire contents of your wallet." The old man scoffed and begrudgingly bought Barend a beer.

"Thanks, old man", Barend said proudly as he sat down next to the old man. He took a sip of his tall beer, then wiped the foam residue from his upper lip. "No need to be angry at those girls now... they were just stating the truth."

"What do you mean?"

"To steal from a bank—it is easy, a mere slip of the hand, especially if you have the required information. And I just happen to know the right man."

The guard turned around and laughed loudly.

"What seems to be so funny?" Barend asked.

The old man kept laughing and took a sip of his beer. "You... you serious?"

The old man stopped as Barend nodded his head. The old man moved closer and talked in a softer voice as he looked around. "Let me give you some news to sober you up... Let's say a man, like yourself, somehow managed to get beyond the guards who watch the doors and the back... and for some miraculous reason make sure none of the tellers can press the panic button... well then, you might have a chance to view the safe..."

Barend nodded. "That's a good start then, right?"

"Wrong... you still have a long way to go then, boy... And believe me, there is no glory in death."

The old man sternly looked back at his now empty glass. "One would be a fool not to try, though... If I was your age... aagh. What does an old man like me know?"

Barend moved closer to the man, preparing himself for persuasion. "A man like yourself knows the flow of money... of the guards and the keeper. A community such as this has quite big farms, and I am sure they do not keep ALL their money hidden under their beds... The bank, of course, cannot keep all the money on the floor, but neither can they keep it all in the safe. That is just not possible. The money has to move from the floor to the vault and vice versa. I am sure that at any given time there should be at least, say, R100,000 or so on the floor, especially with all these farmers banking there."

The old man nodded, grunting with a grin on his face. "Well... uh...you will still have to disable the alarms to have a chance to escape, and that is no mere matter of cutting wires now... I only know the combination because—"

Barend's eyes glistened. The old man slowly got up. "Wait, wait, wait..." Barend pulled the man back slowly.

"I have already said too much," the old man replied, waving his arm. "One will have to be a fool, strong and quick, to even attempt it that way."

"But it is possible?" Barend asked.

The man shook his head. "No... it's not impossible, but... No need to throw your life away for some money." The old man sighed and quickly stood up, as if to avoid conversating any further about the matter. Barend instinctively grabbed his arm to stop him from leaving just yet.

"What if you are wrong... what if someone can make it out with the cash flow... I will make you a deal," Barend replied, with a promising expression. "You help me with the wiring, and I will give you 15 percent..."

"Fifteen percent?" The man scoffed once more and replied in a sarcastic voice, "Well, that is just too kind of you. And if you get caught, which is most likely... I might find myself in a predicament with the police." The man stood up and took his hat. "Your gold can't give an old man his dreams," he said with a sad tone. "What if I could help you with these... dreams," Barend asked persuasively.

The old man stopped in his tracks. "You really believe this could change it all?" he asked in an unbelieving tone.

Barend smiled as the feint streams of sunlight coming through the bar windows caught his face.... "Well, I would certainly like to find out."

"Say that I happen to tell you, I will need you to do me one favor."

"I am all ears," Barend replied, eagerly leaning forward.

The old man sat down and moved his chair closer, as if to whisper a secret. "I have a friend, a dear man who needs help."

"Tell me the address and details, and I will gladly assist after I manage to get the money."

"Sorry, but can't do... firstly, I do not know whether you can be trusted... how do I know you will even return?" the old man frowned.

"What type of thief do you take me for?" Barend asked in a rather offended tone.

"An interesting one, but even so, the situation does not allow me to gamble on my instinct and feelings. He might not live long enough to wait," the old man said, making a noose with his hands, as if he was hanging.

Barend coughed, nearly spewing out the beer he was sipping on. "You want me to save his neck? From jail? And how do you suppose I could do that... just get myself caught, thrown in jail, and walk out with him side by side, smiling? Maybe I can also bring you a souvenir while I am at it."

"That sounds good." the man replied, smirking.

"You are crazy, old man... If there is one place I will never get myself into, it is prison. No, no, no... for no one and nobody."

The old man sighed deeply. "Very well then. I can respect that." He started walking out slowly, limping slightly. Barend sat on the bar chair with his chin resting on his fist, watching the old man disappear into the dark, cold night. He sipped down his glass of beer and shook his head in disbelief.

The old man reached his car door, but the door was slammed closed by Barend before he could get in. "Can't you give an old man a rest then? It is late, and my wife is waiting." He stood there frowning at Barend with his hands on his hips, clearly not impressed by his interference.

"Say I do bring him back, alive that is ..." Barend asked before the old man could protest any further.

"Well, then you will have yourself a deal, and I ain't no man to break my word." he reassured Barend, who stared the old man straight in the eyes and walked away.

"His name is Vuyo, but everyone calls him 'Reverend,'" the old man shouted, flustered and heaving with slight exhaustion as the sun baked his khaki suit.

"Reverend?" Barend asked, apparently slightly confused by the title.

"Long story... he is a man with a good heart..." The old man ripped out a photo of himself and Vuyo from his jacket. Barend looked attentively at the black-and-white photo of the two serious characters before he turned around and started walking away.

"He is kept at Kimberley Prison."

"Remember you have till the 5th at noon ..." the old man shouted. Barend waved with his hand dismissing the old man's instructions.

Again Barend waved dismissively, recounting the last words between himself and the old man as he sat opposite Samantha. His eyes reflected the dim light of the interview room. "Now they say that chasing after the rainbow can make a man lose his mind... I, however, knew exactly what I was doing... somehow. As if I was born for days like that. Since I was a very young boy, I had to find ways to survive. I learned early on that life was not what they preached... and it is definitely not what you make of it... no, no. It is what you take from it. Even in my earliest days, I learned this hard lesson."

Samantha leaned forward with an intrigued yet serious expression. "How come you believed this? You were not born into a family of crime, were you?"

Barend's smile was enigmatic. He looked away for a moment before answering her, his voice suddenly dampened with a hint of sadness. "Well, people who are cut from the cloth are not always that much different, you know. They just have the right words to make it all seem just and holy, but in the end, they end up serving themselves just as criminals do."

The air in the room seemed to thicken with unspoken truths and hidden agendas. Awkward silence is broken by Samantha scribbling furiously in her notepad, trying to unravel the complexities behind Barend's words. There was more to this man than just a criminal past; there was a philosophy deeply rooted in survival, shaped by a life of navigating through shadows and deceptions.

As the interview continued, Samantha sensed that beneath Barend's calm exterior lay a disturbing torrent of stories, each one more elusive and compelling than the last. She was determined to uncover the depths of his tale, even if it meant that she had to probe him continually in order to unearth the darkest corners of his past.

Their exchange crackled with tension, like a shaky stack of wooden logs in a fire, waiting to collapse. It was as if they were playing a game of chess where each word was a move towards unraveling a mystery that could shake the foundations of what she thought she knew about crime, justice, and the human spirit.

Barend's voice trembled as he recounted the harrowing memories. His childhood at the Christian orphanage was clearly defined by its cold walls and floors, rigid rules and harsh punishments, a stark contrast to the warmth and family he craved. "All I ever wanted was to be part of a normal family, a place to belong," he recounted to Samantha, his voice tinged with both sorrow and defiance. "But instead I was placed in an orphanage where the rules were written in fire and brimstone, enforced with the burning stick of the reverend's judgment."

Here, we were taught to adhere to the Bible in a strict manner—do not talk back nor dare to stand up against the authority of God. We were surely punished for any 'unholy' trespasses. We were children, bound to grow into mischief. Even the smallest transgressions led to severe punishment. We had to write out scriptures repetitively and, at times…

the burning." The heaviness became almost tangible in the atmosphere, at these words.

Samantha's curiosity peaked at the mention of "the burning." Again, as always, she pursed her lips before proceeding "What was 'the burning'?"

Barend sadly glanced down at his rough, scarred hands, showing her a white mark stark against his weathered skin. Barend's gaze fell sadly to his scarred hands, the memory vivid in his mind. "A religious act—a symbol of divine retribution. He would use a burning stick, placing us on a chair in front of everyone to shame us, as if this was some kind of freak show. He would then threaten us with flames, preaching about sin and repentance. As the flame drew closer, you could feel the heat, hear his voice condemning you for sinning against the Most High. No one dared defy him, not even the toughest among us. I certainly didn't... until... the day Howie entered my life."

Samantha listened intently while resting her chin on clasped hands, sensing the weight of Barend's words. "What happened that day...?"

Barend hesitated and paused, trying his utmost to hide his grief at first, reflecting on the day as if transported back to that moment. "Under most circumstances, I believed in right and wrong, good and evil— that's all I knew. One day, while taking out the trash, He discovered the hungry puppy whimpering near the scrapyard. "I wasn't supposed to engage with anyone or anything without permission. But there he was—a wounded soul like me...this little poor fellar, hungry and hurt, caught my attention..." His eyes softened as he remembered offering Howie scraps, the beginning of an unlikely friendship that defied the orphanage's rules.

He recounted with a mix of sorrow and tenderness, "I offered it bones, scraps from my meager meals, dry bread morsels... It was hesitant to come closer at first, but soon, we developed a bond. I named him Howie. He became my secret friend, a glimpse of warmth and companionship in a cold, regimented world."

Barend's lips curled with distaste as he mentioned the reverend's son, a boy who took pleasure in others' suffering, like his father. "He was a chip off the old block...", Barend remarked with disgust.

"Greef didn't understand kindness one little bit," Barend explained, frustration evident in his voice. "He saw Howie as just another nuisance, another excuse to exert his power."

Barend's voice faltered as he continued, "I had to be extremely careful, sneaking away to feed him, playing with him in the shadows of the hallways, only once everyone was resting late at night. One night a dark, thunderstorm approached."

Barend, knowing the basement offered temporary refuge, quickly took Howie into hiding there despite the risks. "I left him with some food scraps in an old margarine container, promising to return," Barend recounted, his voice thick with regret. "But when I came back, I heard Howie growling—unusual, more than playful, until I noticed Greef and his cronies cornering him."

Barend's fists clenched involuntarily as he described the confrontation. Sweat droplets started surfacing on his forehead as he recounted the dreadful experience. "I pleaded with Greef to spare Howie, to let him stay inside until the storm passed. But Greef stared himself blind against my so-called disobedience and used the situation as an opportunity to assert his dominance."

He recalled Greef's sneering offer of chocolate—a luxury strictly denied to the orphans unless earned through strict adherence to the reverend's rules. "It was a bribe to lure Howie...," Barend admitted bitterly, remembering how Greef's greed for power overshadowed any empathy.

Samantha gasped, sensing the tragedy that unfolded. "What happened next?"

"Greef's cruelty knew no bounds," Barend continued, his voice catching with emotion. "When Howie defended himself against the hard leather boots kicking him in the ribs, Greef's retaliation was brutal. He got one of his accomplices to hold Howie in a vice grip by his neck, while he violently kicked and beat Howie. Ther rest of his friends restrained me from fighting back, as I reacted to Howie's high-pitched yelps."

Tears welled up in Barend's tired eyes as he described his futile attempts to free himself from their grip and to intervene. He couldn't save his only friend from this brutal senseless violence. "I tried my best to fight back," he confessed, his voice cracking as he remembered the pain and anger. "I fought Greef with all the strength I had in me, fueled by years of unjust treatment and the newfound love I had developed for little Howie."

Despite his desperation to save his little friend, the reverend's intervention brought an abrupt end to Barend's desperate struggle. "He violently pushed me away into a corner of the dark attic, accusing us of behaving like sinners," Barend spat out the words bitterly. "He dismissed Howie's suffering as God's will, a lesson in divine justice."

A warm tear rolled down Barend's cheek as he relived the heartbreaking memory. Barend's anger flared anew as he recounted the reverend's callous disregard for Howie's life. "He abruptly ordered me to take Howie outside, forcing me to abandon the poor thing in the storm, telling me it was a lesson in kindness, that God's ways couldn't be questioned.

"I simply couldn't do it," Barend admitted ashamedly, his voice trembling with defiance and sorrow. "I stayed there in the attic after Greef mockingly left us. He kept shouting threats as he walked up the steps of the attic, his comrades following him and nodding with him in agreement as they sneered at me. After they left, I cried uncontrollably and clung to Howie through the entire night, praying for a miracle, until I eventually fell into a deep sleep from exhaustion. But in the morning, Howie was no longer in my arms. I anxiously ran up the stairs and starting questioning the young men in the other dorms. Most of them looked confused. Nobody could answer me. I couldn't stand the awkward silence. "Where is he…!?" I shouted as I ran from dorm to dorm. When one of my peers finally came out with the truth, it struck my heart like an arrow and I began to break on the inside. Howie was forever gone… his lifeless body a cruel testament to the reverend's harsh teachings… My screams of despair echoed through the hallways in vain, as I collapsed into a little pathetic heap on the cold floor sobbing. As I tried wiping my face, the dust from the floors transferred onto my cheeks, leaving muddy tear stains. At that moment I hated every part of my life. I hated the mouldy familiar smell of the orphanage and what it had put me through. I hated the fact that I was placed there to begin with. Yet nobody seemed to care."

The pain in his voice was palpable as Barend continued, "As I buried Howie in the storm, my tears mingling with raindrops on my cheeks, I swore silently to myself. I vowed to defy their twisted version of righteousness," he told Samantha, his voice firm with resolve. "I made an oath to myself, to find my own path, where kindness and compassion are not considered as crimes."

I marked his grave with my shirt and walked away with a broken heart. That day, my faith in the reverend shattered. My whole being questioned God about all of this horror. How could God allow His servant to be so cruel? How could God allow such suffering?"

Samantha was spellbound, witnessing Barend's raw emotions as the tears that could no longer be contained splashed on the table in front of him. She listened, her heart heavy with the weight of Barend's devastating story. She discovered in him a courage that defied the oppressive walls of the orphanage, an unshakable resilience born from the pain of love and the loss thereof. Barend's tale was not just one of childhood abuse and cruelty, but of the enduring bond between a boy and his dog, and the courage to stand against injustice, even in the face of overwhelming evil authority.

"And then... What happened after that?"

Barend's gaze turned distant, haunted by the past. With his face still bowed down with despair, he finally answered her.

With grief and anger swirling inside me like a hurricane, I entered the classroom that fateful morning. My eyes were red from tears, yet I knew there was no escaping th wrath to come. I had to face what awaited at the front. The classroom, usually buzzing with whispered chatter and nervous energy, was unusually cold and quiet on this particular morning. Even Greef, who reveled in others' misfortunes, was subdued in eerie quietness. At the front of the classroom, the reverend waited solemnly at his old wooden table for all the students to settle, a staunch figure of authority draped in the robes of righteousness.

He took a deep breath, the weight of his memories heavy in the room. Even the guard that was standing nearby overhearing bits and pieces of the story, sighed heavily within himself. "That day changed me completely. I realized that sometimes, the greatest sin is not in breaking rules but in remaining silent in the face of injustice. Howie taught me this truth. He was my first real friend, my first lesson in standing up against tyranny, even if it meant facing punishment."

Silence hung in the air as Samantha processed Barend's story and looked down at her folded hands on the table. She saw beyond the tough criminal facade, a man shaped by a dysfunctional childhood of harsh realities and poignant lessons. Barend's journey was far from over, his past a maze of pain and resilience, each twist and turn of his story revealing a new layer of his complex character.

He proceeded to reveal the details of the tragic event of that day.

"As customary, we began with a ritualistic prayer, recited in unison but with heavy hearts, knowing what was to come.

"Dear Lord, guide us in your ways, forgive our transgressions, and teach us to be righteous in your sight," we chanted mechanically.

The reverend's voice sharply pierced the silence that followed. "This house is a house of order," he began preaching, his tone authoritative and unyielding. "And those who disobey must... be punished. Do we all agree with this statement?"

The room echoed in agreement, a chorus of fearful young males, forced to consent to an injustice too great to stand against.

"Now... an unpardonable sin has been committed," the reverend continued, his sharp gaze settling on me with a mix of feigned disappointment and resolve. "Barend, please step forward."

I stood up and my wooden chair scraped backwards on the floor, almost knocking the desk behind me. Trembling slightly, yet shaken with fear within, I slowly walked to the chair placed before the class. I could have sworn the workers and creatures of the farmlands outside probably heard my footsteps. One schoolshoe after another, I approached my doom. As I sat on the wooden chair in front of him, the wrath of the burning stick awaited—a tool of punishment and repentance.

"Do you confess and repent of your sinful, rebellious ways?" the reverend asked tauntingly, yet his voice stern.

"I confess," I replied, my voice wavering with emotion as I continued with words that were not expected to be uttered, "...for... for wanting to help, for trying to save the helpless dog."

"Do you confess for breaking the rules of the house of God?" the reverend shouted right in front of my face as his livid eyes bore into mine, demanding obedience.

Tears welled up as I suddenly felt the heat of the flame inching ever closer to my hand. "I prayed to God…" I started defending myself, my voice cracking with sorrow, "I asked Him to save poor Howie and to protect him… how can that be considered as…"

"You committed a sin!" the reverend quickly interrupted with an angry and unwavering voice. "You broke the rules, young man! God sees all that we do."

"And how does kicking… killing a helpless little animal conveniently escape His sight?" I retorted boldly, my gaze defiantly meeting Greef's. The reverend pursed his lips, then huffed out of sheer frustration, surprised by my boldness and what he saw as utter disrespect. His eyes went larger and fear gripped me.

"Repent or feel the flame, son. Your choice… Choose carefully!," he commanded finally, his patience wearing thin. As he stood there with his hands on his hips in front of me, I cried bitterly while detesting the sight of his kempt appearance in his professional suit. "Fine…", I uttered hysterically.

He came nearer with an evil smirk and the flame started scorching my skin, yet I clenched the stick ever tighter, refusing at all to let it go as a sure sign of my bravery and forced self-sacrifice. Tears streamed down my reddened cheeks, mingling with the sheer embarrassment and showcasing my horrific pain. I remember looking up at the old eggshell coloured ceiling, where a painting of Jesus suffering on the cross hung, with Mary kneeling at His feet. In that moment, I realized even having the purest of intentions could be useless, just as Mary was unable to save the one she loved.

As the fire ate at my flesh, searing through my resolve, the reverend slapped me so hard across the face that I instantly fell off the chair and collapsed onto the cold, dirty untiled floor. In the motion he snatched the burning stick from my hand, dropping it again to the floor. The other boys gasped in astonishment, afraid and unsure of what would come next. They looked at each other disillusioned and some of the younger, sensitive ones were already in tears. The reverend spat in my face as I lay there on the floor, almost unconscious with pain and confusion. Through my blurry vision I noticed his abrupt hand signal for me to leave the room, his usual confidence shaken by my defiance.

It was at that very moment that I knew without a shadow of a doubt — there was absolutely no way that I could stay in that place any longer… that excuse of an orphanage where cruelty masqueraded as righteousness. If Howie's unjust death served any purpose, it had surely shown me the truth: I simply had to find a way to escape, to start afresh and find a new life beyond those walls.

With careful planning and determination, I meticulously plotted my way of escape, ensuring that my plan was fool-proof so that Greef and his companions wouldn't interfere. He luxuriated in his privileges, his own room was tucked away at the far end of the orphanage. I wanted him to remember the pain he'd inflicted, to be haunted by it, yet I confided in no one about my plans to take revenge, because it was far too risky to expose. Everyday after lunch when the boys had some "free time" to play, I snuck out to the back of the yard to go and sit there near the chicken shed. This was the only place I could go to be all by myself … to think. Whether the weather brought humidity, scorching heat or rain, I didn't skip a day. Every afternoon I would go and sit there to think about my strategy. Some days I had managed to roll a joint with some stolen tobacco from Greef's workers' rooms. As I indulged in the guilty pleasure of smoking, my thoughts became even darker with every inhalation. One Thursday morning I managed to bunk maths class and I went there to my secret hide-out once more. I noticed the truck carrying the food deliveries every Thursday morning and I instantly knew… this would be my ticket out.

Fast forward a few weeks later… I got up that Thursday morning with an intense knot of anxiety in my stomach for what I was about to accomplish. The early morning air was thick with fog, the silence of the house oppressive. In Greef's room, he slept soundly, obliviously snoring and totally unaware of the retribution brewing. Swiftly and silently, I bound him with rope, gagging him with a cloth sprayed with insect repllant to stifle any cry for help as he struggled fruitlessly against his bonds. My hand gripped the old horse whip, a cruel tool that had once been used on us. His angry grunts and attempts at gasping for air were futile. I proceeded to whip him with the very tool of punishment he had dished out. With each strike of the horse whip, I unleashed my fury upon Greef's bound and helpless figure, his back bearing the brunt of my wrath, blood seeping through his shirt.

When I finally decided it was enough, realizing that tarrying too long would place me at risk, I coerced him into the basement where Howie had met his fate, securing him with rusted chains against the old meat wall, where hooks and wires threatened any attempt at escape. I left him struggling, his threats of retribution echoing behind me.

I dropped the whip and seized my bag, my hands trembled with adrenaline...

I quietly yet frantically fled outside, finding cautious concealment in the shadows, knowing that discovery by any of the authorities would mean utter ruin. I kept muttering a feeble prayer under my breath, a hopeless plea for mercy out of my innermost being.

I dared to look back at the terrible building once more, leaving behind the life of oppression and cruelty. As Samantha listened to my tale, understanding the depths of my resolve, she nodded in silent support.

As the small truck approached in the early morning hours while the dawn was not fully in sight, I shifted deftly in the darkness, slipping to the opposite side of the driver unnoticed. Moments later, with the driver's return, I had positioned myself suavely in order to cling to the truck's back door, my figure clothed in black clinging desperately to the dark green truck as it rumbled away. The wind whipped past, and the grip of my sore, tired hands weakened until I could no longer hold on, dropping to the side of the dusty road with a heavy thud as the truck sped on without me.

Heaving, I picked myself up, flippantly dusted my black clothing off as best I could and retrieved my bag. I looked all around me to see if anyone had noticed my arrival, but realized the coast was clear and quickly started sprinting into the distance. I paced relentlessly, my heart drumming in my chest like a panicked rabbit. Fear and adrenaline mixed together gave me the energy to keep running, despite the pain in my muscles. There were no towns nearby for kilometers, just veld, dry grass and dusty roads filled with pebbles polluted with litter here and there. Although the road looked long and exhausting with no promise of refreshment, let alone a new life, I knew I needed to put as much possible distance between myself and Greef before anyone could catch wind of my escape.

I took little 1 min breaks between the sprints about every 30 min, but my anxious mind probed me to keep persevering. When sunset eventually started seeping in, I finally halted my weary legs, bowing forward and hyper-ventilating mercilessly. The timely break forced me to collapse onto a patch of cold, moist and hard ground. Every sinew in my body screamed with exhaustion, a testament to the brutal journey I'd just embarked upon. Nearby, the twinkling white and golden lights of a town beckoned like distant stars in the darkened horizon. Nearly hypnotized by the glimmering, I felt the hope rise in my heart momentarily.

Shaking my head in disbelief while still leaning forward, I realized the enormity of my escape. With only a change of clothes, a scant supply of day-old bread, a blunt knife, and a dwindling metal flask of water, I knew survival was a precarious thread in these unfamiliar lands.

The town sprawled before me, aglow with hope as the warm, inviting lights of shops, houses and bakeries shimmered all over the place. The tantalizing scent of freshly baked bread and sweet confections wafted through the cold night air, teasing my empty stomach. I walked past an old bakery, its exterior looking forlorn, yet firmly established as a favourite of the community. Through its large vintage window, I beheld a dizzying array of treats—doughnuts in various flavours, cookies of all shapes and sizes, with and without sprinkles and other tempting sugary delights I'd only heard of in whispers.

Reluctant to draw attention to myself, I skirted around to the back-end of the shop, hoping to find discarded scraps. Begging was certainly not an option; it would only draw suspicious glares and ensnare me to return straight back to the very life I'd left behind.

The damp night air wrapped around me like a clammy shroud, chilling me to the bone as I lay awake in a little obscure corner near the back of a pawn shop, shivering under its merciless weight. Doubt gnawed at my resolve as I felt my muscles starting to ache from the cold, tempting me with thoughts of retreat to the safety of my former home.

Yet, I knew deep down that I would need to discard those thoughts immediately. Returning there was out of the question and would surely be a fatal mistake.

As dawn painted the landscape with various hues of khaki and green, I ventured cautiously through the streets, staying ever vigilant and blending into the throng of townsfolk. I scavenged here and there for sustenance, keeping a watchful eye for any sign of suspicion, all the while navigating the delicate balance between extreme hunger and the desperate need to remain free and unhindered.

"Why am I telling you this?" I finally asked rhetorically, meeting Samantha's concerned gaze. "Because sometimes, standing up for what's right means standing all alone."

The echoes of Samantha's promise lingered in Barend's mind as he returned to the solitude of his cell that night. Sitting on the cold, creaking steel bed, he felt a surge of hope amidst the despair that had clouded his days for so long. The memory of his beloved Katelyn Lombaard, the daughter he had lost, flickered in his mind like a candle of hope fighting against the darkness of his circumstances.

"I need to find her," Barend whispered to himself, as if reaffirming a solemn, binding oath to himself. The photograph he had slid under the bars lay on the floor of Samantha's office, a visual testament to his unwavering determination. In the stillness of his cell, the image of a young Katelyn smiled back at him, frozen in time.

With a heavy heart and a mind racing with many questions, Barend's thoughts wandered back to the day he last held her little figure in his arms. The warmth of her tiny fingers wrapped around his, the joyous sound of her child-like laughter echoing in his mind—these memories were the only souvenirs he had left. But now, armed with Samantha's promise, a glimmer of hope ignited within him once more, like a fire starting.

In the darkness of the night, Barend knelt on the cold, hard untitled floor beside his bed, clasping his hands together in fervent prayer. "Please, God," he murmured, his whispers barely audible in the stillness of the prison cell, "Let me find her. Let her know that I never forgot her, that I've always loved her, and always will..."

As sleep eluded him, Barend's mind replayed the fond moments from Katelyn's childhood—her first steps, her first words. He wondered how much she had grown up, and what kind of woman she had become. Did she remember him at all? Did she long to know her father, just as he yearned to hold his daughter close once more?

Morning broke through the small, barred window of his cell, casting the faint light of a cloudy day upon the gray brick walls that had become his harsh, unyielding reality. Determination hardened his resolve as Barend rose from the bed, every fiber of his being focused on his greatest goal ahead of him. He had to find her before time erased the last traces of hope from his grasp.

Throughout the day, he waited with bated breath for any news, for any sign that Samantha had uncovered a lead. As he stared at the prison clock in the cafeteria, each passing hour felt like an eternity. However, Barend knew that patience was his greatest ally now. He dare not let go of the hope within him to find his daughter at last. Earnestly he clung to the memory of the photograph in his mind's eye, willing to guide Samantha to the truth he sought.

When the guard finally appeared at his cell door that afternoon, a glimmer of anticipation lit up Barend's eyes. "You have a visitor," the guard announced gruffly, his voice echoing down the narrow corridor.

With a heart racing with hope, Barend followed the guard through the maze of corridors until they reached Samantha's office once more. There, seated at the wooden desk, Samantha looked up with a reassuring smile. Her energetic appearance in the black and white floral dress came as a refreshing surprise. In her delicate pale hands, she held a large file, her eyes shining with a mix of empathy and determination.

"Barend," she began gently, gesturing for him to sit down at her desk, "I've started the search. It may take a great deal of time, but I promise you, I will do everything in my power to find Katelyn Lombaard."

Tears welled up in Barend's eyes as relief washed over him. "Thank you," he managed to utter feintly, almost choking at the weight of emotions that threatened to consume him. "Thank you for giving me hope."

Samantha nodded kindly, her expression earnest. "We'll find her, Barend. Don't you worry…," she assured him, her voice unwavering. "I'll definitely keep you updated on any progress."

As Barend slowly walked back to his cell that evening, a renewed sense of purpose filled his heart with every footstep forward. For the first time in years, the prison walls seemed less confining, less oppressive, as if he was no longer bound, but almost free again. With each passing moment, he held onto the belief that somewhere out there, his daughter was somehow still alive and this alone was enough to keep him going each day.

The next day dawned with a sense of urgency in Samantha's office. She sat at her desk, meticulously studying the file she had assembled overnight. The sun streamed through the window, casting a warm glow over the photos and documents spread out before her. Her thoughts were so pre-occupied, that her coffee had gotten cold for the umpteenth time. However, Samantha's focus was unwavering as she awaited Barend's arrival, holding onto the hope that she could bring him closer to finding his daughter.

When Barend finally entered the room, there was a palpable tension in the air. His serious eyes were fixed on Samantha, silently pleading for any news that could lead him to Katelyn. He sat down opposite her, his hands gripping the edge of the chair in anticipation.

Samantha wasted no time, pushing the heavy file across the desk towards Barend. "I've gathered some promising information," she began, her voice steady despite the weight of the moment. "Here are the three Katelyn Lombaards I found."

Barend leaned stared at her, leaning forward, his heart pounding with a mix of hope and fear. His eyes scanned the contents of the file as Samantha pointed to each entry.

"The first," Samantha explained, "is Katelyn La Cock. She's married and lives in Cape Town, involved in a book reading society with her husband who owns a game ranch."

Barend winced slightly. "La Cock," he muttered to himself quietly, shaking his head. The name didn't sit right with him, conjuring images that felt out of place for the daughter he remembered.

Samantha didn't pay any attention to his comments, but continued, her finger tracing to the next entry. "The second Katelyn Lombaard tragically passed away at a young age from an overdose. Sadly, she had struggled with bipolar disorder and alcoholism…" she said while sighing, awaiting Barend's response.

Barend frowned as his heart sank, but he refused to accept this as his daughter's fate. "No…" he replied firmly, his voice tinged with determination. "That's not her."

Again, Samantha continued, ignoring his previous statement. "And the third," Samantha moved on, "is Katelyn Taylor. She's a lawyer at the Cape High Court, married to Mr. Donovan Taylor, an architect. They have two children and she's also involved in charity work at an orphanage."

Barend's eyes widened as Samantha described Katelyn Taylor's life, exploring the idea of his daughter being this kind pf person. These descriptions seemed so far removed from the memories he held of his dear daughter, yet he couldn't deny the possibility. "Could she be living such a completely different life now?" he wondered aloud, his mind racing with questions.

Samantha glanced up from the file, her tender eyes meeting Barend's gaze with empathy. "Finding her won't be easy," she admitted softly. "Especially without more concrete information."

Barend nodded sadly yet thoughtfully, his mind searching for any detail that could narrow down the search. "She has butter blonde hair, like her mother," he began, trying to picture Katelyn's face in his mind. "And the most brilliant blue eyes. She has a unique, joyful laugh, quite infectious." Barend chuckled softly, as he attempting to mimic his daughter's laughter, earning a puzzled look from the guard nearby. Samantha looked slightly amused but kept her pose.

"She also underwent a kidney transplant when she was young," Barend added, folding his arms, his voice tinged with both pride and concern. "I can give you the details of the hospital she went to for the operation—anything that might help."

Samantha nodded and swiftly jotted down the details in her little black notebook, her pale & solemn expression appearing focused and determined. "Thank you, Barend. This information will be invaluable."

She closed the file gently, meeting Barend's gaze once more. "As I told you before…I'll do absolutely everything I can to find her. But it may very well take some time."

Barend nodded, a sense of gratitude washing over him despite the uncertainty ahead. "Thank you, Samantha," he said sincerely as a half-grin graced his expression for a brief moment. He continued…his voice thick with emotion. "Thank you…For giving me hope."

Samantha smiled and asked Barend what happened to him after he escaped the orphanage, before he could change the subject or conclude the conversation. Barend sighed deeply as he looked her straight in the eyes, ready to unfold another intriguing part of his story…

The sun ascended, casting a dusty heat across the road leading to the circus grounds. In the distance, the red and white tent stood tall amidst the bustling activity of packing and moving.

Little Brad, the boy who had led me here, guided me straight to Master Greg's trailer. Uncertainty gnawed at me, casusing a nervous knot in my stomach as I stood before the weathered door, unsure of what lay ahead. The boy initiated the meeting, reassuring me of good fortune. A hesitant knock echoed, and a deep, strict voice from within beckoned, "Step inside."

I entered cautiously to find Master Greg seated at a sturdy wooden table, his thick arms rippled with muscles that bespoke years of labor. A piece of rich red tapestry hung from the edge of the table, lending an air of faded grandeur to the humble surroundings.

"Well, Little Brad," Master Greg's voice was laced with sarcasm but tempered with a hint of fondness. "You've returned to us. And this time you've brought an accomplice…"

"I always come back, don't I?" Little Brad piped up proudly, posing a bold statement rather than a question.

Master Greg grabbed a knife on the side of his table and sliced open a pomegranate with deliberate care, his keen gaze shifting from Little Brad to me. His scrutiny was thorough, every detail measured and cataloged in his mind. To be honest, the awkward silence made me even more nervous.

"And you..?" Master Greg's voice was calm, commanding attention without urgency. He waited, his patience a silent challenge.

I met his gaze squarely, refusing to falter under his penetrating scrutiny. A half-smile tugged at the corner of my mouth, a testament to my resolve.

"Where is your father, young lad?" The question hung heavy in the air, laden with unspoken implications.

Time stretched taut as I wrestled with the truth within. Finally, I shook my head, unable to meet Master Greg's eyes.

"Left behind…" I admitted quietly, the weight of those words settling heavily upon me in the silence of the trailer.

Master gestured with two fingers for me to approach, and I moved closer, feeling the weight of his gaze as he examined the makeshift bandages on my hands. With gentle hands weathered by years of hard labor, he unwrapped them to reveal the burnt marks beneath. It stung as he applied a pasty green ointment from a nearby jar.

"Most of us here..," Master began, his voice carrying the weight of shared histories, "tell a story quite similar to yours. But here, we find an unique family together. Of course, you'll need to prove yourself first. Can't join the circus without any talents now..."

I nodded silently, the ache in my body a testament to the nights spent running and the bone-chilling cold endured in desperate solitude.

Barend, standing nearby, nodded in agreement with all of the Master's words.

"Brad, take him with you," Master instructed, his voice firm yet kind. "Find him a trailer and something to eat. It seems this boy is an orphan and needs some grub. Take care of that too." With a casual flick of his hand, he tossed a few coins onto the floor as a generous gesture of care.

It was an inevitable moment in my life, a crossroads I had reached which I sensed held the promise of destiny. Here, I knew everything familiar was destined to change. Previously, fear had driven my every action, a constant battle to avoid missteps and consequences.

Now, I found myself embraced by a peculiar yet humble family… a nomadic tribe of sorts, a traveling sanctuary where the extraordinary mingled with the mundane. It was an Olympic camp on the move, a haven of magic, creativity, laughter, and diversion from the harsh realities beyond its borders.

49

Walking past the rusty cages housing the circus animals and the shabby, colorful trailers that housed its inhabitants, I glimpsed a tapestry of humanity. An old lady with thinned out purple-grey hair and a bedazzled black hat smiled mischievously, yet warmly as she read tarot cards. Her weathered face lit with a kind familiarity that echoed the acceptance I hoped to find among these new companions.

Ever so often, my mind drifted back to the faces of those I had left behind at the orphanage. I hoped fervently that they, too, would someday find the courage and means to somehow escape that stifling place. Little Brad led me through the bustling circus grounds to a modest coach. Inside, he handed me a bowl of warm mieliepap topped with melting butter. The sight of butter stirred a pang of nostalgia as I felt my stomach churn with hunger pangs. I couldn't remember the last time I had tasted it.

"Thanks," I murmured to Brad, who hurried off to attend to his duties.

Above the hubbub of preparations, Master's voice boomed across the camp, and over a loudspeaker to bring us to attention every once in a while. It was time to move on to the next town, a routine that felt both thrilling and daunting in equal measure.

Despite the overwhelming desire to let go of all duties and collapse into sleep, I knew that proving myself was crucial. Gathering my resolve, I made my way to the front of the camp to offer my help. The air was humid yet alive with a sense of urgency as performers and crew readied the caravans, tended to the animals, and secured equipment for the journey ahead. It was a whirlwind of crazy activity, yet amidst the chaos, there was an underlying rhythm, a shared purpose that bound this diverse group of wanderers together.

Under the fading light of dusk, I found myself vigorously assisting with loading supplies onto one of the old wagons. Sacks of grain, barrels of water, and crates of equipment were gathered in a row and meticulously stacked and secured. Each task I completed earned a nod of approval or a brief word of instruction from the seasoned performers around me. It was more than hard work, but the sense of camaraderie and the thrill of being part of something larger than myself fueled my determination and gave me the strength I needed to see every task through.

As night descended and the last preparations were made, I felt a surge of anticipation mixed with apprehension. The circus was my new reality, a world of colourful wonders, techniques and uncertainties, where each day promised adventure and a new opportunity to prove myself worthy of belonging.

That evening, we set up camp on the outskirts of the next town, nestled beneath a sky streaked with the remnants of a fiery sunset. Each passing day marked a deeper rift between my tragic past at the orphanage and the uncertain future ahead. The burn on my hand, once raw and painful, now transformed into a brown scar etched with Greg's magical green ointment, its healing properties a testament to the circus's unconventional remedies.

As twilight draped its dusky orange and purple veil over the camp, I wandered around the periphery, reflecting on my newfound journey. It was then that I suddenly caught sight of her… a young girl, draped in a vibrant gypsy dress of deep purples and fiery reds. The velvety fabric cascaded freely, revealing a glimpse of olive-toned skin and lustrous black hair that spilled over her shoulders like a waterfall.

Caught in a moment of disbelief, I approached cautiously. "I did not expect to encounter someone so…" My voice faltered as I nervously swallowed my words, trailing off as our eyes locked in mutual curiosity.

She regarded me with a mixture of intrigue and suspicion, her gaze probing. "So what?" Her tone was guarded yet tinged with a hint of curiosity.

Barend hesitated, unsure of how to articulate the thoughts swirling in his mind. "So captivating," he finally managed, a hint of shy admiration coloring his words as he smiled shyly.

Her lips curved into a faint, demure smile too, the corner of her mouth quirking up in amusement or perhaps something more enigmatic. "Captivating, huh?" It seemed as if she enjoyed hearing such a remark. Her voice held a musical quality, carrying with it a hint of mystery that piqued Barend's interest further.

Caught off guard by her intrigued response, Barend found himself at a loss for words, grappling with the unfamiliar sensation of interest mingled with uncertainty. The encounter lingered in the cool night air between them, an unspoken magical connection forged amidst the transient beauty of their nomadic existence.

The evening settled around the makeshift camp, casting long shadows that danced in the fading light. Tamarah's presence had an unexpected weight, a mixture of curiosity and apprehension that stirred within me as she approached, demanding my attention.

"Tamarah," she boldly introduced herself, her voice carrying a hint of mystery. "There are a few secrets here. May I sit down here with you?"

Before I could respond, she settled beside me on the old wooden boxes stacked outside, her deep gaze unwavering. The directness of her stare unnerved me; back at the orphanage, interaction with girls was strictly limited, our worlds segregated except for the occasional classroom proximity.

"What is your name?" Her inquiry was straightforward, cutting through the silence that lingered between us.

I paused, swallowing the last bite of mieliepap. "Barend... Visagie." There was something about Tamarah's presence that compelled me to engage, to delve deeper into a meaningful conversation. Perhaps she held the key to understanding this strange new world.

"Why is it that you live here?" I ventured, eager to learn more about her life amidst the transient circus existence.

"Well... My mother is the cook here," she began, her voice tinged with a hint of sadness. "As for my father, he's absent, to put it politely."

I wondered about her age, her story... about each and every detail she revealed. She painted an intricate picture of an unconventional life intertwined with the traveling circus's nomadic journey.

"I think everyone finds something different here than what they initially expect," Tamarah continued, as she stared into the distance with her deep dark eyes, leaving me mesmerized along with her lingering words. "So, what did you have to leave behind?"

Her question suddenly pierced a vulnerable area of my psyche, probing deeper than mere curiosity. I hesitated, debating in my mind whether to fabricate a story or retreat into silence. But there was something about Tamarah's earnest gaze that invited honesty and trust.

I carefully began to speak, omitting names and specific places, recounting fragments of my former life: the absence of parents, the confines of the restrictive orphanage, and the main characters that had left their inevitable scars on my heart… Little Howie, Greef, and others who were once my companions.

Tamarah listened intently, with her chin resting on her hand, offering a few interruptions but her eyes never straying from mine. Inbetween the details of my story, she lit a candle which she took out of her pocket and placed it neatly on a wooden crate in front of us. The flame provided much more than light. Its vibrance created a soft inviting ambience, a safe place to share all the struggles I had encountered. As darkness enveloped the sky, signaling the end of our conversation, she bid me goodnight, waving with a soft sincerity.

"Good night, Barend."

Beneath the canopy of stars, amidst the rustling of leaves and the distant murmur of the circus settling into slumber, I found myself fondly pondering the significance of our encounter as Tamara moved away toward her tent. This was a moment to remember, a rare connection in a world where strangers often passed like ships in the night.

The circus wasn't just a spectacle. It was a labyrinth of unspoken rules and silent agreements that bound its inhabitants together like differing threads in a grand colourful tapestry.

Under the canvas of the Big Top, where the air crackled with excitement and the smell of popcorn and sawdust mingled, we performers understood our roles with clarity born of years of tradition and necessity.

Rule number one echoed in every ringmaster's command and every performer's heartbeat: "The show must go on." No matter the obstacles… be it rain-soaked tents threatening to collapse or internal discord simmering beneath the surface… each act, each performance, had to dazzle, to captivate, to transport the audience into a realm of wonder and disbelief.

Yet, amidst the razzle-dazzle and the gasps of curious spectators, another rule held steadfast: "Never steal from someone visiting the circus." Our livelihood depended on the goodwill and curiosity of those who dared to wander into our world. To betray their trust was to jeopardize not only our fleeting patronage but also the delicate balance of our nomadic existence.

"You are only as good as your last act," the unspoken mantra whispered in the shadows backstage. Applause was currency, and our reputation our shield. Each tightrope walk, each lion's roar, each form of cunning trickery, each contortionist's bend… all etched in memory and critique, shaping our standing within the circus community.

And then there was the final verdict that loomed over us like a specter: "You could only stay till you are 18." The transient nature of circus life dictated that youth was both our strength and our limitation. As the years spun by like the turning of a Ferris wheel, we knew our time under the tent was finite, a countdown to adulthood and departure.

Within this colourful swirling universe of spectacle and secrecy, we forged strong bonds, traded epic stories, and shared the burden of our clandestine missions to "collect goods," euphemism for acquiring what we needed to sustain our wandering community. In this world, where every smile covered an untold story and every laugh concealed a heartbreaking sorrow, these rules were not just guidelines. They were the glue that bound the fibre of our beings together, making us an unique family in a way that no traditional home ever could.

In the mysterious world of the circus, where every eloquent act was a tightrope walk between fatal danger and spectacle, we lived by a code that outsiders could scarcely fathom. Contrary to popular belief, we were not mere jesters or entertainers; we were engineers of wonder, guardians of thrill, and masters of our own fate.

Master Greg stood resplendent in his crimson satin robe, adorned with silk and sequins that shimmered under the dim glow behind the canvas wall. It was moments before the grand spectacle would unfold, and the audience's anticipation crackled in the air like electricity.

It was the night of my initiation, and I was a silent observer in this grand theater of marvels.

As the lights dimmed, the audience hushed in anticipation, settling themselves and their children, knowing that the show was about to begin. From my vantage point, I witnessed the orchestrated chaos unfold with meticulous precision and grace. A lion tamer dressed in skin-tight blue and red uniform, fearless and commanding, danced with his majestic beast, weaving a mesmerizing dance of trust and looming danger. Dogs leaped onto the backs of fierce galloping horses, their agility and coordination a testament to months of tireless training.

But it was Ava who stole the breath of every soul under the tent. Suspended high above on a gossamer thread, she defied gravity with every graceful movement, making the impossible seem effortless. Her aerial ballet enraptured the audience, drawing gasps of awe and thunderous applause.

As the final act concluded eventually, Master Greg emerged, his presence commanding the stage. With a flourish, he acknowledged the audience's adulation, taking a slow, magnetic bow that echoed with immediate applause and admiration. In that very moment, I understood... I wasn't just witnessing a spectacular show; I was part of a legacy, a creative family bound by shared dreams and the pursuit of enchantment.

The circus wasn't just a spectacle; it was a sort of sanctuary where the ordinary gave way to the extraordinary, where danger danced with regal beauty, and where each performance was a testament to our unstoppable courage and skill. And now, with each heartbeat resonating with the rhythm of the applause, I knew I had found my place in this world of wonder and adventure.

After the thick red curtain fell and the applause died down, I found myself being handed a broom, swiftly tasked with cleaning the animal cages under the dim glow of the moonlit night. It was a humbling task, but one that tethered me to this strange new world I had stumbled into.

Scrubbing and sweeping the dirty surfaces, I toiled into the late hours in complete solitude, save for the sounds of a few restless animals growling here and there and the occasional distant cackling from the performers' tents. It was in the silence of this moment that I first encountered Little Brad again, his presence a silent beckoning into the clandestine side of circus life.

"How are you, Barend...?", he stood there smirking with arms folded, but my exhausted expression was enough of a response.

Following him through the maze of canvas and rope, we gathered with others at Master Greg's room, a sanctum where secrets were shared and fortunes were unveiled. The air was thick with anticipation as bags were opened, revealing a treasure trove of stolen jewels and assorted goods. Amongst the loot, I could see everything from half-empty cigarette boxes to chewing gum and womens' cosmetics. It was a stark reminder that this was no ordinary circus; it was a carefully constructed haven for thieves, performers by day and "deceivers" by night.

Master Greg's stern steely gaze surveyed each loot with a mix of pride and calculation. I stood on the periphery, a newcomer drawn into a world where boundaries blurred between performance and plunder. It didn't take long for me to be initiated into this dual existence... performing feats of wonder under the spotlight by day, and cautiously slipping through the shadows to acquire riches by night.

Under the cloak of darkness, we moved with utter precision and stealth, breaking into homes and liberating valuables with practiced efficiency. Silence was our ally, and anonymity our shield. Should one of us get caught, the unspoken rule was clear: keep silent, become almost invisible and protect the circus at all costs, for the show must go on.

Within the span of a few nights, I learned more about survival and cunning trickery than I ever did in the stifling confines of the orphanage. Each heist, each act of deception, forged bonds tighter than blood among us night crawlers. We were a family of misfits and thieves, united by necessity and bound by the unspoken rules of our unconventional trade.

As dawn broke over the horizon, casting a fragile light on our nocturnal exploits, I realized that I had found my place in this world of shadows and spectacle. In the circus, where illusion and reality danced in tandem, I discovered that one's survival meant embracing both the spotlight and the shadows with equal measure.

Life in the circus was a whirlwind of vibrant hues, tireless labor, unwavering focus, and enchantment. To those outside the canvas walls, it appeared as a spectacle... a mere evening's entertainment, a larger-than-life display of skill and daring. They queued for hours, eager to pay the price to witness the magic that unfolded under the big top.

Within this bustling world, there existed an unspoken camaraderie. We were much more than mere performers; instead we were a family bound by a shared rhythm and a deep-seated intuition. Master Greg often spoke about being centered, attuned to the subtle energies that ebbed and flowed within our troupe. There were moments when a performer would step into the ring unexpectedly, draped in a robe over their costume. It was as if we sensed it coming, an intuition that pulsed through our veins like an unspoken signal.

Amidst the orchestrated chaos, we had a dual responsibility: to perform stunning death-defying acts with the utmost precision and grace, and to remain sensitive to the pulse and temperature of the audience. It was a delicate dance between illusion and reality, where each act concealed meticulous preparation and practiced spontaneity.

Behind the curtain, before the eager eyes of the audience, we transformed into grandiosity. Acrobats soared through the air with breathtaking agility, animated clowns elicited spontaneous laughter with their antics, and animals normally found in the wild performed feats that defied their nature. Every act was a testament to our discipline and daring nature, executed with a seamless blend of skill and showmanship.

Yet, amidst the eruptions of applause and the gasps of awe, there was an invisible thread that bound us together... the shared understanding that each performance was a glorious culmination of tireless effort and unwavering dedication. We watched out for each other, attuned to the slightest shifts in demeanor or energy, ensuring that every member of our troupe stood ready to shine under the spotlight.

In this world of fleeting enchantment and ephemeral wonder, we navigated our journey with grace and agility, ever mindful of the responsibility to entertain, captivate, and leave our audience spellbound. It was a life driven by passion, colored by camaraderie, and woven with the golden threads of magic that only the circus could conjure.

As the seasons turned and various audiences came and went, the circus thrived like a beacon of wonder in each town it visited. Yet, beneath the facade of glittering performances and applause, shadows began to close in on the group.

Rumors whispered through the ranks—a tightening grip of scrutiny from local authorities, whispers of investigations into missing valuables coinciding with the circus's visits. Still, we pressed on, the show must go on, as Master Greg reminded us. But the tension simmered beneath the surface, an invisible weight that hung over our once jubilant troupe.

One fateful night, as the tent billowed under a stormy sky, tragedy struck without warning. The authorities suddenly descended upon us, their accusations loud and damning. Loud sirens broke through our usual festive melodies and brought the entire crew to a panic-stricken halt. They had found evidence - stolen goods hidden in trailers, whispers of accomplices amongst our ranks. Anxious questions rippled through our makeshift family, faces etched with fear and betrayal.

Master Greg, adorned in his magnificent robe that once commanded applause, now stood there frowning at the center of chaos, his voice barely a whisper against the storm outside. He urgently gathered us under one tent, his performers, his family, and delivered the grim truth. We had to face the reality that we were compromised. The circus was no longer a sanctuary of creativity but a target, a scapegoat for crimes we had not all committed.

In the flickering lantern light, decisions had to be made swiftly. Some of the artists packed up their goods at once, shoving their clothes into their leather cases in a somewhat disorderly fashion. They fled into the night, escaping their tyranny and disappearing like ghosts into the darkness. Others, like myself, lingered in disbelief, grappling with the shattered illusion of our safe haven. I, Barend, once a newcomer finding solace and purpose within these ranks, now stood at the precipice of a harsh reality.

Tamarah, her dark eyes filled with anger and sorrow, approached him amidst the turmoil. "Barend," she whispered gravely, her voice trembling with unspoken words. "They won't stop until they find us all. You must go."

He stood there and looked at her with his hands on his hips, pursing his lips and nodding, a silent acknowledgment of the bond forged in adversity and fleeting joy. Their eyes locked, communicating a shared understanding of the harsh truth. Both of them knew that they could no longer stay there. The circus, their haven of magic and camaraderie, was instantly crumbling around them.

With a heavy heart, Barend uttered a soft, "Yes... I know...". He knew what he had to do. Packing only essentials - a change of clothes, a knife, an old forlorn notebook and the memories that weighed heavier than any possession, he hugged Tamarah one last time and slipped away into the night, leaving behind the only family he had known.

As he swiftly disappeared into the shadows, the echoes of applause and laughter faded into the howling wind. Barend stopped for a moment and looked back at the flickering lights which were becoming more dim with every step. The circus, once a realm of dreams and illusions, now lay there in ruins... a casualty of circumstance and the harsh realities of the hidden world beyond its canvas walls. And Barend, now alone and adrift, knew he had no option but to venture forth into an uncertain future, forever marked by the bittersweet memories of a life he could no longer call his own.

Samantha knew from her years of experience that to get to the information she was interested to hear, she had to win Barend's devotion, to accept even his craziest stories and need to share, so that he would trust her without hesitance. "All in good time..." she thought to herself. Knowing that she has cracked even the craziest of criminals before, she reassured herself that Barend would be no different.

As they parted ways, Barend walked calmly towards his cell with a renewed sense of hope and purpose. He knew that Samantha's task was certainly not an easy one, but he held onto the belief that somewhere out there, Katelyn Taylor, his beloved daughter, was waiting to be discovered. Each passing moment, each conversation with Samantha brought him closer to the possibility of a reunion, and Barend clung to that hope with unwavering determination.

At each meeting, Samantha meticulously recorded every detail Barend provided about his daughter. Her fancy pen moved swiftly across the pages of her brown moleskin notebook, capturing the specifics of Katelyn's appearance, medical history, and any potential leads that could aid in locating her.

"Good," Samantha affirmed once she had finished jotting down the last piece of information. She closed her notebook, sighed and leaned back into her chair with a stern, determined expression, her mind already strategizing the next steps in the search for Katelyn. "I will look into this thoroughly. Now, let's focus on the rest of your story, Barend..."

"And then we were two," Samantha's voice crackled over the phone, a stark reminder of the high stakes they faced. The mission was clear as daylight - save a man from the clutches of death row in exchange for the elusive bank code that promised freedom.

Barend listened intently, his mind racing through the implications. "Locked up? No chance," he muttered to himself, pacing the dimly lit room. His plan had taken shape from whispered rumors and clandestine conversations. A chance encounter had revealed the critical flaw in the prison's security, a detail that could tip the scales in their favor.

Parking his old blue-grey Ford bakkie discreetly along the desolate stretch of road, Barend transformed himself into an elderly woman, a mauve cloak and shawl, plus tinted glasses covering his masculine appearance and hiding his true identity. The sun's early rays at dawn cast a golden hue over the landscape as he awaited the inevitable - a police van approaching in the distance, its disturbing siren piercing the morning calm and causing a few stray hadidas to shriek and flap away into the distance .

With practiced precision, Barend flagged down the vehicle, his voice trembling in a well-rehearsed falsetto. "Good day, sir," he greeted the approaching officer with hands clasping beneath the steering wheel to avoid revealing them too much, sighing and feigning distress over his supposedly overheated car. Suspicion lingered in the air as the officer raised his eyebrows and circled the vehicle, inspecting the faux mechanical failure.

"I'm alone, needing to reach town," Barend continued, weaving a tale of urgency and helplessness, his heart pounding beneath the disguise. The officer's scrutiny intensified, as he stood still every once in a while to stare intently, probing for any sign of deception amidst the smoke and shadows.

The scene hung in delicate balance, a precarious dance of deception and desperation, as Barend anxiously awaited the moment of truth, knowing that one misstep could shatter the fragile facade he'd meticulously constructed.

In the rugged expanse where shadows stretched long over the parched earth, Barend's resolve burned brighter than the rising sun.

The weight of a daring mission pressed upon him, a quest forged in desperation and tinged with the promise of redemption.

"I am alone," Barend's voice quivered with practiced desperation as he faced the advancing police van, its headlights carving through the early morning mist like blades of judgement. "I need to get to town for our weekly prayer meeting," he pleaded, his words weaving a web of urgency around the unsuspecting officer, whose resolve wavered under the morning's golden light.

A nod, a gesture of compliance, and the officer moved closer with his dark frowning moustache, his steps echoing a solemn march of duty. "Open up, please," his strict voice rumbled, commanding authority mingled with suspicion. With a feigned sigh of relief, Barend obliged, hood released to unleash a torrent of smoke... a calculated ruse, a gambit in the game of shadows.

As the officer's focus narrowed on the billowing fog, Barend struck with the swift precision of a hunting cat. A blow, swift and sure, silenced the officer's doubts, sending the old man crumpling to the earth... a solitary sentinel fallen in the path of fate.

"One down," Barend's voice echoed softly in the stillness, a whisper of triumph amidst the swirling chaos. "One more to go."

With a deft twist of fate, Barend pulled off the elderly disguise and swung open the rear door of the police van, revealing its cargo of chained men. Sitting there in contorted postures were three rugged souls bound by the iron will of justice, their eyes reflecting a tapestry of fear and fleeting hope.

"Which one of you is the reverend?" Barend's voice pierced the air, his eyes scanning the trio whose tongues danced in the tongue of Xhosa - a symphony of words foreign to his ears, secrets whispered in the twilight tongue of the land.

Grim resolve etched upon his features, Barend produced a photograph, a snapshot of fate, held aloft to gauge truth amidst the deceit. "Too young," he murmured, his eyes narrowing with the weight of judgment, "too long a nose."

Yet it was the last man who met his gaze with unflinching resolve, a silent testament to the spirit unbroken by the specter of death. The barrel of Barend's gun pressed against weathered skin, a fragile dance upon the precipice of destiny.

A desperate utterance of "Hayi, hayi..." proceeded from the other two men reacting out of pure shock.

"Thula!", the one under threat silenced them as if his authority was never questioned, then looked straight back at Barend. "If you are going to shoot," the old man's Xhosa-infused accent resonated with a quiet strength, "Then make it quick."

A sly smile momentarily played upon Barend's lips, a fleeting dance of reverence for the brave. Then a shot shattered the silence, a chain severed amidst the clatter of freedom's song. "Time to dance," Barend's voice resonated with a quiet command, the echoes of liberation reverberating through the barren landscape.

Shots rang out, a symphony of liberation as the bewildered prisoners fled into the embrace of the unknown, their hearts racing with newfound hope, their shackles cast aside in the dance of defiance against the tyranny of fate.

Barend's adrenaline-soaked breath hung heavy in the cool morning air, his mind racing with the weight of his newfound fortune and the burden of a man chained to destiny. The old man, stoic in the face of liberation, followed Barend's lead with a solemn nod - a dance orchestrated by fate itself.

"Your friend asked me to come say hello for him," Barend's voice broke the silence, a fragile thread weaving through the quiet tension. "So no funny moves now, right?"

The old man's deep brown eyes held a glint of understanding, a silent agreement forged in the crucible of their shared desperation. He shuffled towards the car with old and dusty broken brown leather shoes, his chains clinking a rhythmic refrain against the stillness of the morning. Barend secured him to the window with a practiced hand, veiling him in cloth and secrecy, overshadowed by the dawn's golden light.

Bags in the back of the van rustled along with the old man's awkwardly seated posture, these treasures weighing heavily with the promise of wealth, their contents whispering tales of freedom and absolution. "Well, I just won myself the lottery ticket," Barend muttered with a smirk, his voice laced with a mix of disbelief and anticipation. "This money would be enough to live a carefree life, to sit back and have others serve me." He smiled to himself, caught up in his own emotion, unbothered by the car's tyres frequently dancing over potholes.

The edge of town loomed in a blur of heat in the distance, a sanctuary beckoning with the allure of finality. When they finally stood stil, Barend got out and opened the back of the van. His fingers deftly untied the old man, handing him a bag. It was like an offering from a phantom of the past. "A gift from an old friend," he murmured, his voice carrying the weight of unspoken gratitude.

Vuyo's dusty weathered hands fumbled with the photo, eyes tracing the contours of a past tethered to the present, a testament to bonds forged in the crucible of captivity. The bag yielded its treasures. His eyes widened momentarily as he saw the gun, money, a pass bearing a name not his own. He froze for a few seconds as he observed the contents of the bag…a lifeline spun from the threads of deception.

"This will keep you going for a while, I presume," Barend's words brought great relief, a sudden parting gift in the dance of fate. "This is my final stop."

Footsteps echoed behind him, a haunting melody of appreciation and obligation, a specter of debts unpaid in the shadows of freedom's embrace. Barend turned, eyes locking with the figure trailing in his wake. The intense silence spoke of the unresolved debt between them.

"What is it, you want to thank me or something?" Barend's voice wavered, uncertainty mingling with the raw edges of relief.

"Appreciation accepted, now scoot," he urged, the words a plea wrapped in the shroud of imminent departure.

Yet the man persisted, a shadow refusing to fade into the morning mist. "Now now… I can't go about having you follow me now," Barend's voice quivered, a plea for closure amidst the chaos of liberation. "I made this deal, to get you out. So… you are out… free like a bird…"

A door creaked open, a silent invitation beckoning the specter within. Barend settled into the sanctuary of his refuge, the man's figure a stark reminder of debts unpaid in the ledger of fate.

"Wait a moment now…" Barend's voice cut through the stillness, a warning etched in steel. "This is no taxi you have here… Come on now!"

Vuyo solemnly met his gaze, eyes betraying his unyielding resolve. "I understand," his voice echoed, a quiet assurance in the face of uncertainty. "But I have made an oath."

An oath, a vow whispered amidst the chaos of liberation… a life bound by the promise of recompense. Barend suddenly stared at him looking half-amused.

"Well… I release you of your obligation," Barend's words were a plea, a lifeline extended in the waning light of forgiveness. "All is good and repaid."

Vuyo's head shook in silent defiance, his arms folded and unyielding… a testament to the chains that bound their destinies. "Can't do," his voice carried the weight of conviction. "It is a life for a life… You saved mine… I need to repay it in the same way."

Barend's shoulders sagged, burdened by the weight of an unexpected twist. "Listen, old man," his voice cracked, a plea mingled with resignation. "This is a one-man show. I seriously don't have the time or patience to carry around an invalid."

"Invalid… Invalid?" Vuyo's voice cut through the lingering doubt, a challenge amidst the tumult of their shared destiny.

The gun, an arbiter of fate, had found its mark, pressed against Barend's temple, a fragile and dangerous moment unfolding. "Go on… shoot then," Barend's laughter carried a bitter edge, a defiance against the unseen threads of fate.

"It's empty," Vuyo's voice held no trace of doubt, quietly reassuring him in the face of the unknown.

"Not blind to be shot in my back by a murderer now," Barend's voice wavered while chewing his gum and staring straight ahead at the road in front of him, uttering a plea for understanding in the midst of the tension.

The air hung heavy, pregnant with the weight of their shared fate - a standoff poised on the knife's edge of absolution and retribution. Yet their loomed a possibilty of liberation amidst the tangled web of destiny's design.

The air hung thick with uncertainty as Barend looked at him once more, wrestling with the dilemma before him. Vuyo, a convicted man with a loaded gun, stood as both a promise of salvation and a threat of betrayal in the twilight of their uncertain alliance. Barend's fingers moved with practiced precision as he loaded his own gun, each metallic click echoing through the stillness of the countryside.

"No funny business now, or I will drop you," Barend's authoritative voice cut through the tension like a blade, his gun leveled unwaveringly at Vuyo's head. The convicted man's response was a smile, one that held more than its share of enigmatic calm. He quietly expressed his defiance against the odds stacked in the fading light.

Without breaking eye contact, Barend climbed out of the car, his movements deliberate and calculated. His gaze swept the landscape, searching for something - a test, perhaps, of Vuyo's loyalty and his own resolve. Fifty meters away, an old farmhouse wall provided the canvas for Barend's silent challenge. Four bottles, weathered by time and neglect, found their place in the unfolding drama - two lined on the side, two perched precariously atop each other.

The first shot shattered the evening's peace, a crack that echoed through the valley. Three more followed in rapid succession, each bottle succumbing to the accuracy of Vuyo's aim. Among the debris lay a fallen bird, proving the precision of a man deemed 'invalid' by circumstance but proven invaluable in moments of dire need.

Barend's proud smile mirrored the satisfaction that bloomed within him, an acknowledgment of Vuyo's unexpected skill. "Not bad for an invalid," Barend's thoughts whispered to himself as he looked down at his own feet with his hands on his hips, nodding to himself in admittance of newfound respect in the face of their shared destiny. "Might be useful," he mused, scratching the scruffy re-growth on his chin while his mind is racing with the implications of their burgeoning partnership.

"So we were two..." The memory of their unlikely alliance reverberated in Barend's mind, a tale woven in the crucible of necessity and desperation. "In planning the heist of the bank, it became clear... we really needed to be three."

The old guard's words lingered, a reminder of the missing link in their audacious plan. "Now I can give you the information," the old guard had conceded with the voice of an old smoker, his wisdom etched in the lines of his weathered face. "But I am unfortunately too old to be of practical use in there. You need someone who is truly fast with their hands, to take out the cabling... without being noticed... while the other distracts the guards."

Barend's determination burned as bright as a fiery flame amidst the dire challenges that lay ahead. "I was not about to give up," he reflected, his resolve unyielding despite the odds. The search for the elusive third member of their crew had become a quest of its own, woven into the very fabric of their preparations within the secluded confines of the old shed.

"We kept on working on the plans," Barend recounted with hands folded, his optimistic tone of voice a testament to their perseverance in the face of adversity. "Out in the old shed, while we searched endlessly for the third man." Their quest led them through the shadows of the town, where bustling, dirty bars served as arenas for false promises and fleeting hopes, each encounter with potential recruits fraught with tension and disappointment.

"Most often ended up in fights... men trying to flaunt their bravery...," Barend recalled as he looked away at the window with a hint of frustration, the memories of futile pursuits etched into his mind. However, each setback fueled their determination even more, a flame that burned brighter with every failed attempt.

But amidst all the trials and setbacks, Barend instictively knew... their quest for the third man was not just about completing their crew, but about finding a partner in crime whose skill and loyalty could match the gravity of their daring heist.

The morning sun cast long drawn-out shadows through the narrow alleys of the city, painting the grey cobblestone streets in a slightly golden hue. Barend, with the aroma of freshly brewed Brazilian coffee lingering in the air around him, moved around purposefully in the small kitchen, trying to maintain a sense of order. Vuyo, still blissfully lost in the embrace of sleep on the couch, was unaware of the impending disruption to their routine.

A faint noise, barely perceptible amidst the morning bustle, pricked Barend's ears. He dismissed it at first, attributing it to the usual mischief of stray cats that roamed the alleys in search of scraps. Little did he know, this day would unfold with an unexpected visitor - no mere feline, but a harbinger of fate in the guise of a nimble intruder.

Returning from the kitchen with two steaming mugs of coffee in hand, Barend's eyes widened in shock as he entered the main room. Their meticulously laid plans, strewn across the table moments ago, were now in disarray. Someone had breached their sanctuary, their haven of secrecy.

In the corner of his eye, Barend caught a glimpse of movement. A fleeting shadow darted through the open window, leaving behind a trail of disruption as papers had dwindled into the carpet along with an empty beer can. Without hesitation, fueled by instinct and urgency, Barend took a deep breath, plonked the coffee mugs down on the kitchen counter and lunged into action. The chase was on.

The streets became a blur of activity as Barend speedily navigated through the labyrinth of market stalls of fruits, vegetables, cigarettes and confectionery populating the alleys, his pursuit hindered by obstacles thrown in his path. Tables and crates, hastily overturned in the commotion, threatened to trip him up as he sprinted after the elusive intruder. With each obstacle leapt over and each corner turned, the gap between them narrowed and widened in turns, the man proving to be a swift and agile adversary.

In a stroke of luck cunningly combined with strategy, Barend cornered the intruder in a dark,narrow street alley. For a fleeting moment, it seemed victory was within grasp as the man found himself as a trapped animal, with nowhere left to flee. But fortune favored the nimble, as the intruder scaled a drainpipe with the dexterity of a seasoned acrobat, disappearing over the rooftop in a matter of heartbeats.

Breathing heavily, adrenaline coursing through his veins, Barend strengthened his resolve and scrambled to follow suit. The drainpipe groaned under his weight as he climbed, determination lending him speed and strength. Yet by the time he reached the rooftop, the intruder had vanished into the labyrinthine depths of the city, leaving Barend to survey the empty skyline from underneath his sun-shielding hand in frustration.

The moment hung heavy with the realization of the dilemma that had transpired. Their plans had been compromised, their secrecy breached, and a shadowy figure now a wild card in the game they were playing. As Barend stood atop the rooftop, catching his breath amidst the urban landscape that sprawled before him, he knew that this encounter marked the beginning of a new chapter in their quest... a chapter fraught with dangerous uncertainty and the relentless pursuit of an elusive third member to complete their heist crew.

In the gritty underbelly of the city, where shadows danced with secrets and every scruffy corner held whispers of untold schemes, Barend and Vuyo found themselves thrust into an unexpected alliance with Lloyd, the nimble street cat who had inadvertently stolen their meticulously crafted plans. With the paperwork clutched tightly in his grasp, Lloyd had sought refuge amidst the rusted carcasses of old forgotten vehicles in a scrapyard, oblivious to the storm he had stirred up.

Barend, fueled by a mixture of fury and determination, tracked Lloyd down to the scrapyard, his heavy footsteps echoing off the skeletal remains of automobiles that stood like silent sentinels. Smoke curled lazily from Lloyd's cigarette as he sat all too comfortable on an old vulnerable piece of scrap metal, leaning back casually on his elbows next to the stolen blueprints secured against the wind by his one hand, his gaze fixed skyward in blissful ignorance of impending retribution.

As Barend quickly closed in, his presence betrayed only by the faintest whisper of movement, Lloyd's smile faltered and he hastily jumped onto all fours, intending to crawl and hide between the metal skeletons. Alas, he was not fast enough, as the weight of Barend's leather boot instantly descended upon Lloyd's outstretched hand, pinning it mercilessly to the ground. The sharp crack of bones underfoot mingled with Lloyd's pained exclamation, yet still, he refused to relinquish the plans.

"You crazy old man," Lloyd spat through gritted teeth, eyes wide with disbelief and pain. "How the hell did you find me?"

Barend's response was as terse as his tightened grip on Lloyd. "Your friends can't keep their mouths shut."

Meanwhile, Vuyo made his appearance behind Barend, gun in hand, ensuring Lloyd's associates, bruised and battered, would not interfere. With a resounding gunshot that split the air like thunder, the two men scattered into the shadows, leaving Barend to confront Lloyd alone.

"So you plan to rob a bank, huh?" Lloyd mused, his hoarse smoker's voice tinged with an unsettling calmness. "Crazy enough to try it. But what if the authorities catch wind? What if someone just happens to sell them the exact plans they need? Justice does pay, as they say…"

Barend's brow furrowed in frustration. "We're not bank robbers. Where do you get these ideas?"

Before Lloyd could answer, a hefty rock soared past him, crashing to a halt just inches from his feet. Barend's voice, deep and commanding, cut through the tension. "Take one more step…"

Frozen in place, Lloyd weighed his options, his gaze flickering from the enraged Barend to the discarded plans lying there within reach, begging him to take a risk. Barend's proposition hung heavy in the air as an offer of alliance, steeped in mistrust yet veiled with the promise of mutual gain.

"What if I could be of help?" Lloyd finally ventured, inching cautiously back towards Barend.

With one raised eyebrow, Barend began encircling him, steadily pacing around him with hands behind his back, yet ever on guard against any potential attempts Lloyd may make to escape. "And how might this benefit me … ?", Barend asked, still heavily distrusting Lloyd's sudden suggestion.

"I've got skills, you know…" Lloyd began, enthusiastically sharing snippets of his former daring criminal behaviour.

A tense negotiation ensued, each word a chess move in the precarious game of trust and deception. Barend's laughter, rough and unforgiving, rippled through the stale air as Lloyd proposed terms that would keep the police at bay and ensure his cut of the spoils.

"Twenty-five percent," Barend asserted, his muscular grip on Lloyd's hand tightening with every counteroffer.

Their accord struck, albeit begrudgingly, Barend released Lloyd's pathetic hand, leaving him nursing throbbing fingers and bruised pride. Reluctantly, the scrawny yet cunning figure fell into step, limping behind Barend and Vuyo, a new member begrudgingly welcomed into their makeshift family bound by greed and necessity.

As Samantha, their confidante, later queried how they managed to pull off the heist against all odds, Barend's response was characteristically enigmatic. "Nothing more than careful planning and a whole lot of luck," he offered with a wry smile, glossing over the intricate dance of alliances and betrayals that had led them to the brink of fortune and peril.

Thus, in the shadows of a city that thrived on vice and ambition, three unlikely comrades embarked on a journey fraught with danger and opportunity. It was certain that this would be a journey that would test their resolve, challenge their loyalty, and leave an indelible mark on the annals of clandestine adventure.

The heist was meticulously planned, every detail ironclad and timed to perfection, reminiscent of a plot straight out of an Ocean's Eleven film. Barend, Vuyo, and Lloyd stood in a dimly lit warehouse, surrounded by pages upon pages of scribbled out blueprints and carefully constructed maps of the bank they were about to infiltrate.

"The plan is simple," Barend began, his voice low yet brimming with confidence. "We move in disguised as police officers during a routine visit. Lloyd, your job is to disable the cables while our friend here…" he nodded towards another figure in the shadows, "…holds up the cashier for the money."

Lloyd leaned forward with arms resting on skinny legs concealed by an old, worn-out baggy jeans, his cat-like green eyes gleaming with an almost unbelievable mix of excitement and apprehension from above his thin, skeleton-like cheekbones. If it were not for the fine lines and semi-grey hair, one would have mistaken him for a teenager from afar. "And what about the panic button?" he quickly asked, tapping his fingers nervously on the little makeshift coffee table in front of him.

Barend smirked, as if the thought had already been carefully calculated. "That's where our smoke bombs come in. Dark smoke, harmless but intimidating. They'll cover our exit strategy. By the time the real cops show up, we'll be long gone."

Vuyo stepped forward out of the shadows, his expression serious. "We can't afford any casualties. Hostages only if absolutely necessary."

Barend leaned on the old barstool in front of him, hands folded, nodding in agreement. "Right. Our escape vehicle is crucial. It needs to blend in… a nondescript old kombi, inconspicuous yet fast. Reinforced steel on the sides for protection, engine souped up for speed. It'll be our ticket out of there."

Lloyd raised an eyebrow, running his fingers over the sides of his scrawny face. "And who, might I ask, is the driver?" he asked arrogantly.

Barend's smile widened. "Someone we can trust. Someone who knows the streets and won't crack under pressure."

In the corner, a stocky figure stepped out of the shadows… a seasoned driver with a weathered face and steely eyes. "That would be me," Vuyo announced, his voice gravelly but confident.

Barend clapped a hand on his shoulder. "Perfect. With you behind the wheel, we've got this."

As they finalized their preparations, tension hung in the air, mixed with a sense of anticipation. With every extra cup of black coffee, and every drag of a cigarette, the clock ticked closer to zero hour, the moment they would finally put their plan into motion and seize their chance at wealth and freedom.

"Sooner or later, you can bet the authorities will show up," Barend muttered under his breath, more to himself than to the others. "But by then, we'll be on our way to the score of a lifetime."

With a final nod of agreement, the team dispersed to their assigned tasks, their minds keenly focused and adrenaline coursing through their veins. The heist was set, the pieces of the plot in place. All they needed now was execution. This would require the precision of a surgeon, the audacity of a thief, and the nerve of a gambler.

In the very heart of the city, under the cover of night, they readied themselves to make their first move. The bank awaited, unsuspecting. And Barend, Lloyd, and their trusted driver, Vuyo were about to rewrite their destinies with one daring stroke of criminal brilliance.

It was a hot bustling afternoon in Beaufort West, seemingly tranquil under the warm sun. Schoolchildren chattered on the sidewalk as they made their way home, and elderly ladies swapped stories over tea at the little local hair salon. But beneath this facade of small-town serenity, Barend, Lloyd, and Vuyo were preparing for a heist that was sure to shake the quiet streets to their core.

Dressed in stolen navy police uniforms, Barend inspected their disguises with a critical eye. The uniforms bore an unfamiliar American insignia which could appear to be suspicious if noticed, but time was of the essence and they could no longer obsess over such details. They simply had to make do. Lloyd flashed a sly confident grin, while barely standing still while Vuyo struggled uncomfortably with his ill-fitting attire.

"Where did you find these costumes?" Barend muttered, shaking his head.

Lloyd shrugged casually, standing confidently with legs wide apart and his arms on his hips. "Stole 'em from Suzie's costume shop. Close enough, right? We'll be in and out before anyone notices. Can't risk lifting a real cop's gear."

Barend nodded half-reluctantly, his eyes fixed on the badges as he adjusted his hat. "Stick to the plan. Reverend, wait for our signal by the car."

The reverend nodded solemnly, and Barend set his stopwatch. "We have exactly five minutes to execute this and get out. Stay low boys, keep your hats down."

With a brief determined nod from his accomplices, Barend made an almost incognito hand signal for Vuyo to join him, and the two strolled confidently toward the bank's entrance. The town seemed unusually quiet that day, but Barend sensed something amiss as they entered the foyer of the building. The air was thick with tension.

As they ventured inside, the scene in front of them was utterly chaotic. Customers lay down bound on the floor, trying to quiet their own panicking voices, eyes wide with fear. Lloyd had already made his way swiftly to the counter, where he found the bank teller bound and helpless. This wasn't just any ordinary robbery, but a well-executed ambush.

Barend's instincts kicked in. Within a split-second and from the corner of his eye, he spotted a figure approaching, head covered, and shouted a warning. "Get down!"

Lloyd reacted swiftly, diving for cover behind the counter just as gunfire erupted. Barend returned fire, hitting one of the masked assailants in the knee. The assailant fell down yelping because of the pain, and chaos erupted as more consecutive shots rang out.

Realizing they were outnumbered and outgunned, Barend acted quickly and decisively. He fired at a nearby glass chandelier, bringing it crashing down with a thunderous noise. The loud distraction gave them a brief moment to run out and escape the firefight inside the bank.

Meanwhile, outside, Vuyo was struggling with a different kind of urgency. He needed the bathroom, but there was no other convenient option, except for the outdoors. As he relieved himself by the car, he forgot to secure the handbrake. The vehicle suddenly rolled backward just as a speeding security truck barreled into their path, shattering glass and halting both vehicles abruptly.

Frustrated and panicked, Vuyo kicked at the van's door in a futile attempt to open it. A security guard emerged, reaching for his weapon. Vuyo, shocked yet simultaneously livid, knocked him out with a swift punch.

"Can't you watch where you're driving?!" Vuyo yelled, his temper flaring along with his nostrils.

As Barend and Lloyd sprinted toward him, Vuyo seized the opportunity to take advantage of the situation. He pushed the unconscious guard aside and commandeered the security van. Barend and Lloyd caught his drift and speedily jumped in, and they raced away with screeching tyres and gunfire echoing in their wake.

"What happened in there?" Vuyo demanded, sweaty and out of breath as he gripped the wheel tightly.

Barend's voice was tense as he replied with sweat droplets running down his face, "Man, don't ask now...Just drive. Put your foot to it!"

The heist had started with such precision, but now they found themselves in an unfortunate race against time, trying to flee the relentless pursuit of law enforcement. Ahead lay the escape route they had meticulously planned. one that promised them either freedom or certain captivity, depending on their next moves.

The transition from smooth tar to dusty dirt road rattled the van as Vuyo skillfully maneuvered off the beaten path, stirring up a cloud of confusion along with the dust behind them. Barend, tense with adrenaline, tapped him vigorously on the shoulder, urging him on impatiently.

"Come on, old man! Step on it! We can't afford to slow down now," Barend barked, his eyes nervously scanning the rearview mirror for any signs of pursuit.

Vuyo grinned, his hands steady on the wheel as they approached a bridge up ahead. Without hesitation, he veered toward it, driving right onto the bridge's weathered planks. Their pursuers, obscured by the dust trail, followed the van's tracks blindly. The sound of their vehicle hitting the bridge echoed loudly behind them, confirming their temporary escape.

As they sped away with a great noise from the scene of the heist, Sergeant Dirk Joubert, highly frustrated and foiled in his attempt to stop them, leaned out the window, ripped off his mask and fired a few futile shots at the van disappearing into the distance.

Later, while seated in a secure location, Samantha listened incredulously to Barend recount the chaotic events that took place.

"So, let me get this straight," Samantha mused as she neatly crossed her legs in the floral dress and folded her hands on her lap, skepticism dripping from her voice. "So you're saying… you stumbled upon a bank already under siege by another group of robbers? In Beaufort West, of all places, at the exact same time?"

Barend met her gaze evenly, his expression unreadable in the dimly lit room.

Samantha chuckled, shaking her head in disbelief. "My, oh my… You're quite the storyteller, Barend. This could turn into a bestseller, I'm sure…"

The buzzer interrupted their conversation, signaling the end of their allotted time. Barend stood abruptly with hands placed in his pockets, a wry smile playing on his lips while staring at her with a face like flint.

"Believe whatever you want, Samantha," he replied cryptically as he turned to leave. "The truth is often stranger than fiction."

With that enigmatic remark, Barend left Samantha on her own to ponder the improbable tale he had spun… a tale of daring heists, unexpected alliances, and narrow escapes that blurred the lines between hero and criminal in the labyrinthine world they inhabited.

Samantha spent her evening in the dimly lit hotel room, with old antique furniture and bland interior, surrounded once again by various scattered news reports and cutouts detailing the audacious bank heist that had gripped Beaufort West. The articles painted a picture of chaos and precision: a gang of ruthless criminals, masked and heavily armed, executing a seamless operation. The police were scrambling, promising swift justice while desperately struggling to uncover any possible leads that could crack the case wide open.

Captain Greef's stern voice echoed in Samantha's mind as she read aloud from one of the reports, "'It's our highest priority to find them and ensure that such acts do not go unpunished.'" His determination was palpable, a stark contrast to the bafflement of eyewitness accounts. Witnesses described a swift and brutal incursion by the armed gang, the malfunctioning of security measures, and the mysterious disappearance of the responding police officers.

"No hostages were harmed, civilians safe…" Samantha muttered, her brow furrowing in concentration as she held the clipping up close. "But fifty million rand in loot… that's a heist of a lifetime."

As she drank her last sip of coffee and immersed herself in the details, a shrill cellphone ring interrupted the silence. Samantha instinctively glanced at the caller ID before answering with a composed tone.

"Yes, sir," Samantha responded and sighed, her voice a mix of confidence and caution. "Progress looks good… I'm getting him to talk."

The voice on the other end crackled with expectation, "You have the story, Samantha?"

"I need a few more days," Samantha replied firmly, sensing the urgency in her editor's tone.

"You've got one week," came the editor's swift reply. "Get the story and get back here."

The call ended abruptly, leaving Samantha nervous and with a sense of urgency. She pursed her lips as she put her phone on the table and proceeded to the kettle for a final cup of coffee, unable to rest yet.

She knew she was close to uncovering the truth behind the heist... the connections to inside jobs, the van's suspicious blockage, and the meticulous planning that had thwarted all security measures.

As she stirred her coffee, surrounded by the remnants of investigative journalism, Samantha's mind raced with possibilities. She knew she needed to dig deeper, follow the breadcrumbs of clues, and unearth the hidden motives behind the heist that had left Beaufort West reeling. With a determined nod, she gathered and set aside the articles and prepared to dive deeper into the heart of the story, where danger lurked around every corner and the truth was waiting to be uncovered.

Back
at the Cell

66 "Hello Barend...", she greeted him. Not receiving any response from him yet, she probed further, now all too familiar with the habitual testing of his silent boundaries at every opportunity.

"How are they treating you?" Samantha asked quietly, leaning against the cold metal bars that separated her from Barend.

Barend glanced up from where he sat on the bunk, his expression weary but resolute. "Prison, Samantha, it's like being stripped of everything. Freedom, dignity, even the simplest things we took for granted..."

"We had no idea what we were getting into," Barend continued, his voice low. "Vuyo had been shot, and we couldn't risk taking him to a hospital without raising suspicions. Lloyd said he knew a doctor who could help."

The cell was dimly lit, the air heavy with the weight of their predicament. Barend recounted their desperate dash to the old man's house late that night, their hope hanging on the promise of a secretive doctor's aid. They found the place unlocked, as small-town homes often were, and inside was a scene that spoke volumes about the doctor.

An old grey bearded man sat heavily in a kitch armchair, surrounded by miscellaneous clutter and the faint aroma of brandy hung in the room almost like an evil presence. The radio blared senseless music in the background, competing with the purring of an ancient overweight cat lapping milk from a glass. Lloyd wasted no time in rousing the doctor, his urgency clear.

"Doc, we've got trouble. He's got lead in his arm," Lloyd declared urgently, with skinny arms resting on his hips, as was his usual mannerism when trying to prove a point.

The doctor, startled from his doze, blinked in recognition at Lloyd. "Little Lloyd, my boy," he greeted warmly, rising slowly. His unkempt appearance and the disorder of his home belied a keen mind and steady hands, evident as he led them to his makeshift clinic.

"Just come in quieter next time, see...?" the doctor chided lightly. "You'll give an old man a heart attack."

With practiced ease, the doctor keenly assessed Vuyo's injury, his manner gruff yet compassionate. He wasted no time in preparing for a makeshift surgery, pouring brandy more for nerves than for numbing.

Vuyo's reluctance to drink was met with understanding silence from Lloyd and a shrug from Barend.

"Can you help him, doc?" Lloyd anxiously pressed him for an answer, while wiping a dirty, sweaty forehead and revealing the concern etching his forlorn features.

The doctor's reply was brief and businesslike, avoiding eye-contact with them as he readied his tools, a hefty blade glinting under the dim light. Barend and Lloyd held Vuyo steady as the procedure began, the air thick with tension and the pungent smell of antiseptics.

"Lucky for you, it missed the main veins," the doctor muttered under his grey moustache, his focus unwavering as he worked. Barend watched tensely, feeling a mix of anxiety and relief wash over him as Vuyo grimaced under the doctor's ministrations.

"Doc, how's the family?" Lloyd interjected, his attempt to lighten the mood falling flat in the gravity of the moment.

The doctor's reply was terse, focused solely on the task at hand. "Talking about the bullet, there it is."

Barend, ever the observer, took in the scene with a mix of awe and desperation. This unexpected turn of events, this makeshift surgery in a cluttered room under the doctor's steady hand, spoke volumes about the lengths they would go to for survival.

After what felt like an eternity, the doctor injected Vuyo with a strong painkiller, and they gathered whatever supplies they could before retreating. Their plans had unraveled, their hopes dashed by the harsh realities of their situation.

As they trudged back to the old farm stall where they had stashed the van, Barend's mind churned with thoughts of their failed heist. The twist of fate that led them to rob a bank already under siege, their escape car destroyed, felt like a cruel joke. Yet something nagged at him, a feeling that wouldn't go away until he gave into the urge to inspect the van once more.

With a heavy heart and a sense of impending doom, Barend approached the battered vehicle. His hand trembled slightly as he reached for the handle, preparing himself for whatever revelation awaited inside.

Unlocking the back of the van marked a pivotal turn in our daring escapade. It felt as though fate had delivered us a gift. Unimaginable wealth that shimmered under the dim lights of the old, decrepit farm shed. For me, it was akin to receiving the first Christmas gift I had ever known, an unexpected rush of euphoria and disbelief coursing warmly through my veins as I beheld the glittering treasure: diamonds, gold bars, and stacks of cash in a few sturdy suitcases neatly packed into the van.

When I alerted my friends and called them to come closer, their eyes enlarged with pure shock. We simply couldn't contain our elation. And so we shouted aloud with joy, our voices echoing off the shed's walls, reverberating like a glorious celebration of triumph over impossible odds. We started clapping rhythmically on a beat and proceeded to dance around the van like little Khoi San children around a bonfire, intoxicated by the sight of wealth that promised each of us a new life, far away from the shackles of ordinary existence.

But amidst the jubilation, Barend's voice cut through the frenzy, tempered with caution and pragmatism. "Hold on boys… This changes everything," he said while panting heavily from the excitement, his eyes scanning the gleaming riches with a mix of awe and apprehension. "Realize that whoever sent this van won't stop until they find us. We're up against the worst… police, their dogs, and the roadblocks. We need a fool-proof plan, and we need it now."

He knelt on the dusty floor of the shed, sketching out a rough map of South Africa with a stick. "I say we ditch this car, get another, and head straight for the border," Barend outlined, his tone resolute yet tinged with urgency.

Lloyd, clutching and flipping through a stack of money and grinning from ear to ear, chimed in eagerly. "So, what's the plan? Split up and make a run for it?"

Barend shook his head firmly. "Nope! No splitting up. We stick together. Avoid Johannesburg and all the main cities… way too risky. We take the back roads through the Karoo, up the coast toward Mozambique. That would be our best shot."

Vuyo, standing there with arms folded at Barend's attention, nodded in agreement, his expression grave but determined. "We can't afford any slip-ups," he added, his eyes darting between the map and the treasure before them.

Lloyd, frustrated but compliant, reluctantly set aside the money. "So, what then… we just sit on it?" he grumbled, his impatience betraying his itch to spend their newfound fortune.

Barend's gaze hardened as he locked eyes with each of us in turn. "For now, yes…" he affirmed, his voice steady. "Until we reach Mozambique, where we can trade these without raising suspicions."

Lloyd aggressively slammed the stack of money down onto the dusty floorboards, his frustration palpable in the dim light of the barn. "You've got to be kidding me," he spat out bitterly. "So, what, do you think we're just going to take a leisurely drive up the coast like some perfect little family?"

The tension in the room thickened with the silence as his words hung in the air. It wasn't just about the treasure anymore; it was about survival in a society fractured by apartheid's iron grip. The 1980s in South Africa were a crucible of civil unrest, protest, and violence, where every street corner and social interaction was colored by the stark divisions of race. Laws dictated where one could live, work, and even walk, with separate beaches, schools, and public facilities segregating communities into worlds apart yet coexisting side by side.

"Well… for us to even take the chance to walk together is asking for trouble," Barend interjected, unaffected by Lloyd's little tantrum, his tone of voice low and calculated. "We're not just facing the law; we're up against a whole system which is religiously designed to keep us apart."

Vuyo nodded solemnly in agreement with Barend, his thoughts mirrored in the gravity of his expression. "And now we've got a van full of wealth that screams trouble," he added, glancing at the stacks of money and precious gems with a mix of awe and apprehension.

Barend sat down on the old forlorn couch, sneezed as his nose caught a whiff of dust and leaned forward, the weight of their predicament pressing down on them like a vice. "The plan was simple: take enough to live comfortably for a while. But what we've stumbled upon," he gestured toward the riches spread before them, "is more than any of us could have ever imagined. It's a fortune that could change our lives for good…That's if we can survive long enough to spend it."

Their gaze fell upon the marked bills, numbered and traceable, symbols of their newfound dilemma. "I hate to admit it, but using any of this money would be suicide," Barend continued, wiping his nose, his voice carrying the weight of their precarious situation. "It would paint a target on our backs, and I, for one, am certainly not willing to exchange freedom for a cell."

Lloyd exhaled sharply, frowning with frustration still etched across his face. "So what's the plan then?" he demanded, folding his arms as his voice revealed a mixture of defiance and uncertainty.

Barend stood up straight again, his gaze steady. "Well, we lay low. We find a way to get another vehicle without drawing attention. We avoid the big cities, take the back roads through the Karoo, up the coast toward Mozambique."

Their eyes met in silent agreement, a tacit understanding of the dangers that lay ahead of them. In the backdrop of racial tension and governmental scrutiny, their journey had suddenly transformed from a heist into a desperate bid for freedom and redemption.

As they prepared to leave the barn, all three of them became awkwardly quiet, each man carried the weight of their decisions, knowing that their path forward was fraught with peril, but also with the tantalizing promise of a future unburdened by the chains of their past.

Under the veil of night, burdened by the weight of their ill-gotten gains, Barend and his companions hurried to secure their escape. A new vehicle was paramount, one that wouldn't draw suspicion, along with a disguise and a meticulously plotted route to the border. They spent the remainder of the night huddled in the dilapidated barn, sipping from a bottle of brandy that they happily discovered amongst the loot, strategizing through the weary hours, their eyes flickering with the greed and fear that drove them onwards.

Morning fractured the silence with the distant growl of an approaching car, immediately setting Barend on edge. Instinctively, he reached for his gun underneath one of the couch's cushions, cautiously seeking cover against the looming threat. Vuyo materialized beside him, wielding a makeshift weapon, ready to defend their fragile sanctuary.

In the periphery, Lloyd arrived in a weathered tan old-school Combi, cigarette in his mouth while scanning the rear-view mirror. Barend stared at him half-amused with arms folded as he watched him moving the vehicle back and forth to find a perfect parking spot on the grass. The three put their heads together and eagerly got to work, renovating the poor old vehicle. Its weary façade soon transformed under their urgent hands. The vehicle shed its identifiers as they hastily removed its number plates, masking it with a coat of midnight black paint. It became a fortress on wheels, fortified with steel bars scavenged from their discarded security van, now consigned to the depths of an abandoned quarry.

Amidst their preparations, Barend lit a cigarette and took a step back, pausing for a moment. His thoughts strayed to the town that held fragments of his shattered life... the hometown of his estranged wife and their beautiful daughter, Katelyn. While Lloyd and Vuyo toiled over their newly armored vehicle, Barend was a million miles away in his imagination. For a moment he thought only of her, resolving to bid farewell to the daughter he scarcely knew, his heart heavy with regret and unresolved longing.

Armed with a second-hand teddy bear, a feeble gesture of paternal affection, Barend navigated the familiar streets, each step of his worn-out leather shoes a silent reckoning with his past. Memories of his dear little Katelyn, distant and poignant, haunted his thoughts as he approached the threshold of a house he once called home.

In the thick, humid air of the afternoon, Barend stood at the threshold of a life he once knew, now a fragile tapestry unraveling before him.

Standing in front of his old house, he saw a "sold" board, a stark reminder of financial upheaval. The bank had come to claim the place, a decision that now seemed shortsighted as it was Beth's name on the deed. The house appeared deserted, lawn unkempt with thick shrubs here and there, the interior a melancholy sight with a few lonely items draped in white cloth scattered about. Barend went up the three little steps and rapped on the door, but there was no answer.

Sitting heavily on the front porch steps smoking yet another cigarette, a poor consolation for his bruised emotions, Barend felt the weight of missed opportunities settle upon him. The situation seemed hopeless until a petite elderly woman ambled down the street, laden with shopping bags too heavy for her own wellbeing.

Barend spotted her, immediately jumped up and squashed the cigarette butt under his shoe, hurrying over to offer his assistance. "Oh.. that's kind of you, young man" the old lady said, her figure shaking slightly from what appeared to be Parkinsons. Her voice carried a trace of gratitude, and her smile shone through her whole wrinkly demeanour. "A pleasure helping a lady such as yourself," Barend replied with a polite smile with his hand resting on her shoulder. "Why, what brings you here, young lad?" she asked with a hint of concern.

"I'm looking for Mrs. Hilda Visagie and her daughter Katelyn, who used to live at number 12," Barend explained, pointing down the street.

"Oh...I knew them well," the woman replied warmly, resting a large wrinkled hand upon his arm "Hilda asked me to look after the little one a few times. What an angel she is. And you are?"

"I'm a cousin passing through town," Barend replied smoothly, hoping to glean information without revealing too much of himself, for fear of looking suspicious.

"I'm sorry to tell you, but they don't live here anymore," the neighbor replied cautiously with a frown that dampened her previous cheerful disposition.

Barend probed gently, planting himself in a very casual stance, with arms folded, "Do you happen to know where I might find them?"

The woman hesitated, her gaze holding secrets Barend needed to uncover for Katelyn's sake. "I'm not one to gossip, you know..."

Barend nodded respectfully. "I understand. Thank you for your time, Miss..."

"Call me Miss Valentine," the woman interjected, patting him heavily on the back and causing Barend to jerk with sudden discomfort.

After a brief retaliation he smiled warmly, leaning forward and almost whispering, his flattery quite evident to the old lady. "Like the saint... The name suits you, Miss Valentine."

Miss Valentine chuckled and turned to unlock her front door, but she suddenly paused, seemingly compelled to share more. "It was a terrible ordeal, you know... for that poor girl. I often stopped by for a quick visit at their house to give Katelyn snacks. To my shock and horror, her mother would sometimes be passed out, and there were times I heard them arguing... everyone in the neighborhood did. It wasn't until the police came over that one evening..."

Barend frowned and listened intently as Miss Valentine recounted their troubled past. "At the end of the day, Hilda went to rehab and pressed charges against the man. But Katelyn... she was left sitting on the porch, all alone. She refused to talk to anyone, not even me. When the social workers came to take her away, she clung to the door, crying that her dad would come for her, that he wouldn't know where to find her if they took her away. It was so... terrible... truly heartbreaking."

Barend's heart sank, the weight of guilt and longing heavy upon him. "I understand," he murmured and looked down at his feet ashamedly, his voice tinged with regret. He quickly re-directed his own thoughts and broke the awkward silence. "Do you happen to know where I might find her? I bought her a present."

Miss Valentine regarded him sympathetically. "I'm so sorry, I don't know where on earth they went. But maybe someone at the local school might have some information for you..."

Barend nodded gratefully and feigned a half-smile, while feeling mildly defeated that he was not able to obtain more details. "Thank you, Miss Valentine. You've been very kind."

Miss Valentine in her floral dress and white woolen jersey, hunched over with old age, started shrinking even more as she felt the chill of the breeze. Barend stood there for a moment longer, almost frozen in time, but contemplating his next move. The quest to find Katelyn had just begun, and he was more determined than ever to uncover the truth and make amends for lost time.

The old woman tugged at the edges of her jersey, hugging her frail figure with her own arms. She lovingly examined the large brown teddy bear with a gentle smile, her eyes softening with a hint of nostalgia.

"She might be at the town orphanage, down Fuschia Street, you know.... That's if they haven't found her a home yet."

Barend nodded gratefully, thanking the old lady for the lead. She slowly lifted her hand and waved goodbye, thereafter retreating into her home. After returning the gesture, Barend walked away knowing full well that there was no time to dwell on the past; regret was a luxury he couldn't afford now. With urgency gnawing at his heels, he knew they had to press on towards the border. But before leaving South Africa for good, he needed closure.

Walking towards the orphanage on this quiet cloudy afternoon, Barend couldn't help but feel a pang of nostalgia, gnawing at him even more severely than his physical hunger. The imposing gates encircling the facility seemed to contain not just the children but also their hopes and dreams. Inside, he adopted the guise of cousin Frederick once more, relying on a fake identity document that had served him well before.

As he signed in at the entrance book, Barend was escorted to a large hall by a chubby nurse in beige uniform. Outside, the clamor of children playing echoed faintly. In a corner under a tree, away from all of the commotion, sat Katelyn, absorbed in writing out Bible verses.

The nurse leaned in, her voice tinged with concern as she recounted recent events.

"One of the children was talking about her family... She kept saying her father loves her, that he's coming to take her home. Little Jonny teased her, said she must be lying. Soon, more children gathered, mocking her. She couldn't take the teasing anymore... lashed out, bit me when I tried to intervene."

The nurse showed Barend the blue discolouring and red bite marks on her arm, evidence of Katelyn's bite mark and clearly some emotional turmoil.

"Just so you know...we certainly don't tolerate that kind of behavior here." the nurse stated assertively.

Barend nodded sympathetically, knowing instinctively that he should not allow his own emotions to interfere, as he was sure to raise suspicion, if he were to do so.

"I understand... It must be challenging to care for all these children."

The nurse smirked and shook her head "They can definitely be little devils at times, but we have our way of dealing with even the most difficult of them..." Her words left Barend with a strange feeling of his own memories, of punishment and not being able to stand up for himself as a child.

With a friendly nod of dismissal, she click-clacked away as graciously as her old-fashioned court shoes could carry her, leaving Barend to approach Katelyn. She sat there, tracing her finger over the words on the page, her expression a mix of innocence and defiance. Barend crouched beside her with folded hands, whispering softly.

Barend: "Daddy's little butterfly..."

Katelyn glanced up, her eyes widening with surprise. Barend quickly motioned for her to keep quiet, placing a finger to his lips, before she could shriek with joy The relief and happiness in Katelyn's eyes spoke volumes. Despite what her mother had said, there was hope and belief in her heart again.

Katelyn: "I knew you would come, Daddy. I told them but...". She looks away clearly not wanting to share the details of the event.

Barend smiled warmly, pulling the bear from behind his back and presenting it to her.

Katelyn's blue eyes lit up with pure delight as she hugged the old brown bear close to her chest.

Katelyn: "Oooh, its so cute and fluffy! Like a real bear."

Barend chuckled softly, his facial expression revealing a very different, tender side of him as he knelt beside her.

Barend: "What's his name?"

Katelyn studied the bear for a moment, her brow furrowed in thought.

Katelyn: "Hmm... Well..."

Barend: "How about Trevis the Great Bear?"

Katelyn shook her head, giggling.

Katelyn: "Nooo..."

Barend grinned.

Barend: "Maybe Oscar the Warrior?"

Katelyn burst into melodic laughter, her joy infectious. Barend glanced sideways and noticed the nurse peeking into the room, shaking her head with a knowing smile.

Katelyn: "No silly, it's a girl."

She smiled brightly.

Katelyn: "I will call her Lucy Bear."

Barend nodded approvingly and smiled.

Barend: "Lucy...? Wow, that's a wonderful name. Will you take good care of Lucy Bear for me, Kate?"

Katelyn nodded enthusiastically. As Barend began to stand, Katelyn's small hands grasped his.

Looking down at her rosy apple-cheeks and innocent beaming eyes, Barend saw his own childhood flash before him, memories of being stuck in an orphanage flooding back. What happened next wasn't planned, perhaps not the wisest choice in hindsight, but it felt right in the moment.

Glancing quickly around and noticing the nurse still occupied with the mischievous children outside, Barend leaned in conspiratorially.

Barend: "Shall we play a game, Kate?"

She leaned in curiously.

Barend: "Do you see that red postbox across the street?"

Katelyn nodded eagerly.

Barend: "Come on... Let's see who can get there first without anyone noticing. It's definitely going to be me".

A mischievous grin spread across Katelyn's face. With her finger in her mouth, she thought about it for a brief moment. Then she glanced at him, clutched Lucy Bear tightly and darted towards the window. The game was on, and the expression on her face clearly showed she was in it to win. Beyond it, a backdoor beckoned from the kitchen. The kitchen, normally busy with staff was empty as they were clearing the lunch tables in the hall.

Around the corner Barend noticed the nurse who brought them in. She was busy marking down the roster for the childrens chores on the wall. Barend softly pushed Katelyn out the back door and quietly closed the backdoor behind them to avoid detection. Barend and Katelyn paused. Katelyn pointed excitedly towards a high fence at the back of the orphanage grounds. Barend smiled and signaled for her to come along with him. Carefully he lifted her up, helping her over the fence, and followed swiftly.

Barend knew it wouldn't be much longer before the staff realized Katelyn was missing. He was already in hot water with the police. But in that moment, seeing the sheer joy and innocence on Katelyn's face, he knew this spontaneous escape was worth every risk. Barend and

Katelyn rushed down the streets, to Barend's surprise she followed without asking the direction. She was holding his hand tight, and Barend pushing to make time before being detected. And as they disappeared from the orphange, her laughter echoing softly in the quiet streets, Barend allowed himself a flicker of hope. For once, he wasn't running away. Instead he was running toward something, what he wasn't sure of yet.

What had possessed me to bring a vulnerable little girl along with us, amidst this crew of criminals? Several times on our journey to the farm, I halted in my tracks, the urge to turn back gnawing at my conscience. Yet, each time, Katelyn's tight grip on my hand and her innocent trust held me fast, propelling us onward through the streets toward the weathered old shed where Vuyo and Lloyd still slept, blissfully unaware of what had transpired in the interim.

Once inside, I set about kindling a fire to boil water, needing to break the news to the rest of the gang. Slowly, the sound of clanging metal roused Lloyd from his slumber. The other two stirred, groggy but eager at the prospect of filling their hungry tummies when they saw me stirring up baked beans and warming bread over the flames for breakfast. I always kept a bag of essentials handy, just in case.

Motioning Katelyn to stay hidden behind the van until I called for her, I joined the others around the crackling fire. Suspicion hung in the air as they eyed me, sensing something was going on.

Lloyd: "So, what's the deal now?"

Barend: "Breakfast. What does it look like?"

Lloyd helped himself to a bite of bread dipped in canned beans, his expression a mix of surprise and amusement.

Lloyd: "Who would've thought... my first millionaire's breakfast."

We devoured our food in silence for a moment, but the tension was palpable. Finally, I cleared my throat, bracing myself for the weight of what I had to say to them next.

Barend's voice cut through the early morning air like a solemn vow, his words laden with the weight of their precarious situation.

"If we were to encounter the police, having a hostage... an innocent, frail someone we can control... might just be our 'get out of jail' card," he murmured, his tone low yet resolute. "Do you agree?"

Lloyd's grin widened knowingly. "*Nou praat jy...* (Now you are talking) But where do you expect to find such a person? The three of us would be shot on sight. We can't use each other."

Barend gestured with a sweep of his hand, and from behind the van emerged the little Katelyn, tentative and unsure. She hesitated, standing there with the teddy bear hanging from her one hand.

"Come, Katelyn...", Barend coaxed and she cautiously started making her way forward into the circle of men. Barend glanced at Lloyd with a stern look.

"You're scaring the girl," he admonished softly before approaching Katelyn and gently lifting her up into his arms.

Katelyn leaned in close to Barend, almost hiding behind him and whispering anxiously, "Who are they, Daddy? They look scary."

Barend stroked her blonde hair reassuringly. "Remember what Mom always said? That Daddy is away..."

Katelyn looked up at him and nodded, her brow furrowing. "That you're in jail?"

"No," Barend corrected gently. "That I work for the special police."

Katelyn sighed softly, and held Lucy Bear close as if to comfort herself, the weight of understanding settling upon her young shoulders. "So this means you'll be gone again."

Barend placed his hand on her shoulder and interrupted gently, a note of warmth in his voice. "This time, you're coming with me. We need you for this mission. But you must promise me something. This is a secret mission, and you can't tell anyone about it, okay? Can you promise me that?"

Excitement sparkled in Katelyn's eyes as she nodded eagerly and smiled. "Pinky promise."

She extended her small pinky, and Barend wrapped his larger one around hers, creating a soft click as they parted.

"Alright," Barend said, his voice firm yet tender. "These are Daddy's partners."

He looked over at Vuyo and Lloyd, a silent understanding passing between them as they prepared for what lay ahead.

Barend pointed a commanding finger at Lloyd, his voice resonating with pride and assurance amidst the morning haze.

"That man over there..." Barend began, re-focusing his gaze steadily on Katelyn, "He is one of the fastest you'll ever see. He can leap over gates without a single hand, and his knife skills? Why, he could strike down a fly in mid-air if he so wished."

Katelyn's eyes widened in awe as she gasped, nearly dropping Lucy Bear on the grass beside her. "Really?"

Lloyd, rising to his feet and resting his hands in his scruffy old denim jeans' pockets. He nodded with a self-assured grin. "Of course," he replied, his chest noticeably swelling with pride.

Barend then turned to the Reverend, his tone softening at once, signaling his reverence for Vuyo. "And this man..." he continued, "This one is as strong as a bear. He's faced ten men in battle and even survived a crocodile."

He lifted Vuyo's shirt to reveal a jagged scar running along his side. "A true cowboy, you see," Barend added with a nod, awaiting Katelyn's reaction to his praise for his accomplices.

Katelyn, overwhelmed, instinctively closed her eyes, her young mind trying to grasp the reality of these men. Barend winked at the Reverend, who chuckled with a raspy voice and took a sip of his coffee.

Lloyd broke the moment with practicality. "Well... Time to hit the road, then. Shall we?"

He walked over to Katelyn, handing her a police badge, speaking with gravity. "You're one of us now, young lass...An undercover. Top secret!"

He placed a finger to his lips in a gesture of secrecy. Katelyn nodded solemnly, concealing the badge Lloyd had given her.

Lloyd stretched out his hand to Katelyn, intending to guide her towards the waiting car. Reluctant at first, she secured Lucy Bear under her other arm, but then agreed to take his hand. Meanwhile, Barend and Vuyo heaved and sweated, eager to finish loading the remaining weapons into the vehicle.

Vuyo, his voice tinged with incredulity, voiced his concern. "A little girl? Are you sure about this, Barend? I get it... that it could be an advantage, but..."

Barend interrupted firmly, his resolve unwavering. "It'll buy us time, trust me. The police won't shoot at her, and I'll ensure she comes to no harm. I promise."

Vuyo, adopting a sarcastic tone, quipped back. "So you just asked this random cute girl nicely to come along? Offered her sweets, maybe? Or how else did you get that right" he probed, almost erupting with a mocking laugh.

Barend's reply was swift and resolute. "She's my daughter," he stated firmly. "And she came of her own free will. Nobody forced her to…"

Vuyo sensing the sensitivity of the matter suddenly hesitated, considering his words carefully. "And her mother… I mean no offense, but you don't exactly strike me as the fatherly type…"

Barend's expression softened briefly, as he sighed within, a flicker of emotion crossing his face. But he said nothing more, the weight of their situation pressing upon them as they prepared to embark on their dangerous journey.

Barend stood amidst the quiet half-misty morning, his mind churning with thoughts that defied his own principles. "Now there were two things that I vowed to myself I would avoid like the black plague… pets and children. And here I am, betraying my own first rule," he muttered to himself, frustration etched on his face. "Maybe you're right," he addressed Vuyo, his voice tinged with resignation. "But I can't just leave her there. Her mother won't be out of rehab for months, and who knows what she'll get into next? Katelyn could end up in another one of those lost children's homes."

Vuyo kindly nodded in understanding, a rare gesture of empathy between them. "So you do have a heart…" he remarked softly.

Barend's response was curt, his resolve returning swiftly. "Hey, don't push it, buddy… We stick to the plan, ne? Let's just get to the border. If we execute this perfectly, we'll be across in three, maybe five days max."

Turning towards the waiting van, Barend formulated the next steps. "We'll use the black food crates and some hay to cover everything up. Make it look like a farmer transporting goods."

Lloyd, ever the optimist, stood nearer as he overheard the conversation, grinning broadly. "Fruits of gold, baby. Fruits of gold."

With that, they set to work, their movements swift and purposeful as they prepared for the journey ahead. It was surely fraught with danger, yet driven by the hope of a new beginning beyond the border.

We embarked on our dangerous journey, a ragtag band of three fugitives and a young girl bound for Mozambique, navigating the arid expanses of the Great Karoo, skirting past Plettenberg Bay, Grahamstown, and the Transkei on our relentless trek towards the Mozambique border. Our strategy was simple yet fraught with risk... never linger in one place too long, leaving behind no trace but the dust kicked up by our hurried steps.

The Karoo stretched out before us, a vast, monotonous desertscape that offered little refuge but rather served as a constant reminder of how exposed we were. Nights were no easier. The chill crept into our bones as we huddled in the stolen car on items of clothing that served as a form of a mattress. Katelyn and I would hold each other to try and keep warm, half-covered by a thin, small excuse of a blanket. The blinding copper sunbeams at dawn would wake us up to our rude reality, along with the crispness of the air. There was no time to sleep late, as it posed too much of a risk. Each passing day pushed us further from civilization and from safety.

Fuel was our lifeline, stolen under the cover of darkness or brazenly siphoned from unsuspecting vehicles left unguarded. Lloyd, with his knack for handling petrol, became our unlikely fuel commander, swiftly transferring the precious liquid to sustain our escape.

He worked with a precision that defied his otherwise laid-back demeanor, wielding the siphon like an artist with a paintbrush. We learned to move like shadows, silent and deliberate, snatching what we needed and vanishing into the distance.

Yet amid the adrenaline-fueled heists and the rush to outpace the law, the reality of our situation settled heavily. We were fugitives, burdened not only with our own survival but with the care of little Katelyn who was thrust into our dangerous escapade.

Every glance at her pale, innocent face tightened the noose of guilt around my neck. She didn't choose this life, yet here she was, caught in the maelstrom of our choices.

"Daddy, I'm hungry," Katelyn's high-pitched voice cut through the tense silence in the car, her small frame swaying as exhaustion crept in.

"We're almost there, my girl… just two more hours," I replied, trying to keep my voice calm and my eyes on the winding road ahead.

"But Daddy, I really need to eat. My teacher said I have low blood sugar," she pleaded, her voice tinged with desperation.

"Low what?" I scoffed, the concept foreign and almost absurd amidst the chaos of our situation.

"Blood sugar," she repeated, her voice trembling now. "Please, Daddy, I'm so hungry... my tummy is sore."

Her words hit me hard, her little voice piercing through the cloud of my frustration and concern. My knuckles whitened on the steering wheel. Finally, at the sight of a roadside café I spotted a *Padstal*, its neon sign glowing faintly like a beacon, and I veered off sharply.

Padstals, scattered across South Africa, were havens for weary travelers. This one looked modest but welcoming, with shelves likely stocked with essentials. It would have to do.

As we got out of the car, I grabbed Katelyn's hand firmly before she could run ahead. As we entered the shop and the automatic doors closed behind her, She came to a sudden halt. Her eyes widened as she took in the colorful display and comforting aromas inside. Sweets, snacks, and toys lined the shelves, beckoning to her like treasures. I sighed and nudged her gently toward the correct aisles.

"Food, Katelyn. Stick to what we need," I said, scanning for affordable options. Bread and cheese would have to be enough.

She followed reluctantly, but her attention drifted back to a rack of toys. A blue pony with colourful hair caught her eye. I hesitated, then decided I would invest in a small indulgence to keep her spirits up, dependant on the money I could get.

The shopkeeper, an elderly man with a weathered face neatly dressed in a grey jersey and a maroon poor-boy cap, glanced up from the counter and greeted respectfully as we approached. His sharp eyes fell on my watch, a silver piece that had been my lifeline in too many scrapes.

"Nice watch you've got there," he remarked casually, his voice gruff but curious. "Real silver, I reckon?"

I hesitated, spinning a story in my head. "This watch belonged to my great-grandfather," I began. "He was a paratrooper in the Second World War. The president himself gave him this for his bravery in Operation Desert Fox."

The tale was pure fabrication, but it sounded believable enough. The shopkeeper tilted his head, a hint of skepticism mixed with intrigue. He leaned forward. "R1000," he offered. "That's all I can give."

For a moment, I thought about refusing, but Katelyn's hungry, hopeful face appeared in my mind, without me needing to look back at her. With a heavy sigh, I unclasped the watch and placed it on the counter before him. The shopkeeper inspected it, then nodded approvingly as he handed me the cash.

With the money in hand, I felt a sense of relief as I stocked up on bread, cheese, and a few other essentials. Katelyn clung to the box with the pony, her eyes sparkling with rare excitement as I nonchalantly handed it to her. "Thank you, Daddy," she whispered, as she at the sealed box, hardly containing her excitement. The sight of her beaming from ear to ear was imprinted in my memory. Suddenly I realized nothing mattered more than keeping her safe and happy, and I would do whatever it took.

We left the shop, walking toward the car. I realized Katelyn had stopped by the curb. I turned back, irritation flickering across my face. "And now?"

She held out her hand, looking up at me solemnly. "I can't cross the road without holding hands. Mom said so."

I muttered under my breath, "Your mommy said many things." But I reached out, taking her small hand in mine. Together, we crossed the road and then Lloyd helped me to load our supplies into the back of the car.

Lloyd observed with curiosity, asking, "Should we dig in?"

Barend shook his head, a knowing smile playing on his lips. "You sure?" Lloyd pressed, gesturing to the array of items now packed in the car.

Barend chuckled, replying with a hint of pride, "Of course. If we pack it with fruit boxes, might as well have some fruits now, right?"

Lloyd raised an eyebrow in disbelief. "But how did you manage to..." he started, trailing off as Barend cut in smoothly, "Let's just say I have a way with words."

Meanwhile, Katelyn sat at the back of the van, tenderly combing her little pony's colorful hair, lost in her own world. Vuyo started the car, the engine roaring to life as they prepared to resume their journey towards Mozambique.

Barend, got in the back of the van with her and made himself as comfortable as possible amongst all the loot in the back. Seeking a moment's respite, he lit up a cigarette. In a swift and unexpected move, Katelyn snatched it from his mouth and threw it out of the open window, scowling at him disapprovingly. "*Sies papa... dit stink,*" (Sis Daddy... that smells) she chided in Afrikaans, her expression filled with disappointment.

Barend, irritated yet determined, reached towards his pocket for another cigarette, but Vuyo's disapproving shake of the head halted him. Sighing, Barend leaned back in his makeshift seat of clothes and bags, reflecting on the strange dichotomy of their current predicament - fleeing from the law yet finding solace in the simple moments shared with his daughter amidst the chaos.

Tuning the radio, we first listened to some Rugby - a sport of immense significance to most Afrikaans men. Rugby was so revered that in 1902, there was even a temporary ceasefire during the Second Boer War to allow a match between British and Boer forces. Now, South Africa's Springboks were playing against The Cavaliers from New Zealand in a crucial rugby match. Despite sanctions related to Apartheid policies, this match was a rare international contest.

"The commentator's voice crackled through the airwaves, Naas Botha with a penalty kick!" exclaimed the voice over the radio. "It puts the Springboks right on the attack. You can hear the crowd in the background shouting, encouraging the Springboks. Naas Botha lines it up... there's the kick for the corner... they're chasing for it. Who will reach it first... aaand ... it's a try!"

Katelyn and Barend, now having swopped places with Vuyo and Lloyd, sat in the front, as Barend drove ahead, fatigued yet determined. Bored by the commentary, she turned the radio dial until she found a children's program. Barend glanced at her disapprovingly and quickly switched the radio back to the rugby game.

"Commentator: Danie Gerber running with the ball... Danie Gerber is going to cut inside... he passes the ball to..." The commentator's voice continued to ramble on.

Suddenly, Barend noticed Katelyn reaching for the dial again. Frustration crept into his voice as he interrupted, "First my cigarette, now the radio... cut it out now! You've got your doll. Play with it."

Her face showed clear displeasure as she climbed over to sit in the back with Lloyd and Vuyo. I glanced at the rearview mirror and caught Lloyd raising his eyebrows. Determined to diffuse the tension, I turned the radio back to the rugby match.

We were traversing through the rolling hills of the Karoo, passing by lands dotted with sheep and game farms, under the watchful gaze of multi-layered mountains that almost seemed to touch the indigo sky. The silence enveloped us, broken only by the faint rustling of Karoo bushes. The three in the backseat soon drifted off to sleep, leaving me alone with my thoughts and the road stretching endlessly ahead. It felt like I was driving a taxi.

Eventually, I pulled the car over to a roadside stop. There wasn't much there besides a small round concrete table and a thornbush tree. The road extended into the distance, disappearing into the horizon. It seemed as good a place as any to take a break.

Katelyn stirred awake, rubbing her eyes and yawning. "Where are we, Daddy?"

"On the way to Mozambique, Katelyn," I replied. "Do you know where that is?"

Katelyn shook her head, her curiosity piqued.

"It's very, very far," Lloyd chimed in, stretching and groaning as he climbed out of the car, his bones cracking audibly.

While enjoying slices of a long French loaf with polony and mayonnaise, Katelyn noticed something slowly approaching. She quickly bent down, placing a piece of polony on the ground. The little dog remained cautious, hiding behind a dustbin, but as Katelyn turned around, it couldn't resist and slowly crept closer. Soon, it was nibbling the polony from her hand, licking her fingers and wagging its tail with excitement.

Katelyn's face lit up with delight as she ran around, the little dog following closely behind. It was clearly a street dog, unkempt and in need of care, but to Katelyn, that didn't matter at all. She had found a friend.

"Daddy, can I keep him?" Katelyn asked eagerly, looking up at Barend with hopeful eyes.

"Pleeeeaaaase, Daddy?", she nagged at his lack of immediate response.

Barend looked at Katelyn and coughed as he swallowed his coffee, his expression stern. He turned away from Katelyn holding the little dog and answered coldly, "No. It's time to pack up and go, get to the car."

"But daddy, we can't just leave Tessa here," Katelyn pleaded, standing as still as a statue, while the dog wiggled excitedly in her arms.

"Tessa?" Barend asked, slightly bemused. "The puppy, daddy..." Katelyn clarified.

"Of course you can. We found him here, and he was perfectly fine," Barend replied firmly.

"But daddy, please, please, please," Katelyn persisted, her voice tinged with desperation.

"Over my dead body," Barend replied seriously, his tone leaving no room for argument.

Katelyn sank down to the floor like a ragdoll, upset by her father's resolute refusal. Lloyd and Vuyo walked towards the car, their conversation interrupted by Lloyd's laughter. "She's got you around her finger now, I see," Lloyd chuckled loudly, taking a bite from his slice of bread. Barend intercepted the bread from Lloyd with a wry smile. "Nothing some polony can't fix."

Barend then enticed the dog with the enticing smell of polony. As the dog approached, Barend tossed the food into the distance, and the dog eagerly chased after it.

"Time to go," Barend declared, lifting Katelyn into his arms and draping her over his shoulder.

"Nooo daddy... I don't want to... let me go!" Katelyn's protests echoed through the quiet countryside as Barend lifted her over his shoulder, her small fists pounding against his back.

Approaching the car, Barend suddenly jerked around, feeling the sharp teeth of the little street dog sink into his ankle. With a muffled curse, he swiftly kicked the dog away, eliciting a low growl from the injured animal.

"You know what they say about street dogs..." Vuyo's voice carried a hint of dark humor.

"And what might that be? Stay away from them, I presume?" Barend retorted with a look of disgust, still eyeing the dog warily.

"No... if they bite you, you need to keep them around... to see if they have any terrible disease or even worse, rabies. If they die within a few days, well, let's just say you've got it coming; if they live, then you're lucky," Vuyo explained nonchalantly, a grin playing on his lips.

"Hogwash... complete nonsense," Barend scoffed as he climbed into the car and started the engine, casting one last glance at the persistent street dog.

"Just remember I did warn you," Vuyo added with a smirk, settling smugly into his seat.

And so, amidst the odd humor and lingering suspense of the moment, the gang of three criminals and one girl grew by an unexpected member... Tessa, the street dog.

Despite the unusual circumstances, Katelyn's face lit up with joy at this unexpected turn of events, while Barend couldn't help but shake his head with a bemused smile as they drove off into the unknown Karoo landscape.

A Holiday
Home

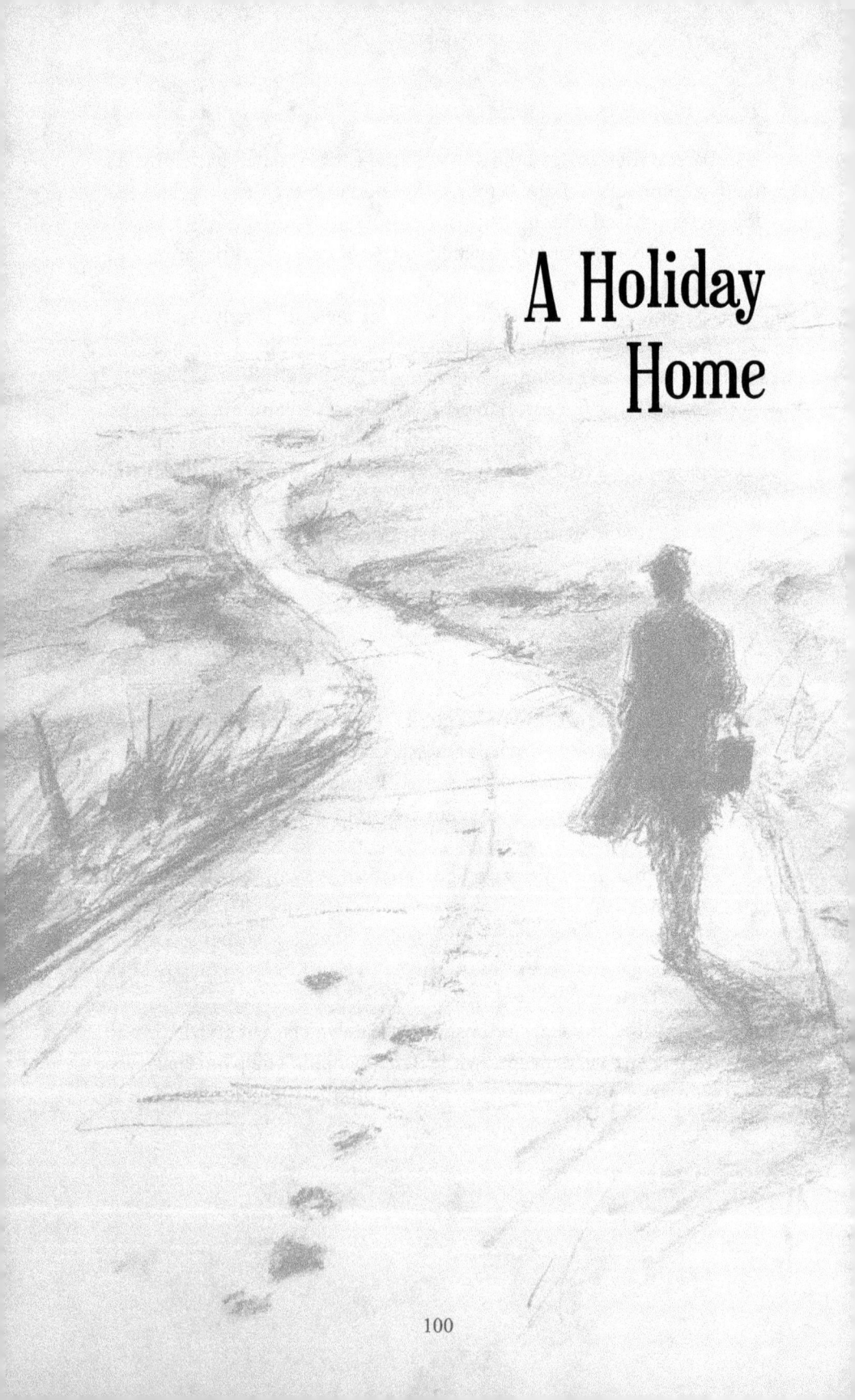

A s criminals on the move, Jeffrey's Bay offered a tempting array of vacant high-end holiday houses. The majority of them were luxurious properties left unattended for most of the year by wealthy owners who indulged in occasional visits. Driving towards the lake, our eyes caught sight of a pristine white double-storey wooden house, a quaint replica of the American dream nestled amidst its own spacious plot. Barend parked the car discreetly down the road, our gaze fixed on the secluded holiday retreat.

Barend circled the property a few times cautiously, his steps silently treading on the gravel path, scanning for any possible signs of occupancy. With practiced precision, he retrieved an old wire from his pocket and expertly manipulated it to unlock the back door. The latch yielded reluctantly with a soft click, allowing us quiet entry into the silent sanctuary of someone else's seasonal escape.

Moments later, the garage door rumbled open, revealing Barend with a satisfied smile. Lloyd maneuvered the car inside with precision before closing the garage door behind us. Katelyn, exhausted from the day's events, had already fallen into a deep sleep on the backseat. Barend carefully lifted her limp form into his arms and ascended the marble staircase, marveling at the opulence that spoke of excessive wealth - open spaces, minimal furnishings aside from the granite countertops, sparkling chandeliers, and floors polished to a sheen. It seemed inconceivable that such a place could remain vacant for most of the year.

As Barend settled Katelyn into a plush double bed in the first room he found upstairs, the young girl stirred, her discomfort apparent even in her sleep. Just as he was about to leave, she called out softly.

Katelyn: Daddy...

Barend paused in his tracks, his concern evident.

Barend: Yes, Katie?

Katelyn: It hurts, Daddy....

Barend knelt beside her, his brow furrowed with worry.

Barend: What do you mean? Where does it hurt, sweetheart?

Katelyn winced, placing her hand over her side.

Katelyn: Here...

Barend: Okay, let me get you some water, alright?

Katelyn's voice trembled.

Katelyn: But I want a doctor, Daddy...

Barend hesitated, trying to reassure her.

Barend: It's late, Katelyn. The doctors are probably asleep now. It's probably just from all the driving today. I'll get you some water, okay?

Katelyn shook her head, tears welling up.

Meanwhile, Lloyd's voice broke the tension from the doorway.

Lloyd: What have you done now?

Barend's frustration spilled over.

Barend: I DON'T KNOW, OKAY! I DON'T KNOW! Ice cream, then ponies, and now I'm supposed to play doctor too...

Katelyn turned away, apparently on the verge of tears, clearly hurt by Barend's words. Lloyd intervened with his usual charm, pulling silly faces to ease her distress. Barend, feeling helpless, stormed out of the room in search of pain relief, rummaging through cabinets in a desperate attempt to find some pain pills.

He then decided to take a stroll through the quiet streets as darkness settled over the town. There were no cars, no pedestrians... just an unsettling tranquility that put him on edge. Wearing a pair of sunglasses, previously stolen at the Padstal, he slipped into the local quick stop, his eyes scanning the mundane aisles until they caught on something chilling: wanted posters, one bearing an uncanny resemblance to Vuyo and Lloyd. He grabbed the Panados and hurried out, wary of attracting attention.

On his return, a sense of being followed prickled at the back of his neck. Footsteps echoed softly behind him, barely audible yet unmistakable in the stillness. A security guard's black vehicle crept along the road, closing in steadily.

"Good evening, officer," Barend feigned a smile and greeted cautiously while pulling up his sunglasses into his hair, so as to portray a facade of transparency.

The security guard rolled down his window, eyes narrowing suspiciously.

"Evening. Where are you headed?" the guard inquired.

Barend's hand hovered near his concealed firearm, a precaution against unseen threats.

"Just needed some pain relief for my daughter," Barend replied calmly. "You know how it is. Thought a walk might clear my head. We're staying nearby for the night."

The guard scrutinized him for a tense moment, then nodded curtly and drove off. Barend let out a slow breath as his head hanged low, the tension in his shoulders easing slightly. The night seemed darker now, shadows elongated and ominous. He hastened his steps back to the holiday home, every sense acutely alert to potential danger lurking in the darkness.

As Barend strolled back toward the holiday home, relief washed over him as the security guard moved on without incident. The night seemed to stretch on, quiet and ominous, but he pushed the unease aside. As he stepped through the back door, the faint strains of music and the acrid scent of burning filled the air, instantly alerting him.

He hurried into the kitchen to find Katelyn, Vuyo, and Lloyd huddled around the stove, each seemingly engrossed in their culinary endeavors.

"What in blazes are you three up to?" Barend exclaimed, taking in the chaotic scene. Pots simmered dangerously on the stove, emitting occasional pops and hisses.

Katelyn turned with a wide grin. "Daddy, we wanted to surprise you with dinner!"

Barend's eyebrows shot up. "Surprise me? Looks like you're trying to burn the house down!"

Vuyo, always quick with a retort, chuckled nervously. "We're just... experimenting. You know, bonding over a hot stove."

Lloyd, wiping sweat from his brow, added, "It's not as easy as it looks."

Barend surveyed the array of interesting ingredients scattered across the counter—some recognizable, others not so much. There were a few cloves of garlic, along with several powders and spices, what looked like a piece of half-defrosted chicken, a handful of potatoes and a bunch of other sauces. Raising his eyebrows he remarked, "Well, I hope this doesn't end with us ordering takeout."

Katelyn tugged at Barend's sleeve. "Daddy, you have to taste the sauce we made!"

Barend slowly walked nearer and glanced skeptically at the bubbling concoction in the pot. "Alright, but let's hope I survive it."

He dipped a spoon into the sauce, took a cautious sip, and tried not to grimace at the unexpected blend of flavors. "Well, it's... certainly a mix of creativity..." He tried to conceal his need to cough, as the chilli flavours were coming through strongly.

The kitchen erupted in laughter as they all shared in the absurdity of the moment. Despite the chaos and the earlier tension, Barend couldn't help but smile at the sight of his makeshift family, bonding over an impromptu cooking adventure.

In the dimly lit dining room of the expansive holiday home, the air was thick with the aroma of an eclectic dinner concocted by Katelyn and her makeshift family. Lloyd, with a bottle of fine whiskey in hand, sauntered into the lounge area, his expression one of contentment mingled with a hint of mischief.

"Quite a collection," he remarked with a grunt, running his fingers along the bottles on display. "One day, I'll have my own room filled with drinks like these."

Barend's voice cut through the moment, firm and commanding. "Reason to celebrate, I presume. Remember... we have to leave early in the morning... not negotiable..."

Lloyd shrugged nonchalantly, a devil-may-care grin on his face as he took a swig of whiskey straight from the bottle. "One night is all I'll need." he mumbled and walked back to the kitchen, avoiding further conversation around the subject.

Meanwhile, Katelyn, wearing an oversized red and white checkered apron that nearly swallowed her petite frame, proudly announced her culinary feat.

"I cooked you some yummy food, Daddy," she beamed, her eyes sparkling with anticipation.

Barend's smile was warm but tinged with apprehension as he took his seat at the head of the table. "Sit down now," he instructed gently, "that's your place there."

Vuyo, ever the mediator, took Katelyn's hands in his own, and she, in turn, reached for Lloyd's. With closed eyes and a solemn expression, Katelyn began their prayer.

"He who parted the heavens and gave life," Vuyo intoned, his voice steady and deep. "We thank you for this day, for this meal."

Katelyn's eyes flickered open, catching Lloyd's gaze fixed upon her, his eyes inadvertently betraying a hint of defiance. She frowned, perturbed by his lack of compliance. Sensing her discomfort, Barend tightened his grip on Lloyd's hand, silently urging him to follow suit and close his eyes.

"Close them," Barend commanded softly yet firmly.

Lloyd complied, shutting his eyes as Barend's voice resonated with solemnity through the room.

"My God, you turn our darkness into light," Barend intoned reverently, pulling from a resource, a Psalm etched in his memory long ago. "Your way is perfect, flawless. You shield those who take refuge in You. You arm us with strength. Your right hand sustains us."

"Amen," Katelyn responded quietly, her voice earnest and respectful.

Barend shifted uneasily, his gaze wandering around the opulent dining room, unsettled by the unexpected prayer.

"Eat up now," Barend redirected, attempting to lighten the solemn mood. "Food's ready, before it gets cold now..."

"Why don't you have some first, little Kate," he suggested gently, trying to coax her into eating.

Katelyn pretended to feed her toy pony, reassuringly declaring, "I'm okay, Daddy. See, little pony loves it too."

Barend glanced around the room, discomfort evident in his demeanor. Vuyo chuckled softly to himself, a subtle sound that filled the air with a touch of camaraderie amidst the lingering tension.

Barend delicately speared a small piece of food with his fork and cautiously brought it to his lips, masking his apprehension with a gentle smile. Katelyn watched him intently, waiting for his reaction. The dish, heavily seasoned with chilli salt and slightly burnt, offered a challenge to his palate.

As Lloyd reached for another sip of brandy, Barend swiftly intercepted the bottle, taking a large gulp to wash down the robust flavors of Katelyn's creation.

"That's... that's great," Barend managed, almost coughing his voice masking the taste with gratitude. "Thank you, Katelyn. Now, if you take these pills, you'll feel even better." he deflected from the conversation about the food, so as to avoid exposing his aversion toward it.

"I'm okay now, Daddy," Katelyn assured, her concern for her father evident in her voice. "The pain comes and goes sometimes."

"Eat up," she insisted, pushing past her own discomfort. "We shouldn't waste any food."

Barend exchanged a glance with Vuyo, who shrugged in response, trying to control his laughter. Lloyd and Vuyo obediently took spoonfuls, their expressions neutral as they sampled the meal before them.

Out of the corner of his eye, Barend noticed little Tessa, the street dog they had taken in, standing there with a wagging tail, eagerly eyeing the food. His authoritative look in her direction, made the dog yield, sitting still and yet eagerly awaiting a bite. With a quick motion, Barend scooped up a generous portion on his fork, ostensibly taking a bite but discreetly dropping it to the floor for Tessa to devour. Katelyn beamed with delight, turning back to the stove.

Tessa bounded over, tail wagging furiously, and happily gobbled up the offering. Barend rose from the table, the scrape of his wooden chair causing everyone to look up momentarily. He glanced at Lloyd and Vuyo who continued to eat cautiously, dipping some bread in the mixture every now and again.

"Now eat up, gents," Barend encouraged them with a mocking smile, patting them both on the shoulder before standing. Katelyn smiled warmly at the small group gathered around the table, her blue eyes bright with relief and affection.

Though the thick curtains shielded them from the outside world, their neighbors that go on their daily walks with dogs of various breeds, had begun to notice the unlikely group dwelling together under one roof. This was a sight that was not only frowned upon but also deemed illegal.

As night settled in and the household slept, Barend stirred awake to the sudden flickering blue lights outside. Carefully, he rose from his bed, mindful not to attract attention, and approached the window. A security van idled nearby, its blue lights casting an eerie glow as two officers looked at one another, then at the house, approaching it with purposeful steps.

The knot in Barend's stomach was apparent, but he acted quickly. He woke Vuyo with a gentle tap, then a shake, urgency in his voice. "Time to split. They must have spotted us somehow. Lloyd, it's time to go. The authorities are closing in." His words were terse, conveying the gravity of the situation.

Barend lifted Katelyn gently, her small form cradled in his arms like a fragile rag doll. She stirred slightly, her eyes fluttering open in the dim moonlight. He silenced her with a finger to his lips, a hushed "shhh" that conveyed urgency without fear. With practiced ease, he settled her into the back of the car, her sleepy gaze questioning.

Once Katelyn was safely inside, Barend retrieved his rifle, the weight of it reassuring in his grip. He turned to Lloyd, the urgency clear in his eyes. "We need a diversion," Barend said quietly, his voice low but firm. "Think you can keep them distracted for a while?"

Lloyd's response was immediate, laced with a hint of skepticism. "You're kidding me right?"

Barend met Lloyd's sweaty, nervous gaze without a hint of amusement. "You can hotbox, start a car?"

Lloyd smirked, a wry grin spreading across his face. "Of course... for a bottle of Jack, a man will do wonders now."

Barend's smile was brief and tight. "Go on now."

Lloyd slipped out the back door, moving stealthily through the shadows, blending into the night. He approached the security vehicle parked nearby, an unexpected gift left open with keys dangling in the ignition... a thief's dream. With deft hands, Lloyd started the car, the engine roaring to life with an eager growl that shattered the stillness.

The sound of squealing tires filled the air as Lloyd peeled away, the sudden noise alerting the security guards who were quick to react. They gave chase, their footsteps pounding after the fleeing vehicle. Lights flickered on in neighboring houses, curious eyes peering through blinds out into the commotion unfolding in their quiet street.

Meanwhile, Barend wasted no time. Arming himself with strength, he swung open the garage door and hit the accelerator, the car roaring to life under his command. The engine's deafening roar echoed through the night as Barend navigated through the winding streets, adrenaline pumping through his veins.

In the distance, Lloyd's luck ran thin. The quiet pursuit turned into a frenzied chase as police cars, with sirens blaring, joined the pursuit. Red and blue lights painted the night as the police closed in, their demands crackling over loudspeakers.

"Pull over the car now, or we will shoot," the authoritative voice warned.

Lloyd's response was swift and risky. He yanked the handbrake, the car spinning wildly as police vehicles surged past in pursuit. Dust and gravel flew as the cars maneuvered through the narrow, congested streets, the chase intensifying with each heartbeat.

It was a gamble, a daring bid for freedom in the face of mounting odds. And as the chase continued to unfold under the cloak of darkness, the stakes only grew higher for Barend and his crew.

Barend, Vuyo, and Katelyn waited in tense silence outside of town, the appointed meeting place shrouded in darkness. An hour had passed since they watched Lloyd disappear into the night with the police hot on his tail. Anxiety hung heavy in the air, each passing minute adding weight to their worries.

"We can't stay much longer," Barend muttered, his voice low but urgent. "It won't take them long to break Lloyd and find out where we are."

"10 more minutes," Vuyo replied, his gaze flickering between the shadows and the road ahead. "We need to give him a chance."

Barend cocked his gun with a determined click. "10 max. We can't afford to take chances. If they trace us here, they won't come in peace...", he said sternly

A sudden crack of a stick behind them shattered the silence, followed by Tessa's sharp high-pitched bark. Barend reacted swiftly, moving into the cover of the bushes with calculated speed. The approaching figure was obscured by darkness, but its rapid approach suggested urgency or danger.

Without hesitation, Barend lunged forward, his trained instincts taking over. He seized the man by the neck and threw him forcefully to the ground, the impact knocking the wind out of him. In the dim moonlight, Barend could see the man struggling beneath him, retaliating with a desperate punch of a scrawny arm that caught Barend square in the face.

Vuyo rushed in, pulling Barend off the man before things escalated further. Barend maintained his hold, keeping the man pinned to the ground with a firm grip, then planting his foot upon his back. It was then that the features of their unexpected visitor became clear as daylight. It was Lloyd… battered and swearing vehemently, spitting out sand and frustration.

"You could have warned us, you idiot!," Barend growled, his voice a mix of relief and reproach. "Told us it was you, at least made some kind of signal."

Lloyd pushed himself up slowly, rubbing his jaw, then his back and glaring up at Barend through gritted teeth. "Damn it, Barend," he muttered hoarsely, dusting himself off. "I was running for my life, last thing I would think of is giving you some stupid signal."

Barend released him with a sigh, tension easing from his shoulders. "We don't have time for mistakes like this," he cautioned, glancing around warily. "Let's move along. We need to regroup and figure out our next move before they catch up."

Lloyd nodded grimly, the gravity of their situation settling over them like a heavy cloak. As they retreated into the cover of darkness, the sound of approaching sirens in the distance reminded them that their window of escape was rapidly closing.

Katelyn's laughter rang out, a brief respite in the tension that had gripped them all. "Silly billies," she teased, her little voice light and merry despite the gravity of their situation.

Lloyd glanced around with a weary smile, grateful for Katelyn's cheerfulness. "At least someone is glad to see me," he remarked, moving closer to her to give an awkward side-hug. "Did you see me drive away with the car…? I was as fast as lightning!"

Katelyn shook her head, her expression apologetic. "Really, you mean I missed all that?"

"I'm sorry, I was sleepy," Katelyn explained, her voice tinged with regret.

Lloyd chuckled softly. "That's alright now. There's always next time."

Barend frowned and interjected with a solemn tone, his gaze focused on the road ahead. "Hopefully, there won't be a next time. We need to find another way. It won't be long before they start spreading their search wider. We were fortunate they had very little to go on except for descriptions from the bank robbery."

The seriousness of Barend's words settled over them like a thick, heavy shroud. They were fugitives now, hunted by both the law and their own mistakes. The night air carried a certain chill that matched the anxiety in their hearts as they contemplated their next move, knowing that each decision could either lead them closer to safety or deeper into danger.

Through the silent expanse of the night, their disguised car crawled forward amidst a snarl of halted vehicles, the result of an unseen calamity further up the road. Barend peered ahead, the kaleidoscope of police lights swirling in the distance, casting an ominous glow against the night sky. The mere sight of law enforcement stirred a latent unease within him, a caution born of years spent navigating the murky waters of survival.

"We'll need to get a closer look," Barend murmured, his voice tight with concern as he assessed the scene unfolding ahead of them. The cars inched forward at a glacial pace, the occupants of each scrutinized by beams of light from vigilant police officers. Any sudden movement could spell trouble, and that was a risk they couldn't afford to take.

Katelyn, snugly nestled between jackets in the front seat, slept peacefully, oblivious to the tension thickening around her. Barend motioned urgently to Lloyd and Vuyo, gesturing for them to hunker down in the back seats. The faint clinking of bottles betrayed Lloyd's impulsive decision to pilfer "souvenirs" along their journey, a move that drew a disapproving shake of Barend's head.

As their car slowly drew nearer to the blockade, Barend's pulse quickened with fear. It wasn't standard procedure; this was no routine traffic stop. Special forces officers, heavily armed and meticulously thorough, stood sentinel beyond the blockade. In their heightened state of alertness, the slightest misstep could lead to catastrophe.

"Fellars, we can't turn back now," Barend muttered tersely, eyeing the officers' meticulous scrutiny of passing vehicles. "They're looking for us … three men, different races, traveling together. But with Katelyn…"

He glanced at his daughter, a beacon of innocence in the front seat, her slumber a stark contrast to the perilous situation unfolding around them.

"Stay low," Barend instructed in a low voice, his eyes flickering to Lloyd and Vuyo in the rearview mirror. "And for God's sake, just keep quiet."

The air hung heavy with anticipation as their car crept forward, each second ticking by fraught with the looming threat of discovery. The night held its breath, waiting to see if their carefully crafted ruse would hold under the unforgiving scrutiny of those searching eyes.

As the line of halted cars inched forward, Barend's heart sank deeper into his chest, a feeling of cold sweat rising through his veins. The police blockade loomed larger with every passing moment, revealing not just the standard issue officers, but a specialized unit, armed to the teeth and alert to every movement. Their weapons gleamed under the harsh glare of floodlights, casting long shadows across the road.

Barend's knuckles whitened on the steering wheel as he caught sight of the armored vehicles and the stern-faced officers beyond. This was no ordinary roadblock; this was a fortress bristling with intent. The mere thought of engaging with such a force sent shivers down his spine.

Behind him, Vuyo's voice broke the tense silence, a prayer whispered on the edge of desperation. "Our father who art in heaven, deliver us in our time of need."

Those words hung in the air, a plea mingling with the hum of engines and the distant murmur of officers coordinating their positions. It was a prayer laden with the weight of imminent danger, a lifeline cast into the uncertain night.

Barend's jaw tightened as he nodded solemnly, acknowledging the gravity of their predicament. His mind raced, calculating their next move amid the mounting pressure. Survival hinged on their ability to evade detection, to slip through the fingers of those who would see them captured.

The seconds stretched into eternity as they inched closer to the blockade, each passing moment heightening the peril. The quiet resolve of Vuyo's prayer echoed in Barend's thoughts, a beacon of hope amidst the encroaching darkness. They were warriors in a battle for their freedom, against odds stacked high and justice closing in.

The officer's approach to the car sent another chill down Barend's spine, along with a hollow feeling in his stomach. His hand trembled imperceptibly as he handed over the forged driver's license he had carried for years, under the alias Johan Du Plessis.

"Identity, please," the officer demanded with a strict tone, scrutinizing the document under the beam of his flashlight. "Johan Du Plessis, huh? What's in your van?"

In the back of the van, Vuyo and Lloyd lay low in a tense atmosphere, their fingers poised on triggers pointed at the officer's head. Their silence was thick with the unspoken threat of pending violence.

"We're just transporting supplies to our farm near Kruger," Barend replied calmly, his voice steady despite the adrenaline coursing through his veins. The officer's flashlight swept into the van, illuminating Katelyn sitting beside Barend. Her eyes fluttered open, weariness etched on her young face.

"She's exhausted. Lost her mother a few days ago," Barend explained softly, hoping to appeal to the officer's empathy. "It's a tremendous loss. Hard for a man to manage alone, raising children and all."

"Difficult to explain to a child," the officer murmured, his tone softened by understanding. The flashlight lingered on Katelyn for a few seconds that felt like an eternity to Barend, before he withdrew it. The tension in the air eased slightly, though the standoff remained palpable.

The night felt like the longest one ever, the weight of their circumstances pressing in from all sides. Barend's heart pounded almost audibly in his chest as he awaited the officer's next move, praying silently that their fabricated story would hold under scrutiny. They were poised on the knife's edge, balancing between escape and capture, their fate hanging on a precarious thread of deception and luck.

"Just a routine check, you'll be out of here in a minute," the officer reassured them, his tone measured but his eyes probing as he aimed his flashlight into the van. Tessa's bark punctuated the air, a nervous response to the tension mounting inside the vehicle.

Barend sat rigidly, his heart hammering against his chest as he watched the officer inspect the covered boxes and supplies scattered within. Buckets, mops, and various food provisions lay in disarray, their mundane appearance a stark contrast to the gravity of the situation unfolding.

"Uh…What are you looking for, officer? Maybe we can be of assistance?" Barend's voice was strong and steady, a mask over his inner turmoil. His mind raced, calculating their odds of slipping past this unforeseen blockade unscathed.

The officer's response shattered any hope of an easy escape. "There's been a bank robbery. We're searching for these three men." He held up sketches, his gaze flicking between the faces of Lloyd and Vuyo, marked with a certainty that chilled Barend to the bone. The third sketch, depicting Barend with his distinctive moustache, was less defined, its details murky and open to interpretation.

Barend's breath caught in his throat as he feigned composure, flipping through the pages slowly, his eyes fixated on the images. The seconds stretched into eternity as he weighed his next move, every nerve on edge.

"Mmm, we really haven't seen anyone resembling these men," Barend finally replied, his voice calm but his thoughts racing. He met the officer's gaze directly, willing himself to appear cooperative and innocent, concealing the turmoil roiling beneath the surface.

The tension in the van thickened, each passing moment intensifying the precariousness of their situation. The officer's scrutiny lingered, his suspicion palpable in the air. Barend held his breath, silently praying that their carefully constructed facade would withstand the scrutiny of law enforcement, even as their chances of slipping past this checkpoint unscathed dwindled with each passing second.

"I know that man," Katelyn pointed decisively at the sketch of Lloyd, her finger hovering over the image. The police officer's gaze shifted curiously from the drawing to Katelyn, his expression turning more intent. "Oh, you do…?"

Barend's heart skipped a beat as he watched his daughter, her innocent face revealing a determination beyond her years. He met her eyes, silently urging her to be cautious. Katelyn nodded subtly, affirming her statement with unwavering certainty.

"Yes, come to think of it," Barend interjected, his voice steady despite the tumultuous thoughts racing through his mind. "We did see a man who looked very much like that in old town. It seemed he was moving house or something—him and a few others, stacking their car to the roof." Barend cast a glance at the officer, gauging his reaction carefully.

The officer's scrutiny intensified as he absorbed Barend's account, his brow furrowing slightly. "And what were you doing in old town, sir?" His tone was polite but probing, leaving no room for evasion.

Barend maintained a composed facade, his mind racing underneath his black beanie to concoct a plausible explanation. "We were dropping off the son of one of our farm workers," he replied smoothly, his voice laced with a hint of disdain. "You know, officer, I can never understand those people. Spending whatever they get on cheap wine and behaving like..." Barend hesitated, choosing his words carefully. "Barbarians."

The officer's expression softened momentarily, a hint of agreement flickering in his eyes. "Can't agree more," he murmured, jotting down notes in his pad. "Thank you, sir, for your cooperation. If you think of anything else, don't hesitate to let us know."

Barend nodded gratefully, a sense of relief washing over him like waves as the officer slowly stepped away. He exchanged a brief glance with Katelyn, a silent acknowledgment passing between them of the peril narrowly averted. The tension in the van eased slightly, but Barend knew their journey was far from over. As they pulled away from the blockade, the road ahead stretched uncertainly, fraught with dangers and uncertainties yet to be faced.

Over the crackling police radio, an urgent directive echoed: "Send a unit to old town immediately. Possible sighting at the township shebeen."

Barend navigated the van through the opened blockade gate, his gaze fixed ahead, betraying no hint of the turmoil brewing within. As they passed through, Barend glimpsed a familiar face in the crowd, a fleeting recognition that sent a shiver down his spine. He kept his head low, unwilling to attract any unnecessary attention. The man's eyes bore into the passing vehicle, a moment of recognition flickering between them before Barend sped away.

In the back of the van, Lloyd's voice broke the tense silence, barely audible over the hum of the engine. "These barbarians," he muttered under his breath.

Barend shot a glance at Lloyd through the rearview mirror, his tone clipped. "It was just chit chat, man," he replied tersely, tension radiating through his words. "I had to get us through. You didn't want to decorate a cell now, do you?"

Lloyd shook his head ruefully, taking a swig from a bottle that appeared seemingly out of thin air. "Where did you get that? I thought I hid it deep down."

Barend's eyes narrowed as he noticed the crate where Lloyd had stashed his contraband, the lid now ajar. "Can't hide the good stuff now," he muttered in his usual raspy voice with a shake of his head, his frustration evident. "I can sniff this out from anywhere."

Meanwhile, Katelyn's voice cut through the tense atmosphere, a reminder of their precarious situation. "Remember what Dad told you," she spoke softly but firmly, her eyes fixed on Lloyd. "We're on a secret mission."

On that note, Barend felt a strong urge to reprimand Katelyn gently for the remark she had innocently made earlier, and to stress the urgency of their situation without making her fearful.

However, the gravity of their predicament hung heavy in the air as they drove on, the road ahead fraught with danger and uncertainty. Each passing moment intensified the need for caution, their mission now more perilous than ever before.

"Yes, Daddy," Katelyn replied softly, sensing the seriousness in her father's voice. His troubled expression did not go unnoticed.

"Is something wrong?" she probed gently, her concern evident.

Barend hesitated, weighing his words carefully. "Nothing... I need you to help me," he finally began, his voice low and urgent. "There are some bad policemen who want to hurt Daddy and his friends."

"Very bad... evil cops," Lloyd interjected, his voice filled with a mixture of anger and fear.

"Now we cannot let them find out anything about our mission," Barend continued, his eyes shifting between Katelyn and Lloyd. "We do not know who of them are good and who are bad, so we can't tell anybody."

Katelyn nodded solemnly as she stared at him, understanding the gravity of the situation. "Not a word," she affirmed quietly, her determination clear despite her young age.

Barend's smile was filled with pride and reassurance. "That's a good girl," he said softly, reaching out to gently pat Katelyn's shoulder. His heart swelled with a mix of paternal love and the weight of their dangerous reality. They were in deep waters now, navigating a treacherous path where trust was a luxury they couldn't afford.

Arts
Festival

We arrived in Grahamstown at an opportune moment, right in the midst of its bustling, colourful arts festival. The town hummed with energy, its streets thronged with curious visitors and locals alike, creating a perfect camouflage for our small group. Amidst the vibrant chaos, blending in would be effortless, a sanctuary where anonymity could shield us from prying eyes and pursuers alike.

"Seems like a good place to disappear, eh?" Barend remarked quietly as he surveyed the lively scene unfolding before them. "And maybe make some money without drawing attention."

Lloyd chuckled incredulously. "What trail?" he quipped, his voice tinged with amusement and skepticism.

Barend ignored the jab and reached into his jacket, producing a set of sketches, clear likenesses of both himself and Lloyd. The sketches were a reminder of the danger that lurked not far behind, the persistent threat of law enforcement tightening its grip with each passing hour.

"I think, we'll split up," Barend continued, his tone more serious now as he laid out their plan. "To avoid suspicion… Stick close to the cargo and take turns."

The plan was clear: earn enough money throughout the day to fund their next move. They needed horses, carts, and supplies for a journey through the rugged terrain leading to the Mozambique border. The mountains would provide cover, but they needed some provisions to sustain them on the arduous journey ahead.

With resolve in their hearts and the weight of their situation pressing down on them, they dispersed into the festival crowds, each with a role to play in securing their escape route. The stakes were high, but so was their determination to outwit their pursuers and forge a new path to freedom.

We were still scraping for cash, every penny needed to be earned legitimately to avoid drawing unnecessary attention. Vuyo, resourceful as ever, navigated the outskirts of the bustling festival, realizing entry wasn't an option for him. Outside the festival grounds sprawled a lively array of market stalls and carnival attractions. The air was thick with the scent of spookasem, vibrant paintings vying for attention, and the distant melodies of cheerful children's songs weaving through the crowd.

Among the colorful chaos, one specific stall captured Vuyo's interest. He couldn't help but notice the shootout game. It beckoned with promises of quick rewards for precise aim. Vuyo fished out his last donkeys, a few coins hiding in his trousers' pockets, and exchanged it for a single ticket. Clearly, this was his chance at some much-needed cash.

Lloyd watched with arms folded, his usual arrogant stance. Vuyo took his shot, his aim as steady and focused as the most skilled, experienced hunter. The tension mounted as the target came into view. With a steady hand and unwavering concentration, Vuyo's shot hit the bullseye dead center.

The crowd erupted in cheers and applause, smiling at one another and gazing at Vuyo. He stood there proudly as the stall owner counted out his winnings. It was quite a modest sum, but enough to keep them going for a while. It was a small victory amidst their larger struggle, a glimmer of hope that they could gather the resources they needed without resorting to illicit means.

"Quite a shot," the man behind the stall remarked, his admiration evident as he reviewed the score. "No one's come close to that today, by far."

Vuyo nodded modestly, scanning his surroundings with caution. The young attendant disappeared briefly and returned with a substantial brown bear, handing it over with a smile. "That's all yours now. Feel free to come back anytime."

"Don't mind if I do," Vuyo replied, his grin widening as he accepted the prize. For him, the remainder of the day became a series of bartering these newfound treasures for modest sums. With practiced skill, he navigated from one stall to the next, exchanging plush bears and other prizes for much-needed coins.

It didn't take long for Vuyo to establish a winning streak, dominating every shooting game the festival had to offer until the stalls began closing one by one at day's end. Returning triumphantly with a pocketful of generous earnings, Vuyo found Barend and Katelyn waiting at a hotdog stand nearby.

The day's success was written all over Vuyo's face as they resumed their journey, the weight of their mission lightened by the small victories they'd achieved amidst the festival's chaotic allure.

Barend and Katelyn wandered through the bustling festival grounds, contemplating their next move to secure funds without attracting unwanted attention. The distant echo of a commotion drew Barend's attention toward the school gymnasium, an offbeat locale away from the main festivities. Despite the holiday, they ventured closer, discovering a young man nursing a blackened eye and a split lip just outside.

"What happened to you?" Katelyn inquired with genuine concern as they approached. Barend's stern eyes signaled for her to wait before speaking any further.

The man looked up, his faint smile masking the discomfort. "An uppercut," he replied nonchalantly.

"You should learn to duck," Barend advised with a hint of humor, though his concern lingered.

The man chuckled weakly. "Well, that's easier said than done."

"Why do you fight?" Katelyn pressed, her curiosity piqued.

"Good money," the man explained, his demeanor a mix of pride and resignation. "Stand for a round, and you've earned a week's wages."

"A week's earnings? Really...?" Barend queried, intrigued by the prospect.

As a gesture of friendliness concealing his sole aim to obtain further information Barend handed the man a cigarette, lighting it for him as they conversed further.

"My next match is in an hour," the man continued, exhaling a plume of smoke. "Against the bullfighter."

"Bullfighter?" Barend echoed as he lit his own cigarette and inhaled deeply, his interest growing at the mention of a formidable opponent.

"One of the best, sir," the man snickered and affirmed, his voice carrying a blend of respect and apprehension.

As they exchanged words, the air around them hummed with anticipation amidst the smoke of their cigarettes, each moment in the unexpected encounter with the bruised fighter bringing them closer to an unforeseen opportunity amidst the carnival's chaotic backdrop.

Barend and Katelyn found themselves at the edge of the school gymnasium, where the tension of anticipation hung heavy in the air. The young man, nursing his bruises, shook his head firmly in response to Barend's suggestion of returning to the ring.

"That would be madness... got enough of a beating for one day," he muttered with a wince.

Barend's attention shifted to the young man's entry number, contemplating his next move. "You mind if I..." He gestured towards the number.

The man nodded, pulling off the entry number and handing it over. "It's strictly for men," he remarked, nodding towards Katelyn.

Barend smiled warmly at his daughter. "How much for your top?" he asked the young man.

Without hesitation, the man hastily peeled off his red hoody and held it out. "Make it R50."

Barend exchanged the money, handing the hoody to Katelyn, who eyed it with hesitation. "Put it on," Barend gently urged, noticing her reluctant stare.

Katelyn shook her head, clearly not keen on wearing the secondhand garment.

Near the entrance, a group of men stood guard, checking tickets diligently. "Ticket, please," one of them requested as Barend and Katelyn approached.

"I'm here to fight," Barend stated confidently, eyeing the men guarding the doorway with a sense of determination.

Inside, the gymnasium was transformed into a makeshift arena, with a small boxing ring at its heart. Noisy spectators crowded around, their voices rising in excitement and anticipation. While boxing itself wasn't illegal, the presence of men taking bets at a nearby table hinted at an underground gambling operation, adding an edge of danger to the already charged atmosphere.

Barend handed over his entry number, a subtle exchange in a place where trouble could brew with a misplaced word. The man at the desk, with a weary look and a badge that glinted under the dim lights, nodded knowingly as Barend indicated his intent.

"Thought you were out," the man remarked, a hint of curiosity in his voice.

Barend's response was cautious but firm. "We want no trouble now."

The man's response was swift and pointed as he flashed his badge and gun. Barend acknowledged the unspoken message with a nod, understanding the implicit threat.

"That way, sir," the man directed, gesturing towards a narrow passage along the wall.

Barend proceeded along the designated path, moving through the buzzing atmosphere of the gymnasium. Men of all shapes and sizes huddled in various corners, some deep in conversation with coaches or fathers, all united by the shared pursuit of money or glory in the ring.

Upon entering the dressing room, Barend took a moment to survey the bustling scene. The air thick with anticipation and the sharp tang of humid sweat. He approached a stocky, muscular man who had just stepped out of the ring, wiping blood from his mouth.

"Hey! Tell me about the bullfighter," Barend inquired, seeking insights into his upcoming opponent.

The man spat into a nearby bucket, wiping his mouth guard before responding. Katelyn, observing the gritty reality of the arena, averted her eyes in mild disgust.

"Your first time?" the man asked, assessing Barend with a mixture of curiosity and camaraderie.

Barend hesitated briefly, then nodded. "You could say that, yeah..."

The man chuckled, understanding the mix of nerves and determination in Barend's voice. "Well, good luck to you then! The bullfighter ain't one to take lightly."

"Better go home then... bullfighter leaves no one standing," the man cautioned as Barend mulled over his decision to stay and fight.

"Oh... and why's that?" Barend queried, his tone reflecting both curiosity and a hint of determination.

"He's got one hell of a right hook," the man explained, a note of respect and caution in his voice. "All the money's on him. He's the reigning champion, never been knocked out."

Barend glanced at the score board displaying the odds, large red digital numbers confirming the bullfighter's dominance in the ring. The odds were heavily stacked against him, but there was something in Barend's eyes that spoke of a fierce resolve to challenge the odds.

"We allowed to bet also?" Barend asked, already mentally preparing himself for the upcoming bout.

The man nodded, acknowledging Barend's intent to bet on himself. With a nod of thanks, Barend made his way towards the betting tables, acutely aware that every eye in the room was sizing him up, gauging his chances against the feared bullfighter.

As Barend proudly approached the boxing ring, the man overseeing the match greeted him with a mixture of encouragement and expectation.

"Hope you're not going to let me down," the man half-joked, half-serious. "I put good money against you, and I'll have a bloody hard time explaining to the wife where that money went."

Barend feigned a faint smile for a second, then sharpened his gaze, a flicker of determination gleaming in his eyes as he stepped into the ring. He was ready as ever to face the bullfighter and defy the odds stacked against him.

Barend approached the betting station with a determined look, pulling out the last of his money and placing a bold bet on himself. He hastily scribbled the name "Richie" on the betting slip, a pseudonym he hoped would keep his identity carefully concealed.

Leading Katelyn aside, Barend draped a hooded top over her head, shielding her from the gritty scene unfolding around them. "This is no place for girls," he murmured, his voice laced with concern. "Please keep yourself covered and stay safe."

The shrill sound of the ring bell resounded through the air, signaling the start of the bout. Before entering the ring, Barend stripped off his black shirt. His body bore the testament of a hard life lived – scars deeply etched into his strong, muscular frame. Each scar told a story of resilience and endurance, a stark contrast to the pristine buff physique of his opponents.

He strode confidently right to the center of the ring, the arena pulsing with the roar of the crowd. Across from him stood a formidable opponent, a man with a massive physique reminiscent of a sumo wrestler, with shiny exaggerated bronze muscles bulging out of his torso, his gloves raised in anticipation. The crowd erupted in rowdy cheers and taunts, energized by the imminent clash.

Barend wasted no time, closing the distance with a burst of speed. He launched a punch aimed at the behemoth's head, only to have it deflected back with startling force, rattling his resolve. Undeterred, Barend adjusted his strategy, targeting the man's exposed sides with calculated strikes.

Each blow landed with precision, but the opponent's layers of bulk absorbed the impact like a fortress. Barend danced nimbly around his large adversary, evading powerful swings that threatened to end the match in a single blow. In between dodges, Barend countered with rapid-fire punches, aiming to wear down his opponent's formidable defenses.

With a tight grip around Barend's neck, the imposing opponent lifted him effortlessly as if he were completely weightless, parading him to the edge of the ring where the ropes awaited. The crowd's roars intensified as they anticipated the final blow.

A wicked smile creased the man's sweaty face as he taunted Barend, relishing his dominance. He swung a heavy fist towards Barend's face, the impact landing with a resounding thud, threatening to shatter Barend's resolve.

"Daddy! Daddy!" Katelyn's panicked cries echoed through the chaos, her voice a desperate plea for her father's safety.

The boxer's attention momentarily shifted, surprised by the unexpected outcry. "A girl?" he muttered incredulously, momentarily distracted.

Seizing the opportunity, Barend summoned his strength, unleashing a powerful counter-attack. With a swift and precise punch, he struck the man squarely on the ear, sending shockwaves of disorientation through his adversary's brain.

"Time to dance," Barend growled through gritted teeth, his determination reignited.

The man retaliated furiously, launching another assault towards Barend, who deftly dodged the incoming blow. In a swift motion,

Barend delivered a forceful kick to the side of the man's knee, causing him to buckle in an instant and drop to one knee.

The towering opponent swung with all his might, aiming to crush Barend under the weight of his powerful blows. Barend stood firm as a rock, bracing himself for the impact. The man's fist connected squarely with Barend's jaw, sending shockwaves through his body. Blood gushed from Barend's nose, dripping onto his denim shorts and staining it crimson, but he gritted his teeth against the pain.

With unwavering resolve, Barend countered swiftly. Channeling all his strength into a decisive uppercut, he unleashed a devastating blow that caught the big man completely off guard. The impact reverberated through the arena as the man crumpled to the ground like a felled tree.

The crowd erupted in a thunderous roar, shouting, cheering and whistling, filling the air with excitement and disbelief. Barend raised his fists triumphantly, adrenaline rapidly coursing through his veins. His heart pounded as he revelled in the sweet victory of overcoming a seemingly insurmountable challenge.

Walking tall and more proud than usual, Barend made his way to the betting station amidst the cheers and applause. He collected his earnings, a bag heavy with the weight of his success, proof of his prowess in the ring and his ability to defy the odds.

As he counted the winnings, a wide grin spread across Barend's bloodied face. This victory wasn't just about gaining money. Additionally it was a testament to his strength, determination, and the unyielding spirit that drove him forward against all odds.

That evening, as dusk settled over Grahamstown, the three companions gathered around a worn wooden table in a dimly lit room. Vuyo opened his little cloth bag and laid out his earnings first, a substantial stack of bills and coins that caught the flickering light from the oil lamp. With a gentle smile, he handed Katelyn a soft brown teddy bear, a small gesture amidst their newfound fortune.

"You made that much… how?" Lloyd queried, his curiosity piqued.

"Let's just say that I have a way with guns," Vuyo smiled and replied cryptically, his eyes glinting with a mixture of pride and caution.

Next, it was Barend's turn. He produced a hefty bag overflowing with crumpled notes, the fruits of his victorious bout in the ring earlier that day. "Took down the bull," Barend announced proudly, positioning himself in a wide-legged stance with folded arms, his grin widening as he recounted his triumph.

Excitement buzzed in the air as they piled their earnings together, the table soon becoming a montage of wealth and possibility. With swift fingers, Vuyo ironed out the crumpled notes and arranged them in neat little groupings. Lloyd, not one to be outdone, reached behind him and heaved a massive sack onto the table with a resounding thud. Coins spilled out in a cascading wave, clattering against the wooden surface and mingling with the paper money.

Vuyo uttered a click of the tongue, uttering his displeasure toward Lloyd for messing up his neat display of notes.

Barend looked at Lloyd, who couldn't care less about the disorder of the loot. He stared intently at Lloyd with a mix of surprise and amusement. "And this...? What's all this?"

"Just outside town, there's this wishing well," Lloyd explained, his smile widening as he recounted his scheme. "People drop money, believing it'll bring them luck. So did I." He gestured proudly to the coins, some still glistening with the remnants of their watery origins.

"Oh well... Money is money, and this will have to do," Barend concluded, his voice tinged with a hint of admiration for Lloyd's ingenuity.

The three men looked at one another, exchanging nods, their eyes glinting with determination and a shared understanding that their collected wealth would pave the way for their next steps. In the flickering candlelight, amidst the clink of coins and rustle of bills, their plans began to take shape against the backdrop of uncertainty that lay ahead.

It was a long nights drive to get closer to Lesotho, a sense of urgency pushing now more than ever.

A Country for Cowboys:

A t the small town here people don't ask too many questions and one can always strike a good deal with a trade. With the car sold for scrap metal, we soon found ourselves in a dusty yard surrounded by horses of all shapes and sizes. It was a scene straight out of the Wild West, but the reality of choosing our mounts was far from romantic.

"Choosing horses is very much like choosing a wife," I remarked to the salesman, scanning the animals skeptically. "You don't know what you've got until you've bought the animal."

The salesman with his neutral cowboy attire chuckled knowingly, launching into his pitch with practiced ease, detailing each horse's strengths and quirks like a seasoned car dealer hawking his wares. I played the part of the discerning buyer, probing about health histories and watching for any signs of discomfort that might reveal hidden flaws.

Meanwhile, Katelyn darted among the horses, running to and fro, her excitement almost contagious as she inspected each one with youthful enthusiasm. "A good father would probably keep his child on a leash," I mused inwardly, watching her fearless exploration. "But I believe you can't protect them forever. You've gotta let them go… Let them grow up strong and have some adventure while they're at it."

Tessa, our loyal little companion, raced alongside Katelyn like a little lively ping pong ball, weaving between the horses' legs with the agility of a seasoned ranch hand, narrowly escaping every foot and hoof. It was enough to make most parents nervous, but in that moment, I couldn't help but admire the fearlessness in both Katelyn and Tessa.

As the sun dipped low over the horizon, casting long shadows across the corral, the decision weighed heavily on me. We definitely needed horses sturdy enough to carry us and our newfound wealth through the rugged terrain ahead. And amidst the dust and the neighs of the horses, our journey into the unknown began to take shape, one hoofbeat at a time.

Walking confidently ahead of the horses, I made a point to test their mettle, spooking a few to gauge their reactions. One particularly spirited horse reared up, kicking its stall in defiance.

Glancing around, I spotted Lloyd and Vuyo, each standing there with hands on hips, navigating the horses cautiously. Lloyd seemed wary, almost nervous and childlike in his apprehension toward the animals. It was a stark contrast to the bravado he often displayed in most other situations.

Focusing on my task, I examined the horses closely, brushing over their glossy hair with my fingers. I peered into their eyes, seeking intelligence and spirit. I checked their teeth and tongue, assessing their health and age. Satisfied with my observations, I selected a sturdy boerperd, a dark brown stallion known for its resilience and speed—a practical choice for the rugged terrain ahead.

Taking the horse for a test run around the yard, I observed its speed in order to confirm whether it would be suitable. Agility and endurance were paramount; there was no room for a show horse on our journey.

Meanwhile, Lloyd had set his sights on a striking white horse adorned with black spots. Approaching him, I noticed the patterns resembling those of a leopard, hence Lloyd had aptly named it "Leopard." Apart from his awkward mannerisms, tugging at his jeans and scratching his greasy hair and beard, he planted himself right in front of the horse and folded his arms. His pathetic grin was infectious as he defended his choice.

"You aiming to join the circus?" I teased, unable to resist poking fun at him.

"Oh… well, you're just sour 'cause you didn't snag this beauty," he shot back, his pride in his new companion evident.

Chuckling, I turned to Vuyo. "Can you handle it?"

"I've handled some stubborn donkeys in my life," Vuyo replied with a grin.

I exchanged a knowing look with him before addressing the salesman with a grin. "We need something sturdy. Got a first-time rider heading into rough terrain."

The salesman winced slightly at the thought, but his professionalism held firm. Each of us had chosen a horse that suited our personalities and needs, marking the beginning of our adventure into the wild unknown.

"Sure, I will go check our stock," the salesman replied cheerfully and nodded, heading off to retrieve more horses.

"I don't need no baby gel," Lloyd remarked with disdain, eyeing his chosen horse confidently. "The two of us are going to be just fine."

Barend scanned the bustling yard, searching for Katelyn. In the corner of his eye, he caught sight of her beside a donkey, dressed in a bright pink halter.

"This one, Daddy, this one!" Katelyn exclaimed, bouncing with excitement in front of the donkey. "She's just like my little pony."

Barend frowned. "It's a donkey, Katie. We actually need a horse, you know…"

"But I want the donkey!" Katelyn insisted. "It's small and so cute, Daddy, please please please."

Barend approached the donkey, noting its weathered appearance. "That one ain't no good," he explained to Katelyn. "It's not a horse."

"But I want it," Katelyn persisted. "She's been hurt, Daddy."

The salesman interjected, offering some insight. "She's a stubborn one, this donkey. She was supposed to take kids out at the festival but refused. They make good babysitters though, herd animals. Once a donkey bonds with a herd, she'll become its protector."

Barend raised an eyebrow, considering the implications. "Protector?" he scoffed.

"But Daddy… she's been hurt," Katelyn pleaded softly, touching the donkey's long ears.

Barend hesitated and sighed, feeling the weight of his daughter's concern. "Alright," he relented, a small smile forming. "We can't leave her here. What if…" Katelyn leaned in and whispered in his ear, "…this man hits her again?"

Katelyn gently stroked the donkey's ears once more, her eyes filled with compassion and determination. "Can it pull some weight?" Barend asked, eyeing the donkey skeptically.

"Sure can," the salesman replied confidently, while chewing a piece of gum. "That horse is as strong as a bull. She'll pull twice the weight of your horse for sure. We use her in the fields mostly. Sometimes dress her up for kiddies' parties or the festival… but I think her showtime is over."

"Why so, she old?" Barend inquired, curious about the donkey's history.

"No, just stubborn like hell," the man chuckled, leaning against the wooden fence

"She got a name?" Barend prompted.

"Jasmine," the man said with a hint of fondness.

"She's perfect," Katelyn declared with enthusiasm, her eyes sparkling as she looked at the donkey.

Barend glanced at Katelyn, quite surprised by her choice. "You sure about this now, Katelyn? This little old donkey..."

"Jasmine..." Katelyn interjected firmly, stroking the donkey's mane. "A real princess."

The donkey seemed to respond well to Katelyn's touch, leaning into her hand affectionately. Barend sighed inwardly, recognizing that while Jasmine might not offer the speed they required, her strength would be invaluable for carrying heavy loads across rough terrain.

"At least she's quite strong, and we will need to carry some heavy weight," Barend conceded, choosing to see the practicality in Katelyn's attachment to the gentle, sturdy donkey.

"If she will walk with you, you can take her... by all means. She's not much use to me anyhow," the owner of the donkey said dismissively.

Barend knew immediately they were taking a wild chance with Jasmine, but Katelyn had set her heart on the donkey and refused any other suggestions they had made for a horse. They loaded up the three horses, evenly distributing the weight, and the seller threw in an old donkey cart to help with the load.

After some time went by where they struggled to get Jasmine moving, Lloyd enticed her with a crisp red apple, successfully luring her to follow him. However, after a few minutes, it became evident that Lloyd was still walking beside his horse.

"What on earth, so are you telling me that you are planning to walk your horse to the border?" Vuyo teased, amused by Lloyd's predicament.

"Shut up, old man," Lloyd retorted, casting a derogatory glance at Vuyo's stark white teeth peering through his grin.

"Hey! Who are you calling old?" Vuyo hissed, trotting his horse closer to Lloyd, who quickly took refuge behind his speckled white horse.

"You two, please get along now, or you lose your cut," Barend interjected firmly, signaling for them to move faster.

Lloyd hesitated but eventually attempted to mount his horse, only to fall flat on his back in the dirt road. His colorful language echoed into the distance as the others moved ahead at a brisk pace. Leopard, Lloyd's horse, trotted after them, leaving Lloyd scrambling desperately, trying to wipe the dirt off the backside of his jeans before running to catch up with them.

Despite the rocky start, they pressed ever onward, with little old Jasmine plodding along steadily with Katelyn beside her. Lloyd finally started settling into the rhythm of the journey, his earlier mishap a humorous memory among the challenges they faced on their daring adventure toward the border.

With Jasmine now part of their team, the trio prepared themselves for the journey ahead, knowing that with her resilience and Katelyn's unwavering trust, they had gained more than just another pack animal. The band had surely gained a loyal companion for the challenges that lay ahead.

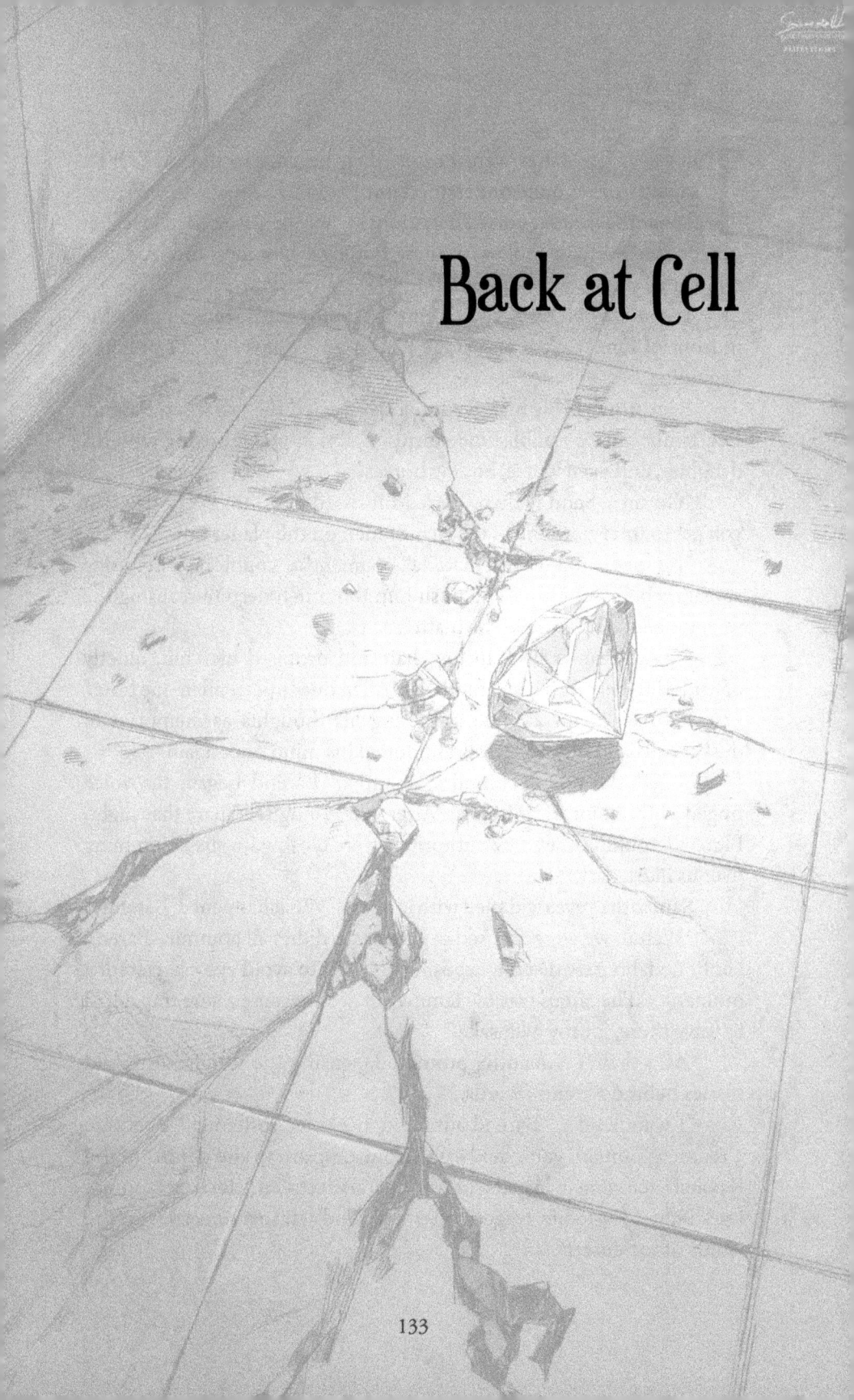

Back at Cell

They say, "If wishes were horses, then beggars would ride." It's a saying I never quite understood until now.

Samantha leaned forward curiously, her pen poised above her notebook. "So, you took your 'new findings' into Lesotho. Are you telling me, that's where one will find it?"

Barend shook his head, nervously tapping his fingers on the table in front of him while a wry smile played on his lips. "That's only the beginning..."

Samantha's brow furrowed slightly. "I need the full story, Barend. I certainly can't go publishing stories of a man going boxing with his daughter, and even worse, buying horses."

"Go on...Send it then," Barend insisted. "It's not every day that you get to interview one of the richest men on the planet now."

"It's not front cover material," Samantha countered, her tone revealing her cautiousness to push him too much despite realising the urgent need for closure in the matter.

Barend leaned back in his chair and dropped his chin, quietly considering her words for a moment. "All in due time... all in due time."

He paused for a while, gathering his thoughts as memories of dusty roads and hidden treasures flooded his mind once again.

"I left the circus behind, Samantha," Barend began, his voice tinged with a hint of nostalgia. "After everything fell apart that night, I knew I couldn't stay. The authorities were closing in, suspicion hung over us like a dark cloud."

Samantha's eyes widened with interest. "What happened, Barend?"

"Well... we were accused of crimes we didn't all commit," Barend continued, his gaze distant, exposing his need to avoid eye-contact for a moment . "The circus was my family, but... it became a sure trap. I had to leave there, for my own sake."

"And then?" Samantha prompted, sensing the weight of untold stories behind Barend's words.

"I wandered..." Barend admitted, his voice softening. "I became a roaming nomad, you could say...from Lesotho to the depths of the Kalahari, chasing whispers of ancient artifacts and lost treasures. I found clues buried in forgotten temples and whispered secrets in the winds of the desert."

Samantha put down her pen for a while and leaned in closer, captivated by the tale unfolding before her. "And so... did you find what you were looking for?"

Barend nodded slowly, a flicker of triumph in his eyes. "I found more than what I bargained for, Samantha. But some treasures are best left buried."

She grabbed the pen again, scribbling furiously in her notebook, hanging on his every word. "So what now, Barend?"

He smiled knowingly, his gaze drifting once again to the window where the sun was beginning to set. "Now... I share my story. The world needs to know that beneath the surface of everyday life, there are still mysteries waiting to be uncovered."

Samantha nodded, her excitement palpable, despite suppressing her smile. "It's a story worth telling..."

Barend chuckled softly and folded his arms calmly yet authoritatively before looking her straight in the eyes, as was his frequent manner. "Just remember, Samantha. Sometimes, the greatest adventures begin with a single wish and the courage to chase after it."

As he spoke, a sense of determination filled the air, carrying with it the echoes of a life lived on the edge of discovery and daring.

The land of King Moshoeshoe:

We were entering the lands known as Basotholand (Lesotho), land of King Moshoeshoe. We clearly understood the risk of entering this land but it was worth clearing the police from our tracks.

Lesotho... Black people needed a special pass to come from this place to South Africa. For a white man to enter into their land... well let's just say you needed to be a bit crazy, or so I thought.

Journey through Lesotho:

Lesotho stretched before us like an emerald carpet beneath the vast blue African sky. The landscape was a departure from the arid savannahs and dense forests I had grown accustomed to in other parts of the continent. Here, green hills rolled endlessly, punctuated only by the occasional rondavel (traditional huts of the Basotho people) and their accompanying herds of cattle grazing lazily in the pastures.

Riding through this serene expanse on horseback, our progress was marked by the quiet rhythm of hoofbeats and the gentle sway of the grasslands under the weight of the wind. The air was crisp and clean, filled with the scent of earth and the distant murmur of mountain streams.

"Quite a different world, isn't it?" Vuyo remarked, his voice carrying a hint of wonder as he observed the tranquil landscape.

I nodded in agreement, marveling at the simplicity and beauty of Lesotho. "No fences, no skyscrapers. Just endless green and those big skies," I replied, breathing deeply and taking in the panoramic view.

Katelyn, perched confidently on her horse beside us, was equally captivated. Her bright blue eyes sparkled with curiosity as she waved enthusiastically at the Basotho villagers tending to their daily chores. "Dumea Ntate! Khotso mé!" *(Praise the Father! My Peace!)* she called out cheerfully, practicing the greetings she had quickly learned.

The villagers responded with warm smiles and waves of their own, their faces painted with expressions of genuine hospitality. It was clear that in this remote corner of Africa, greetings were more than mere pleasantries. They were a cultural currency, a way to establish trust and respect among neighbors.

As we continued our journey, I couldn't help but admire the resilience of these mountain people. For generations, they had defended their herds and their land against raiders, forging a strong sense of community and mutual support. Their endurance and pride shimmered in the fields, as constant as the wind.

"We should find a place to rest soon," I suggested, glancing around at the approaching dusk. "Somewhere we can take shelter for the night. My voice was low, aware that nightfall here carried its own quiet mysteries.

Vuyo nodded in agreement, his eyes scanning the horizon for a suitable spot. "I saw a cluster of rondavels just ahead," he pointed out. "We might find hospitality there."

We gently guided our horses towards the village, where smoke from cooking fires curled lazily into the evening sky. As we dismounted and approached, the villagers welcomed us with open arms, their faces lit with curiosity and kindness. The amber glow of lanterns and bonfires here and there spread warm light across the village, making the moment feel strangely intimate.

"Kea leboha," *(Thank you)* I said gratefully, expressing my thanks in Sesotho as we were offered a place to stay for the night. The warmth of the fire, the aroma of cooking vegetables, meat and maize, and the laughter of children playing nearby filled the air, wrapping us in a sense of belonging amid unfamiliar surroundings.

Tomorrow would bring new adventures in this land of big skies and open hearts... a journey that promised to deepen our understanding of Lesotho's rich culture and its resilient people.

In the highlands of Lesotho, our journey unfolded amidst the rugged beauty of rocky hillsides and the humble warmth of its people. The donkey adorned in pink became a familiar sight, often drawing a crowd of curious children eager to pet the gentle creature.

"The aloe flowers here are said to be sacred," Vuyo remarked, his gaze tenderly fixed on the vibrant orange blooms standing out against the rocky terrain.

"Reminds me of home," I mused, noting the similarities to the wildflowers back in our own lands.

A sense of quiet serenity enveloped us as we navigated through this picturesque landscape. It wasn't long before Lloyd, always with an eye for the unusual, stumbled upon *hlahla se maele...* the trickster plant, as the locals called it. Its resemblance to *cannabis* didn't escape my notice, though here its use seemed more ceremonial than recreational.

As we journeyed deeper into the heart of Lesotho, the warm greetings of the locals greeted us like a gentle breeze. We bartered goods for food and fresh water, relying on Vuyo's rudimentary grasp of the native language to facilitate our exchanges.

"Ha ke na chelate *(I have no money),*" Vuyo would say with authority softened by a friendly smile, politely declining any requests for money from beggars who crossed our path.

The sense of safety from local authorities was a relief, but our idyllic surroundings belied occasional reminders of the outside world's intrusion. Outsiders, drawn perhaps by the same allure that brought us here, occasionally disrupted the tranquility of these lands. The distant rumble of a truck or the flash of strange eyes over a hill could jolt us back into a wariness we tried hard to shake off.

"We'll need to stay vigilant," I cautioned, casting a wary glance at the horizon where unfamiliar figures sometimes appeared.

Vuyo nodded in agreement, his expression earnest. "Agreed. We've come this far; we can't afford to let our guard down now."

The journey through Lesotho was proving to be both enchanting and challenging. We encountered the resilience of its people and the untamed beauty of its landscapes. As we pressed on, I couldn't help but feel a deep sense of gratitude for the opportunity to experience this corner of the world, even amidst its complexities and uncertainties.

The kingdom of Lesotho sprawled endlessly before us, a vast expanse of untamed wilderness where the horizon seemed to merge seamlessly with the heavens. Here, there were no boundaries set by fences, only an unbroken landscape that stretched as far as the eye could possibly see, showcasing nature's dominion over this rugged terrain.

Our bodies were intensely fatigued from days of relentless riding. Ankles, knees, hips, and backs protested with every movement, chafed and sore from the unforgiving journey towards the border. Yet, despite our discomfort, we pressed onward, driven by the urgency of our mission and the unyielding determination to reach our destination.

Pausing to take a rest and replenish our dwindling supplies, we stumbled upon an elderly Basotho man seated tranquilly outside his rondavel. His attire was a wide straw hat atop his head and a blanket displaying a vast array of colours knitted together which was draped around his shoulders. These items spoke of a simple yet dignified life in harmony with the land.

Though initially reticent, the old man eventually emerged from his modest dwelling bearing a weathered photograph in his wrinkled hand. In it, three young men in British military uniforms stood proudly, captured in a moment of youth and courage. With a weathered finger, he pointed to the figure on the far left, then to himself, mumbling half-words one could hardly pronouce... a poignant gesture that spoke volumes without words.

Vuyo, with his natural gift for languages, translated the man's tale. These were his comrades, fellow Basotho men who had been conscripted to fight in the Second World War. It was a conflict that thrust them far from their rural homeland into the very heart of global strife. For those who had never ventured beyond their mountainous sanctuary, the war was a bewildering journey into the unknown, taking many to distant lands like Italy and North Africa, never to return again.

Moved by the man's story and touched by his hospitality, we bartered our meager belongings for much-needed supplies, our necessary drinking water and other essentials that would sustain us on our arduous trek. Our provisions were diminishing very quickly, yet our burdens remained heavy as we resumed our journey, carrying not just our physical loads but also the weight of history and the resilience of the Basotho people etched into our hearts.

Barend withdrew a cigarette from his pocket as he rested against a sturdy tree, taking respite from the rigors of tending to the horses. Nearby, a group of young Basotho girls approached, their voices animated and curious. One girl, emboldened, smiled and suddenly seated herself next to Barend while Vuyo as well as the girl's friends stood there observing the scenario and chuckling from a distance, quite astonished at her brazen move.

Barend, glancing from the corner of his eye and feeling somewhat uneasy under the scrutiny, greeted the girl tentatively. It was evident they had likely never encountered a white person up close before, their fascination palpable as they reached out to touch Barend's arm, marveling at the fine hairs that adorned it, a feature that was clearly uncommon among the locals.

In this remote corner of Lesotho, superstitions held sway over daily life, and it didn't take long for Barend to discern this aspect of their culture. The girl beside him plucked a few strands of his arm hair before he could protest, a mischievous act that prompted laughter from her companions as they playfully scattered away. Vuyo, thoroughly amused by the scene, shook his head and joined Barend, sharing in the light-hearted moment amidst the vast, serene landscape.

"What was that all about?" Barend asked, a bemused expression playing on his face as he took a drag from his cigarette.

"White gold," Vuyo replied with a chuckle.

"White gold?" Barend raised an eyebrow and looked at him inquisitively.

"Yes, its your arm hair," Vuyo explained. "Around here, some of the witchdoctors claim that the hairs of a Caucasian, mixed with traditional medicine, can bring wealth."

Barend exhaled a puff of smoke thoughtfully. "Well, I'll keep that in mind next time we trade," he said with a smirk. Vuyo, bending over to rest his hands on his knees, erupted in uncontrollable laughter, the sound echoing through the quiet hillsides.

Meanwhile, Lloyd had found his own way to pass the time, playing games with the local children. darting around as energetically as his weary, skinny legs could carry him. It looked more like they were playfully ganging up on him, attempting to topple his pathetic figure to the ground in a heap of hysterical laughter and playful scuffles. Katelyn, not far away, giggled as she proudly displayed her donkey to some other young girls who were fascinated by the adorned animal. The scene was a blend of camaraderie and innocent mischief, set against the backdrop of Lesotho's expansive and tranquil landscapes.

The sun dipped below the horizon, casting a warm glow across the campsite where we gathered around the crackling fire. Katelyn, her face adorned with white dots arranged around her eyes in constellation-like patterns by the older Basotho women, continued to giggle gleefully as she played with Jasmine nearby.

Above us, the sky stretched out in a vast canvas of midnight blue, adorned with a breathtaking display of stars that seemed to pierce through the darkness. It was a clear night, and even other galaxies were visible to the naked eye, shimmering with distant light. Yet, despite the celestial beauty, the chill of the approaching night air began to settle around us.

Barend draped a karos, a thick wool blanket traded from the Basotho people, over Katelyn's shoulders, coaxing her to settle down. Nearby, a cooking pot hung over the fire, steam rising from its brim as the aroma of a simple yet comforting meal of meat, vegetables, water and herbs filled the air.

Lloyd lay on his side, propped up by his elbow. Barend, noticing his discomfort, leaned over and asked, "You okay, bro?"

Lloyd chuckled softly, his voice tinged with fatigue. "Ja, *ag*... my calves just a little stiff, you know. Too much exercise today..."

Barend offered him a jar of horse gel. "You maybe need this?"

Lloyd nodded gratefully. "My back and inner legs burn like hell, man... I hurt in places I never knew I had before."

The campfire crackled softly, casting flickering shadows across our weary faces as we sat on makeshift benches of tree trunk, settling in for the night under the expansive starlit sky of Lesotho.

"So... is it gonna be some sort of Irish soup?" Lloyd asked with a mischievous grin, eyeing the cooking pot.

Vuyo glanced over at Lloyd, raising an eyebrow. "What do you mean?"

Lloyd leaned in, brandishing a bottle he had been keeping close. "You add in some sort of liquor now," he teased, nudging the bottle towards the pot.

Vuyo chuckled and gently pushed the bottle aside. "I think it's ready."

Carefully ladling the hearty brown soup into four bowls, Vuyo passed them around the circle of weary travelers gathered around the crackling fire. The aroma of simmering ingredients filled the air, blending with the smoky scent of the campfire.

As tradition dictated, we closed our eyes in reverence, taking hands. Katelyn, her youthful voice soft but earnest, led us in a prayer: "Thank you God for the world so sweet, thank you for the food we eat. Thank you for the birds that sing, thank you God for everything. Amen."

We echoed her sentiment with quiet 'amens' before picking up our spoons. Steam rose from the bowls, carrying the rich fragrance of the soup cooked to perfection over the open flame.

Katelyn took the first sip, her face lighting up with a smile. "Hot but good... nice and salty," she remarked with satisfaction, her cheeks flushed from the warmth of the soup and the fire. Lloyd poured a generous splash of liquor into his soup with a mischievous grin. "Irish soup... just how I like it."

Around the fire, our makeshift family in this vast and unfamiliar land of Lesotho, we savored the simple pleasure of a warm meal shared under the canopy of stars, finding comfort and sustenance in each other's company.

Katelyn leaned forward, her eyes bright with curiosity as the fire crackled beside them, casting dancing shadows on the faces gathered around.

"What did you want to be... when you were like me?" she asked, her voice carrying a youthful innocence that contrasted with the ruggedness of their surroundings.

Lloyd chuckled, his eyes narrowing playfully. "A girl? I was never a girl," he quipped, his voice rough yet lighthearted.

"No man, silly," Katelyn giggled, shaking her head at his jest. "When you were a child..."

Lloyd's expression softened, contemplating her question for a moment before replying. "Who told you I was a child?"

"You really are a clown, silly Billy," Katelyn teased, her smile wide as she glanced at him playfully.

Lloyd suddenly fell silent, taking a sip of whiskey as he mused over her words. Before he could respond, a deep voice interjected from the side.

"Probably a cowboy, like John West," Vuyo declared, his voice carrying a hint of nostalgia. "Riding to the east on my steady horse, fighting for the good of humanity."

"So you became a super detective," Katelyn quipped, her eyes sparkling with admiration as she turned to Vuyo and folded her hands.

Barend, sitting nearby, joined in with a proud grin. "But of course, one of the finest," he added, smiling and nodding in agreement with Vuyo's declaration.

Katelyn's attention then turned to Lloyd, her gaze expectant. "And you?"

Lloyd paused, his eyes glinting with a touch of whimsy. "A magician... I wanted to make things disappear," he confessed with a grin, proud of himself for giving such an original answer.

With a flourish of his hands, he made the bottle of whiskey vanish. Katelyn gasped in delight, immediately reaching out to check his pockets, finding nothing.

"Where did it go?" she asked, her eyes wide with wonder.

Lloyd chuckled, repeating his magic gesture, and the bottle reappeared in his hand.

"*Abra kadabra,*" he said with a flourish, causing Katelyn to burst into high-pitched laughter as the bottle materialized once more.

"So why didn't you?" Katelyn asked between giggles, her eyes twinkling mischievously.

Lloyd took another big gulp from his bottle, his rough laughter contrasting hers in the warmth of the firelight as they shared this fleeting moment of magic and camaraderie under the vast expanse of the starlit sky.

"Didn't I what?" Lloyd's voice broke through the quiet night air, his words carrying a hint of amusement.

"Become a magician," Katelyn pressed, her eyes sparkling with curiosity as she turned to him.

Lloyd leaned back with his hands on the piece of tree trunk behind him, a wry smile playing on his lips. "Well, I did kind of, in a way. I still make things disappear, come to think of it."

Barend's gaze sharpened, his stern expression directed at Lloyd. Before Barend could interject, Lloyd quickly amended his statement. "It's my specialty, in my unit of course, at the special forces."

Katelyn's attention shifted to Barend, her eyes wide with expectation. "And you, Daddy?"

Barend's face softened momentarily, contemplating her question. "Filthy rich... a life with no worries, to be completely free," he answered, his voice tinged with a hint of longing.

"Free from what, Daddy?" Katelyn persisted, her youthful curiosity driving her to understand.

Barend hesitated before answering, his eyes scanning the flickering flames of the campfire. "Free from all this... running around, trying to survive," he finally replied, his tone tinged with resignation. "You won't understand, you're still a child."

"But am I free, Daddy?" Katelyn asked softly, her voice carrying a poignant note of innocence as she stared into his soul.

Barend sighed deeply, unsure what to answer, a strange quiet settling between them as he stroked her hair. Moments passed in the gentle crackle of the fire before Lloyd abruptly broke the silence.

"How about a little story?" Lloyd suggested, his tone lighter, aiming to change the subject and shift the mood.

"A story, yes… yaih!!!!" Katelyn exclaimed, her smile returning as she leaned forward eagerly.

Barend's features relaxed slightly, his eyes glancing from Katelyn to Lloyd. The firelight danced across their faces, casting shadows that seemed to weave their own tales beneath the vast canvas of the starlit sky.

"Now, when I was a child, my parents used to tell me about a strange man, or thing, that walks with a dress and a covered head," Barend began, his voice low and deliberate, the crackling fire punctuating his words. "No one who saw his face ever lived to tell the tale. So my mom always made sure I went to bed when she told me to, because that way he couldn't see me. They called him Antjie Somers... and we were warned to beware of him, or he'd put you in his big dark bag if you didn't listen to your father."

Katelyn's eyes widened with fear in the flickering firelight, her gaze darting nervously around the dark night. "That's not a real story, is it?"

Lloyd shrugged, a hint of mischief in his eyes. "Well, no one really knows for sure. But there were reports of missing children in these mountains a few years back."

"Good night," Lloyd declared abruptly, turning away with a mischievous smile.

Barend shot Lloyd a disapproving glance. "What? My dad used to scare us with that tale all the time," Lloyd explained, defending his choice of story.

The fire crackled softly, casting dancing shadows around them as the night pressed in. The air was crisp and cool, filled with the distant sounds of wildlife and the occasional rustle of wind through the trees. Above them, the stars twinkled brightly against the deep, velvety sky, casting a tranquil aura over the campsite.

"Barend, you turned out mighty fine," Lloyd nodded confidently.

"Of course," Barend replied with a shake of his head. "If she has any nightmares, then you don't have to worry about Antjie Somer." He punctuated his words with a hearty punch to Lloyd's shoulder.

Lloyd winced slightly, but grinned in response. "Thanks for the reassurance."

Vuyo, who had been lying on his back and quietly gazing up at the stars, spoke up then. His voice was soft yet resonant in the stillness of the night. "My people used to believe that one could communicate with the spirits of the mountains. There's a tale about the mountain of Thaba Bosiu in Lesotho, where King Moshoeshoe sought refuge from his enemies."

He paused for a moment, his amber eyes reflecting the flickering flames of the fire. "Legend has it that during a fierce battle, the mountain itself rose up and shielded the king's warriors, allowing them to surprise their attackers and secure the victory."

Barend and Lloyd listened intently, drawn in by Vuyo's colourful storytelling. The crackling fire and the distant sounds of the night served as a backdrop to his tale, weaving a sense of ancient mystery and reverence around them.

Barend took the first watch of the night, his eyes scanning the vast expanse of sky speckled with stars. The loot, carefully concealed amidst hay stacks and containers on the back of the donkey cart, remained carefully hidden from prying eyes. The animals were tethered a few meters away, sheltered behind a small hill that provided a modicum of protection against the brisk wind sweeping across the Lesotho landscape.

Although the sky was clear, Barend couldn't shake off a nagging sense of unease. Lesotho had offered them respite from the relentless pursuit of the authorities, but the recent quietness unsettled him to a degree. His mind wandered to the man at the bank, the one who had fired shots. There was something about him, something familiar in his eyes, although the majority of his face was hidden under a balaclava. Barend hoped fervently that the man hadn't recognized him in return.

With a deep breath, Barend resolved to push these thoughts aside. There was still a long journey ahead, and he needed proper rest. He stretched and made his way over to where Lloyd sat by the crackling fire, stirring a pot of soup.

"You're on," Barend said firmly, nodding towards the darkness beyond the firelight. "See you in the morning, bro. The horses are around the back."

Lloyd acknowledged with a consenting nod, clumsily getting to his feet as he prepared to take over watch duty. The night enveloped them in its quiet embrace, broken only by the faint rustling of leaves in the wind and the occasional snort of a horse nearby.

Stubborn Donkey

The cool misty morning enveloped the campsite, casting a tranquil haze over the landscape as Barend stirred awake. The ground beneath his feet was damp from the night's dew, a tangible reminder of the chill that clung to the early hours. Nearby, Katelyn lay curled up, nestled in the warmth of her blanket. Barend moved quietly, careful not to disturb her peaceful slumber, and gently draped the thick blue blanket back over her.

A deep sigh escaped Barend's lips as he reached for his first cigarette, the glowing tip briefly illuminating his face in the dim light. "A cigarette before the princess awakes," he mused to himself, the smoke curling lazily into the crisp morning air.

Vuyo, ever observant, spoke up from across the campfire. "Makes a person think sometimes, right?" he offered, his voice carrying a hint of contemplation.

Barend shook his head lightly, exhaling a plume of smoke. "Nothing really to think about," he replied stoically. "Just a few more days, one border... and a new life."

Vuyo rose from his seat, stretching and pulling his shirt right. A knowing smile played on his lips as he surveyed the mist-shrouded surroundings. The promise of a fresh start hung in the air, mingling with the scent of damp earth and the quiet rustle of leaves stirring in the breeze.

Barend's eyes twitched with a mix of disbelief and anger as he surveyed the scene for the second time. The cut rope lay on the ground, a stark testament to the thieves' precision. It wasn't just the horses that were gone; their precious cargo of hay stacks, their loot, had all vanished into thin air.

Making his way over to where Lloyd should have been keeping watch, Barend's frustration boiled over. He found his comrade sprawled on the ground, mouth agape, clearly under the influence of his beloved "Irish soup." Without a moment's hesitation, Barend grabbed a bucket nearby, walked back to him and splashed cold water over Lloyd's face, jolting him awake with a shock.

"What the...?! Can't a man rest in peace..." Lloyd muttered groggily, only to freeze as he took in the sight of the missing horses.

"Darnit..." Lloyd cursed, his speech slurred. He looked down to find part of the cut rope still gripped in his hand. "I tied my hand..."

With a furious roar, Lloyd instantly sprang to his feet, kicking up dust and hurling rocks in a fit of rage. "Bastards! They took my finest brandy right from under me... those damn crooks! When I find them, I'll break their limbs, starting with their fingers... and owww..."

Amidst the commotion, Katelyn stirred awake, making puppy-like little sighs. Her tender voice cut through the tension like a beacon of innocence amidst chaos. "Daddy, where is Jasmine?"

Barend's heart sank momentarily. "I'm not sure right now, Katelyn, but give me a minute. We'll find them."

And Lucy?" she asked again, this time with heightened concern.

"Lucy was on the back with Jasmine and the rest of our cargo," Barend explained, his mind racing with possibilities. "All that's left is a bag of food next to us at the fire. They'll realize what they have soon enough, unless that's exactly what they came for."

"It's going to be fine, Katie," Barend tried to reassure her as calmly as possible, though his own resolve was tinged with fury. "I'll make sure I find Lucy Bear and whoever did this."

Barend clenched his fists together, every muscle in his body rigid with pure anger. But he knew this was not the time to vent his frustrations. They needed a plan of action, and they needed to act upon it swiftly. The thieves wouldn't have gone very far, not with their horses, especially Jasmine and with the heavy cargo of loot. Justice would be swift, and Barend was determined to ensure it.

They pressed on, urgency driving their every step as they followed the trail left by the thieves. Hours passed by, marked only by the relentless advance of the sun overhead, casting their pursuit in a grueling heat.

"We can't possibly catch them on foot," Barend muttered to himself, though the determination in his voice was unwavering. "But we can't give up now..." His jaw clenched, anger and worry twisting in his gut.

They marched on, the land unfurling endlessly before them. Every now and then, they spotted some heaps of horse dung, fresh tracks, and remnants of hay strewn along the path, reassuring signs that they were on the right track. But the absence of any sign of the thieves themselves weighed heavily on their spirits.

The sun beat down mercilessly, sapping their strength with every passing minute. They realized they had no more drinking water left, and the parched landscape offered no respite. Still, they continued to push forward, driven by the desperate need to reclaim what was stolen.

"I really can't go on, Daddy... It hurts..." Katelyn's voice trembled with exhaustion as her knees toppled, causing her to sink down onto the ground, her small frame unable to endure the relentless march any longer.

Barend's heart clenched at the sight of his daughter faltering. He knelt beside her, gently brushing sweat-soaked hair from her forehead and feeling her high temperature with the back of his hand. "Hang in there, Katie... Daddy will get you through this...," he murmured, his own fatigue and worry etched across his face. "We'll rest for a moment, then we keep going. We have to find Lucy and Jasmine."

He glanced at Vuyo and Lloyd, their faces etched with determination and weariness alike. "We're definitely not giving up," Barend declared, his voice carrying a resolve that echoed across the desolate landscape. "Not until we find them."

"This isn't the time for tears, my girl..." Barend's voice was firm, though filled with a tenderness that only a father could muster in such dire circumstances. "Don't worry...We're going to find Jasmine and Lucy Bear, okay?"

Katelyn looked up at her father, her eyes brimming with worry and pools of tears. "Promise, Daddy?" she whispered softly, her little voice quivering.

Barend's jaw tightened as he fought to contain his own emotions. "If it's the last thing I do," he muttered to himself, his fierce determination a palpable force in the air.

Seated on a rock nearby, Katelyn's small figure seemed so fragile and lonely amidst the rugged wilderness they found themselves in. Her tear-streaked face and unkempt hair spoke volumes about her exhaustion and fear.

"Okay, let me take a look at that..." Barend sighed, kneeling beside her. It was clear the journey had taken its toll on his daughter; her feet were blistered, her otherwise subtly rosy cheeks flushed a deeper shade with fever.

"Daddy, my side hurts so much," Katelyn whimpered, pointing to her abdomen.

Barend gently touched her forehead, feeling the heat radiating from her skin. "You're burning up, Katie," he murmured, worry creasing his brow. "Here, drink a last sip of water. You're probably just dehydrated."

Katelyn took a long sip from the canteen, tears still glistening in her eyes. "But Daddy... Lucy can't sleep without me," she choked out, her voice shaking between the sobs. "And what if that masked man comes and takes her away?"

Barend's heart clenched at his daughter's sheer distress. Failing at words, he gathered her into his arms, holding her close against his chest. "Shh, it's going to be okay, baby," he whispered, his voice hoarse with emotion. "Daddy won't let anything happen to Lucy.... I promise you."

He rocked her gently, the weight of their predicament pressing down on him like a heavy burden. In the vast expanse of the ruthless wilderness, with uncertainty stretching out before them, Barend found solace in the warmth of his daughter's embrace, a beacon of hope amidst their darkest hour.

"And Jasmine, Daddy?" Katelyn's voice was earnest, her eyes pleading for reassurance.

Barend nodded solemnly, his expression grave yet resolute. "And Jasmine. I promise, Katie."

"Now you stay here," Barend instructed gently, trying to temper his daughter's insistence.

Katelyn shook her head defiantly. "I can help, Daddy. Jasmine will only go with me."

Barend sighed inwardly, frustration tugging at his resolve. "This donkey has been nothing but trouble from the start. If it weren't for Katelyn..."

"But I can help, Daddy, please," Katelyn persisted, her voice wavering between determination and pleading as she stood up. "I'm a big girl now, see.,,"

"I said no, alright?" Barend's voice hardened, his gaze piercing. "No arguments."

Katelyn's lower lip trembled as she fought back another wave of tears, her disappointment palpable. With a frustrated kick at the dusty ground, she turned away, her small form silhouetted against the stark landscape.

"Lloyd, you stay here with Katelyn," Barend instructed, redirecting his attention to his grumbling companion.

Lloyd shook his head adamantly, his tone stubborn. "No way. I didn't sign up for babysitting, bro." He gathered his gear and started to move forward. "What if you don't come back?"

Barend's eyes narrowed, his patience wearing thin. "Then you drop her off at the first orphanage you find. They always have space for one more."

"She's your problem, not mine," Lloyd retorted, his frustration mirroring Barend's.

"You watch your mouth, boy!," Barend warned sharply, his voice low and dangerous. "Before you say something you'll regret."

Lloyd fell silent, his expression mutinous but subdued. With a last defiant glance at Barend, he grumbled and reluctantly followed, the weight of their uncertain journey pressing heavily upon them all.

Lloyd's severe irritation simmered visibly, his eyes locked defiantly onto Barend's. "Make my day," he muttered through clenched teeth, a challenge clear in his tone.

Barend's patience suddenly snapped. With a swift motion, he lunged at Lloyd, grabbing him by the collar and throwing him hard onto the dusty ground. Tessa, sensing the tension, barked fiercely, her teeth snapping at Lloyd's pant legs as if trying to intervene.

Lloyd reacted instinctively, pulling a knife from his belt and slashing towards Barend. With practiced reflexes, Barend deftly deflected the blade, his hand moving as quick as lightning to strike Lloyd across the face with a powerful punch. Lloyd stumbled backward, blood streaming from his split lip, mixing with the dry earth beneath him.

Tears welled up in Katelyn's eyes as she ran closer, gaping at the terrible scene in front of her. Her voice was trembling with desperation. "Stop it! Please, just stop!"

Barend stood there towering over Lloyd, his chest heaving with adrenaline and frustration. He kicked the knife away angrily, his gaze hardening as he glared down at his injured companion. "You've made enough of a mess for one day, Lloyd."

Lloyd's mouth twisted in pain and defiance as he slowly regained his footing, dusting himself off and wiping the sweat and blood from his face. He stood there panting, glaring back at Barend with resentment burning in his eyes.

Meanwhile, Katelyn sobbed bitterly, her distress evident as Barend approached her, his hand reaching out to comfort her. But she recoiled, pulling away from his touch. "I didn't mean that, Katie," Barend murmured softly, regret coloring his tone.

The tension hung heavily in the air, the silence broken only by Tessa's subdued whimpers as she hovered protectively nearby, trotting to and fro. The day's events had taken their toll, leaving wounds both physical and emotional, their resolve tested against the unforgiving landscape and the dangers that lurked within it.

Tears streamed down Katelyn's face as she sat there with her head bowed, resting on her arms, her voice choked with anguish. "Leave me alone!" she cried when Barend tried to console her, her words sharp with hurt. "I wish you never picked me up."

Barend winced at her words, his own heart heavy with guilt and frustration. He turned to face her, trying to compose himself while the wilderness around them was quiet except for the soft whispers of the wind through the grass. "At least mom would not fight like this," she continued grievously, her voice trembling with every word.

Barend's brows furrowed, a pang of sadness and regret gripping tightly at his chest. "Well, where do you think she is now, huh? Looking for you?" he retorted, his voice tinged with bitterness. "No... she left you. What a great mom, huh?"

"I'm all you have, like it or not..." Barend continued, his tone softer now, pleading. "And I'm trying my best to take good care of you..."

Katelyn shook her head vehemently while sniffing and wiping the tears, her gaze filled with hurt and defiance. "No... Go away! I don't need you..."

Barend's heart sank like a heavy rock in the ocean as her piercing words hung in the air. He turned away from her, his jaw clenched tight, struggling to contain the turmoil of emotions within him. The silence between them carried on for what felt like an eternity, heavy with unspoken words and unresolved pain.

By now, Barend felt the weight of their situation like the oppressive heat of the sun above. The landscape stretched out barren and unyielding, as quiet as can be, except for the high-pitched hum of the sun beetles. The harsh heat of the day was starting to sap their last energy.

Barend and Vuyo cautiously signaled for them to press on, moving at a brisk pace, their determination driving them forward like relentless hunters on the trail of their prey. Barend's mind was a whirlwind of conflicting emotions, the echoes of Katelyn's hurtful words still haunting him.

"She didn't mean what she said, Barend," Vuyo remarked gently, breaking the silence that hung heavy between them. "She's just a small girl, you know. Tell me ... what does she know about life?"

Barend, still quiet with disillusionment glanced at Vuyo, his expression gravely troubled. "Maybe she's right, though ..." he mused aloud, his voice tinged with doubt.

Vuyo shook his head firmly. "Don't get sentimental now, Barend. We have a plan. Let's just make sure we get to the border, and you can give your daughter the life ... any life that you want. You can start fresh, umhlobo (*friend*)..."

"That was the point after all, right?" Barend replied quietly, a flicker of hope reigniting like the small flame of a candle within him.

Barend nodded resolutely, his jaw set in determination. They continued their relentless pace despite the exhausting heat, each step bringing them closer to the border that promised a new beginning, yet weighed heavily with the uncertainty of what lay ahead.

Barend squinted through the dim glow of the campfire at Vuyo, his curiosity piqued after days of shared hardship and silent camaraderie.

"You never told me what were you in for?" Barend's voice was low, edged with a mix of caution and genuine interest.

Vuyo met his gaze boldly and evenly, the flickering light casting shadows across his weathered face. "You never asked," he replied simply, his voice tinged with a hint of resignation.

"So I'm asking you now. What is it you were going to be hanged for?" Barend pressed, his tone earnest yet cautious.

"Murder," Vuyo answered without hesitation, his eyes flickering briefly downward.

Barend's brow furrowed slightly, processing the admission. "Thought so, but you sure don't act or look like no cold-blooded killer if I may say. What happened? Target practice gone wrong?" he asked, attempting to lighten the weight of the revelation.

Vuyo sighed heavily, his gaze distant. "Love can make a man do crazy things, Barend," he finally offered, his voice tinged with regret and a hint of sadness. He looked down and picked a little sheath of grass, trying to busy his mind with something other than the painful memories of the past.

Barend nodded slowly, understanding the complexities of human nature all too well. "Agree to that," he muttered, a flicker of his own past pain surfacing briefly. "That's why I keep from it like a pest."

"So where you from then? How come you're so good with that gun of yours?" Barend inquired, changing the subject to learn more about the man beside him.

"Well, I grew up on a farm," Vuyo began, his voice softening with memories. "My mother worked at a preschool, very religious, always at every prayer meeting possible." He paused, his expression darkening. "My father, on the other hand, well… let's just say he was not an easy man. Hardworking, fun-loving, but he had his days. He was like… a hard task master" Vuyo continued, his words tinged with the weight of old wounds. "And my mother's body showed the marks of his aggression clearly."

Barend listened intently as the flame reflected in his eyes, his own childhood scars resonating with Vuyo's words.

He was a big fan of the old westerns, cowboy movies, especially John Wayne. Barend's eyes sparkled with nostalgia as he shared this with Vuyo, the fire crackling softly in the cool night air.

"I knew all the lines," Vuyo continued, a fond smile tugging at his lips. "It was my favorite time watching it with him and playing to be a cowboy. He even taught me to shoot like one, and shooting, I was real good at. I was even a better shot than the farmer's sons. I shot literally everything... cleared the birds, cans..." Vuyo chuckled, remembering the mischief of his youth. "To my mother's contempt, naturally. She believed my gift of shooting was a curse, that it was the devil's instrument. And I could hear them fighting at night."

Barend leaned forward, his expression solemn as he absorbed Vuyo's story. "And then... what happened?" he prompted gently, sensing there was more.

Vuyo hesitated, a shadow passing over his features. "I came out from my bedroom after I heard the quarrel and the door slamming as my father walked out. A few bottles lie on the floor," he recounted, his voice softer now, filled with the weight of memory. "Approaching my mother, I find her crying, lying in the passageway, her mouth bleeding and clothing torn." Vuyo's gaze lowered, reliving the pain of that moment.

Barend's eyes darkened with understanding, the lines of his face etched with empathy. "I walked closer to touch her face, but she pulled away from me," Vuyo murmured, the memory still raw after all these years.

Barend nodded solemnly, hanging on every word.

"It was not long before my mother placed me into my uncle's care when she became sick," Vuyo continued, the fire casting flickering shadows across their faces. "My uncle was an Anglican priest, and I followed in his footsteps."

His silence spoke volumes, a shared understanding passing between them of the wounds that shaped their lives.

As they sat around the crackling fire, Vuyo's voice wavered slightly as he recounted his time as a priest, his words hanging heavy in the night air.

"Working as a priest, you see many things," Vuyo began, his eyes distant as he gazed into the fire. "I met a young woman, Therene... a beautiful blonde girl with soft brown eyes and a heart just as kind as her eyes..." He paused, as if searching for the right words to capture the depth of his feelings.

"At first, she came to visit to drop off old clothing for the church child care projects," Vuyo continued, his voice softening with nostalgia. "But the more I saw her, I could not help..." He trailed off, a hint of melancholy coloring his tone.

"It was as if she was everywhere I went, and the more I tried to suppress it, the more I felt it." Vuyo's gaze flickered towards Barend, who sat there silently, still listening intently.

"But she was to marry Andre Myburgh, the mayor's son," Vuyo sighed, his shoulders sagging with the weight of unspoken regret. "On the wedding day, I saw her one final time." He spoke slowly, each word laden with emotion. "I could see her beautiful appearance through the window of the guest house. I brought her flowers but did not have the heart to give them to her, so I just left them at the door."

Barend nodded understandingly, his expression unreadable in the flickering firelight. The night seemed to hold its breath as Vuyo continued, his voice betraying the ache of a heart torn asunder.

"My heart was torn from the inside," Vuyo confessed, his eyes clouded with memories. "On the day the woman I loved... the woman I dreamed of my whole life... she married another. I was speaking at a funeral, but felt like I was in the coffin myself." He shook his head bitterly, as if trying to dispel the painful recollections.

"And what was I supposed to do?" Vuyo's voice was tinged with frustration. "Marrying a man of a different color was not only illegal, but an act against God, some said... so they believed." He sighed heavily, swallowing the tears, his hands clenched into fists.

"I thought it would go away," Vuyo admitted quietly, his gaze fixed on the dancing flames. "But it became only more difficult."

Vuyo remained silent, the crackling of the fire punctuating the heaviness of the moment. The stars above bore witness to their shared silence, the weight of unspoken dreams and shattered hopes hanging between them like a veil of mist over the rugged landscape.

After that, I threw myself into the works of the church," Vuyo continued, his voice tinged with a mixture of resolve and lingering pain. The fire crackled as if echoing the emotions in his tale. "It became somewhat easier with time, focusing on the hurts of others. I avoided seeing her at all costs."

"But it was not long before she returned," Vuyo sighed heavily, his eyes distant as he recalled the vivid memories. "At first, with blue marks on her arm, clearly from aggressive handling. She didn't want me to do anything about it. She only came to drop off some clothing." His fingers traced an invisible path over his arm, as if recounting the touch of her bruised skin brought forth a rush of old feelings.

"Andre," Vuyo continued, his voice hardening slightly, "was acutely uneasy if she was absent from home, always suspecting her. Meanwhile, he didn't make much of a big deal about the evenings he spent outside of the house, to say the least." Vuyo's jaw tensed, the lines of his face etched with a mixture of concern and disapproval. "He would come back home late at night, and well... let's just say he had a way with women." He paused, his gaze flickering towards Barend, who listened ever intently.

"Even with his behavior, sometimes drunken anger that he took out on her, she remained devoted, faithful," Vuyo admitted with a mixture of admiration and sadness. The complexities of human relationships were laid bare in his words, each sentence carrying the weight of unspoken truths.

"Therene offered to help at the soup kitchen at the church," Vuyo added, a hint of pride in his voice despite the family's disapproval. "Much to her family's despise." He shook his head slightly, a rueful smile touching his lips. "But she was determined to make a difference, despite everything."

It was late Friday evening, the air thick with tension as Vuyo approached Therene's house. The routine visit to collect clothing and food supplies from the community took a somber turn as he prepared to leave. As he made his way to the back door, he heard Andre stumble in through the frontdoor with a loud noise.

"Therene! Therene... waar draai jy? *(where are you)*" Andre's voice echoed harshly through the house. "Kom hier, jou mooi ding! *(Come here, you beautiful thing!)*"

Therene nervously made her appearance, holding a glass of brandy tightly, her face a mask of calm composure. "Ek kan ruik hy was hier! Dit stink soos... *(I can smell he was here, it smells like...)*" Her words trailed off as Andre barged toward her.

With a gentle touch, she slowly placed a finger on his lips. "Shhhh, kom, kom, sit hier by my *(shhh, come, come and sit here with me)*." But Andre pushed her away roughly, the crystal glass slipping from her hand at once and shattering on the floor. Vuyo's heart clenched at the sound of her cries, the anguish in her voice cutting through the stillness of the night.

"The town people are talking," Andre accused, his voice thick with suspicion. "And I will never let a black man have his way with my wife."

"Andre, I have never been unfaithful to you," Therene pleaded, her words desperate yet firm. "Even when I knew about those girls..."

"You're crazy! There is nobody else," Andre insisted, advancing toward her with evil intent that sent a shiver down Vuyo's spine. He hesitated, torn between the urge to intervene and the knowledge that it was not his place to do so.

"Christa, Petra..." Therene's voice quivered as she spoke, her eyes darting nervously around the room. "I heard all the stories and I can smell their perfume on you..." She leaned in, hesitating for a moment before inhaling deeply from Andre's shirt. "A woman's perfume... like the ones you used to buy me when we first met."

Andre chuckled mockingly, taking her hand in his. "It must be yours then," he said with a smirk, "Haven't had any for a long while..."

As Andre drew closer, breathing brandy fumes, intent on kissing her, Vuyo's resolve hardened.

Therene, infuriated by his actions, attempted to pull her hand away, but Andre's grip tightened, forcing her down to the floor. Before he could strike her again, the door burst open with a crash. Vuyo stood framed in the doorway, his presence filling the room with a tense energy.

He boldly stepped forward, his voice cutting through the tense air like a knife. "That's enough now, Andre."

"Well, well, well ... Look who we have here," Andre declared coolly, stepping forward. "If it isn't Superman, or should I say, 'Reverend Man.'"

He was shocked yet livid to find Vuyo standing there, his expression dark with determination. "Stay out of this, Vuyo!" he shouted loudly, his voice tinged with both fear and anger.

But Vuyo held his ground. "Not when you're hurting her," he said firmly with arms folded, his gaze steady on Andre's.

Therene's eyes flickered with a mixture of relief and fear as Vuyo's presence seemed to momentarily halt Andre's advance. The room filled with an uneasy silence, broken only by the soft sound of the wind outside and the distant murmur of voices from the town beyond.

Andre's face twisted into a sneer as he grabbed his hunting rifle from the wall. Slowly, he approached Vuyo, the rifle held ominously in his grip. "There's no need for violence," Vuyo interjected calmly, trying to diffuse the escalating tension.

Andre turned the rifle towards Vuyo, the cold metal of the barrel inches from Vuyo's face. He chuckled darkly. "I didn't ask for a home visit or a sermon in my own house," Andre retorted, his voice laced with menace. "You're throwing breadcrumbs to the crows."

"Even a crow will eat when it's hungry," Vuyo countered evenly, his gaze steady despite the threat before him.

In a sudden twist, Therene launched herself at Andre, her desperation turning to fury as she struggled to wrestle the gun away. She sank her teeth into his arm, drawing a cry of pain as Andre dropped the rifle to the floor. Anger flashing in his eyes, he struck out with his free hand, the blow landing on Therene's face. She crumpled onto the floor into the corner, gasping for breath, tears streaming down her cheeks.

Vuyo's jaw clenched as he watched the scene unfold, his resolve hardening. He knew this confrontation was far from over, and the stakes had never been higher.

Andre continued kicking aggressively at her without pausing for a moment. Instinctively, Vuyo runs toward Andre, grabbing the nearest heavy object he could find on the coffee table... a large glass ornament. With adrenaline coursing through him, he swings it hard, landing a devastating blow to Andre's head. The impact is audible, and Andre crumples to the floor, blood spilling from the wound.

Vuyo lets the ornament drop from his grip, the weight of what he's done sinking in. Therene lies half-unconscious on the floor, her breathing shallow. Vuyo staggers to his feet, wiping blood and sweat from his forehead, and kneels beside her, checking her pulse.

Outside, the noise of approaching footsteps and raised voices grew louder. People were already on their way there, drawn by the commotion. Vuyo leans over Therene, pressing a quick kiss to her forehead. In that very moment, he knew his life would never be the same again.

Deciding swiftly, Vuyo understands his best chance is to flee. He knows all too well the odds stacked against a black man in such a situation, especially without any guarantees that Therene will testify against her husband. With a heavy heart, he resolves to run, seeking any way to prove his innocence and buy himself time.

From town to town, Vuyo moves, always a step ahead but never quite far enough. Trouble finds him wherever he goes, reminding him that some prayers go unanswered. In desperation, he finds himself answering other people's prayers, often with his own hands.

Vuyo sighs heavily, the weight of his choices and the harsh realities settling on his shoulders.

"I realized that you can't save both the butterfly and the spider," Vuyo began, his voice tinged with weariness as they sat around the fire. Barend looked at him, intrigued.

"What do you mean by that?" Barend asked, his brow furrowed in thought.

"The spider survives by preying on the weak, while the butterfly lives off the flowers to survive," Vuyo explained. "You can't save both because their survival depends on different things. So, I took care of some spiders in my life."

Barend considered this, his gaze flickering into the fire's flickering light. "So why didn't you take care of me then?" he asked quietly, a hint of hurt in his voice.

Vuyo met Barend's eyes squarely. "Well, fact is… you're not a spider," he said with a faint smile. "You have a good heart, Barend."

Barend chuckled lightly while lighting another cigarette, the tension easing a bit. "You just don't see that," he said, shaking his head. "But she does…" he remarked, inhaling deeply from his cigarette

"If we can get over the border," Barend said, his tone more serious now, "I can change. It can all be different, I'm sure of it."

Vuyo nodded solemnly and rubbed his hands together, the fire casting shadows on his face. They both knew crossing the border would mean more than just escaping the past. It would be a chance for redemption and a new beginning, a hope they both desperately clung to in the darkness of the night.

The sun dipped low on the horizon, casting long shadows across the rugged landscape. Barend and Vuyo trudged forward, their steps heavy with exhaustion and uncertainty. The land ahead seemed endless, with no clear trail to guide them.

"Barend, I think it's time we stop and turn around," Vuyo suggested, his voice tinged with concern. "We might lose track of where we are."

Barend remained silent, his jaw set in determination as he pressed on, each step a struggle against the encroaching night. The chill of evening descended upon them, a reminder of their vulnerable position in the vast wilderness.

"It's getting dark, you know..." Vuyo remarked, his tone edged with worry. "Those thieves could be miles ahead by now, or worse, they've found our things hidden among the hay."

Just then, a faint voice echoed through the valleys in the distance. Barend halted, straining to hear over the rustling wind. The voice carried a sense of urgency, mingled with the eerie solitude of the surroundings.

"Barend," Vuyo whispered, his eyes scanning the horizon for any sign of movement. "Did you hear that?"

Barend nodded, his senses heightened as he focused on the direction of the sound. It was a call that pierced the silence, beckoning them into the unknown. With each passing moment, the urgency to find its source grew stronger, driving them onward into the gathering dusk.

The young man scowled at the stubborn donkey, kicking up dust in frustration. "Damn donkey, should have killed it and left it long ago," he muttered under his breath and stood bent over, catching his breath.

The donkey, unmoved by his threats and rough treatment, continued to resist, stubbornly refusing to move forward. Despite its defiance, the donkey carried their precious cargo... hay stacks and all kinds of precious stolen goods plundered by the thieves.

"It's our lucky streak, this one," remarked the red-haired long-bearded man, his voice gravelly as he returned to the campfire. "Got our loot right on its back."

"We'll get moving tomorrow," he continued, warming a fire poker in the flames and brandishing it playfully at Jasmine. "And if it won't walk, I say we make it run."

Across the fire, a younger man tended to their meal, stirring a pot of beans and eggs over the flames.

In the meantime, Barend and Vuyo conspired together in quietness. Their plan was to wait until darkness cloaked the land, then sneak back for their stolen horses, just as the thieves had done to them.

"Or," Vuyo interrupted, a mischievous grin spreading across his face as he approached the fire, "we can teach them a lesson."

Barend's eyes lit up mischievously at the suggestion, his smile matching Vuyo's. The two criminal brothers tensed, sensing trouble as they lifted their guns, wary of Vuyo's approaching shadow.

"Looks like we're about to have ourselves a little showdown," Barend said, his voice low but filled with authority and anticipation.

"Put your hands up," the older brother demanded, his voice gruff and authoritative.

Vuyo approached cautiously, his hands held slightly away from his sides in a gesture of surrender. "Thank heavens I found you," he began, his voice animating weariness. "I'm just a hungry old soul looking for some warmth around the fire. It's been days since I last ate."

The older criminal scoffed, his expression hardening. "Beat it, old man. This ain't no soup kitchen."

Vuyo persisted, undeterred. "Some water then, if I may," he requested politely.

Without a word, the older brother grabbed an old cup, turned away, unzipped his trousers and urinated into it. He placed the foul cup in front of Vuyo on a little makeshift table they had stolen along with the other goods and sneered. "All yours now," he jeered, sharing a laugh with his younger companion.

Vuyo stared at the cup in disgust, his jaw tightening in restrained anger. The two brothers continued to laugh, clearly intoxicated from Lloyd's special bottles.

"May I have your name?" Vuyo asked suddenly, his voice steady despite the situation.

"What for?" the younger brother scoffed, slurring slightly. "It's not like you'll remember it."

Vuyo's eyes narrowed slightly. "I want to write it on your graves," he replied calmly, his words cutting through the drunken haze.

Enraged, the older brother reached for his gun, intending to silence Vuyo permanently. Before he could react, Barend surged forward with lightning speed. With a swift and powerful movement, he tackled the older brother to the ground. The gun clattered to the dirt, forgotten as the sole of Barend's leather boot connected solidly with the man's face, rendering him unconscious in an instant.

The younger brother staggered back, shock and fear flashing across his face as he realized the sudden turn of events. Vuyo stood tall, his gaze steady and unwavering.

"Next time," Vuyo said calmly, "think twice before you underestimate an old man."

A crackling fire cast flickering shadows in the gathering darkness as the young criminal stirred awake to the sight of his older brother being ruthlessly beaten.

"You gonna talk, son?" Lloyd taunted, twirling a hefty stick with a sinister grin. "Or shall we do this the hard way?"

The older brother glared defiantly at Barend, blood dripping from his split lip to stain the dirt beneath him. "You don't know who you're messing with," he growled hoarsely. "Better watch your back."

Barend shook his head slowly, a mix of disappointment and resignation evident in his voice. "What a pity," he murmured aloud.

With deliberate calmness, Barend withdrew a page from his pocket and held it out to both brothers. "If it were up to me, I'd put an end to this right here and now," he began, his voice carrying a weight of finality. "But my friend here," he gestured towards Vuyo, "he's got a conscience."

The younger brother's face lit up with a relieved smile. "Thank you," he muttered gratefully, his words thick with emotion. "Thank you."

Addressing the paper to the younger brother, Barend wrote in clear, deliberate strokes, his hand steady despite the tense atmosphere. The fire crackled nearby, casting dancing shadows on the scene as the older criminal smirked and crumpled his own paper, tossing it disdainfully into the flames.

"Barend... fine, have it your way," the older brother sneered, his voice laced with defiance.

Ignoring the older brother's theatrics, Barend turned his attention to the younger one, who dutifully began scribbling his details on the paper. With practiced efficiency, Barend seized the older brother's arm and hauled him roughly away from the fire, while Vuyo secured the younger brother's wrists with tight knots.

"Don't go running into them bushes now," Barend warned gruffly, his gaze unwavering as he glanced at the bound younger brother. "I've got a steady hand, and I'd hate to waste bullets on you tonight."

The sun sank below the horizon, casting the landscape into deepening shadows. Barend positioned the older brother, his face etched with a grim resolve, and the crack of a gunshot shattered the eerie silence. The younger brother, helpless and restrained, watched in horror as his older sibling crumpled to the ground in the distance.

Enraged and desperate, the younger brother thrashed against his bindings, kicking and squirming in a futile attempt to break free.

Barend stood over the trembling young man, his gaze piercing through the dim light of the dying fire. The young thief looked up at him, his voice quivering with fear and desperation.

"Please don't... I... I beg you," the young man stammered fearfully, his face drained of color.

Barend's expression remained stern. "Who sent you?" he demanded.

"Nobody," the young man blurted out quickly. "We're just two thieves... we saw your horses and... well, we thought..."

Before he could finish, Barend delivered a swift kick to the man's knees, sending him crashing to the ground.

"I beg you, sir, for mercy," the young man pleaded, his voice choked with emotion. "I have a wife back home, and a baby boy..."

"You should have thought about that long ago," Barend interrupted, his tone cold and unwavering.

He loaded his gun methodically, the sound of each bullet sliding into place echoing in the tense silence. A faint smile played on Barend's lips as he raised the gun, aiming directly at the man's face. The gunshot reverberated through the valley, followed by a moment of eerie stillness.

The young man opened his eyes, expecting the worst, only to find himself still alive. Barend's voice cut through the lingering echoes.

"See this as your second chance," Barend said authoritatively. "Go to your wife, tell her you love her, and take care of your child. Raise your boy to be a better man... But if I ever see you again..."

The young man swallowed and nodded fervently, his gratitude palpable despite the fear still etched on his face.

"You have my word," he whispered, his voice trembling with relief and newfound resolve.

Barend stood wide-legged over the fallen older brother, who lay subdued on the ground with a cloth gagging his protests. Vuyo knelt beside him, his heavy knee pressing into the man's back to keep him pinned down.

Barend turned to Vuyo, his eyes narrowing with a mix of determination and dark humor. "Shall we feed him to the crows?" he asked, his voice carrying a cold edge.

The older brother struggled against Vuyo's restraint, muffled sounds of defiance barely escaping the cloth which they secured in his mouth. Vuyo glanced at Barend and smirked, his grip tightening just enough to remind the man of his precarious situation.

"Should have written that letter now," Vuyo quipped, his tone laced with irony.

Barend nodded in acknowledgment, his gaze flickering briefly towards the horizon where the last remnants of daylight faded into dusk. He considered the implications of their choices, weighing justice against mercy in the harsh landscape that surrounded them.

After a moment's contemplation, Barend stepped forward, his presence commanding as he looked down at the older brother with a mixture of disdain and resolve. "Leave him…" Barend commanded tersely to Vuyo. "We've dealt with enough tonight."

Vuyo released his grip reluctantly, cautiously rising from the older brother's back as Barend turned away, walking back towards their campfire, lighting a cigarette. The air hung heavy with the echoes of their encounter, the distant cawing of crows mingling with the fading cries of the defeated.

As they retreated into the encroaching darkness, leaving the would-be thieves behind, their journey continued with the weight of their actions settling heavily upon them, knowing that their choices had shaped the path ahead in ways both unforeseen and irreversible.

The early morning air was crisp as Vuyo and Barend rode back on horseback, their hearts buoyed by the sight of Jasmine and their recovered treasures. But their relief was short-lived as they approached the spot where they had left Lloyd and Katelyn, only to find emptiness and silence.

In the distance, a voice broke the quietude. Lloyd's frantic shouts echoed across the hillside, the desperation in his tone unmistakable. He was calling for Katelyn, his voice carrying a desperate plea that sent shivers down Barend's spine.

As Barend and Vuyo drew nearer, Lloyd spotted them and walked toward them, wiping sweaty hair out of his face. He immediately began a nervous attempt at explanation, his steps faltering as he walked backward.

"I see you found the horses... that's very good, and the gold?" Lloyd stammered, trying to deflect from the issue at hand, his eyes darting nervously.

Barend dismounted slowly, his gaze fixed on Lloyd with a mix of intense concern and growing anger. "All there," Barend replied tersely, his voice betraying the worry that gnawed at him.

Lloyd continued to evade Barend's piercing stare, his movements awkward and uneasy. "This side? All is good... all is good," he muttered, hands on hips as usual, avoiding eye contact.

Barend's patience wore thin as he pressed Lloyd for answers. "So where is my daughter, Lloyd?" he demanded, his voice rising with each word.

Lloyd hesitated, his eyes shifting uncomfortably. "She is here... somewhere..." he mumbled, nervously scratching his head while scanning the surroundings as if hoping Katelyn would miraculously appear.

Growing increasingly agitated, Barend seized Lloyd by the shoulders, his grip firm and unforgiving. "Katelyn, come out now! Your father found Jasmine. The game is over!" Barend called out desperately, his voice tinged with a mixture of fear and urgency.

Lloyd's face fell, a mix of guilt and fear clouding his features as he struggled to find the right words. "She was right there, man. I'm telling you the truth," he pleaded, his voice trembling.

Unable to contain his frustration any longer, Barend stormed over to his bag, retrieving his gun with a determined resolve. The weight of the situation bore down heavily on him as he faced Lloyd with steely resolve.

"What exactly did you expect me to do, tie her to a tree?" Lloyd blurted out defensively, his words a feeble attempt to justify his failure.

Barend's hand tightened around the gun, his eyes narrowing with a fierce intensity. "At least then she would be here. I asked you to do one thing... one thing," he growled, his voice thick with disappointment and anger.

With a frustrated kick, Barend sent a discarded bottle rolling across the ground, the clanging sound echoing the turmoil within him. The morning sun cast long shadows around them, but all Barend could see was the enormous void left by his missing daughter, the echoes of Lloyd's excuses fading into the chill morning air.

The hills stretched out around Katelyn, their rolling expanses devoid of landmarks or any signs of civilization. She had been wandering around alone for what felt like hours, calling desperately for Jasmine, her voice becoming hoarse with each cry. The harsh sun beat down mercilessly, casting long shadows that offered no respite from the heat.

Exhausted and very hungry, Katelyn finally sank down onto a patch of dry grass, sobbing bitterly, her tears streaming down her dusty cheeks. She clutched a few pieces of biltong her father had given her, her only source of sustenance in this barren landscape. Despair weighed heavily on her young shoulders as she struggled to recall which direction she had come from.

Amidst her cries, a faint sound suddenly reached her ears. It was a soft mewing that initially sounded like a kitten. Startled, Katelyn turned, her eyes widening as she saw two fluffy leopard cubs cautiously approaching her. Her heart raced with a mix of fear and wonder. She had heard tales of leopards roaming these hills, elusive and powerful creatures that commanded both respect and fear.

Carefully, Katelyn scanned her surroundings for any sign of the cubs' mother, but there was none in sight. Taking a deep belly breath, she remembered her father's teachings about animals and cautiously extended a piece of biltong towards them. The cubs sniffed the air, slowly creeping closer, their curiosity piqued by the scent of the dried meat.

The sun dipped below the horizon, casting long shadows across the rugged landscape. Katelyn sat in solitude amidst the rolling hills, the two leopard cubs now her companions in the gathering dusk. Their playful antics had momentarily lifted her spirits, but as darkness quickly started descending, a chilling sense of isolation settled over her.

"Awww... You hungry and alone too?" Katelyn whispered softly, offering another piece of biltong to the cubs. They eagerly accepted, their tiny jaws crunching on the dried meat. The warmth of their furry bodies provided some comfort as Katelyn stroked them gently, their purrs a soothing melody amidst the encroaching silence.

But with the onset of the night, Katelyn's initial sense of wonder turned into a growing unease. The sky darkened swiftly, its hues fading from vibrant blues to ominous shades of black. Panic gnawed at her as she anxiously attempted to emulate her father's fire-making skills with two white rocks, but her efforts yielded only sparks that quickly fizzled out.

Frustration mingled with fear as the cold air seeped through her clothes, chilling her to the bone. She huddled closer to the cubs, their warmth a meager defense against the night's embrace. The distant cries of nocturnal creatures such as owls and even jackals echoed through the silence of the hills, their eerie calls heightening Katelyn's sense of vulnerability.

Lying next to the cubs on the grass, Katelyn shivered despite her efforts to stay calm. Her mind raced with thoughts of Jasmine, lost somewhere in this vast wilderness. She whispered silent prayers for her father and Vuyo, hoping against hope that they were out there searching for her, that they hadn't given up yet.

The flickering stars above offered very little solace as Katelyn fought internally against the fear threatening to overwhelm her. She clung to the presence of the leopard cubs, their companionship a fragile lifeline in the darkness. Exhaustion tugged at her eyelids, but she dared not sleep, afraid of what may be lurking in the shadows.

As the night wore on, Katelyn's resolve hardened. She told herself that she couldn't afford to give up now. With renewed determination, she vowed to survive until morning, when she would resume her quest for Jasmine with unwavering determination. The hills whispered ancient secrets around her along with the crickets and owls, their echoes urging her to persevere amidst the wild unknown.

The once tranquil night shattered into chaos as the distant howls of hyenas pierced the air. Katelyn's heart raced as she scanned the moonlit horizon, her hand gripping a makeshift weapon… a stout branch torn from a nearby bush. The leopard cubs, sensing the danger, scurried away, retreating into the safety of their mother's burrow, leaving Katelyn all by herself to confront the approaching threat.

"Don't be scared now," Katelyn murmured to herself, her voice trembling with fear as she watched the doglike figures draw nearer. The hyenas' eyes gleamed ominously in the moonlight, their sharp teeth glistening in the darkness. Instinctively, Katelyn secured her grip on the stick, her knuckles turning white as the knot in her stomach tightened too.

The sly hyenas prowled closer, almost camouflaged between the bushes, their movements stealthy and deliberate. Katelyn's mind raced with thoughts of her father and Vuyo, wondering if they were searching for her, if they were even aware of the danger she faced. She swung the stick in wide arcs, hoping to intimidate the predators, but they continued their advance with eerie persistence.

A primal growl erupted from the lead hyena, sending shivers down Katelyn's spine. Panic threatened to overwhelm her, but she fought to remain resolute, knowing she had to protect herself and the vulnerable cubs. With each step the hyenas took, Katelyn's breath quickened, her eyes darting between the encroaching predators and the distant hills.

Then, a desperate cry shattered the tension. One so loud and sudden that it pierced through the night and echoed across the hills.

"Daddy!!!" Katelyn screamed aloud, her voice laced with terror and desperation. Tears welled up in her eyes as she prayed for her father's swift arrival, for his strong arms to shield her from this nightmare.

The hyenas hesitated momentarily at the sound, their ears twitching as if unsure whether to press their attack. Katelyn's heart pounded in her chest as she held her ground, the stick trembling in her grasp. She could only hope and wait, willing her father to come, to rescue her from the jaws of the predators closing in around her.

The day had dragged on relentlessly without a trace of Katelyn. Barend, Vuyo, and Lloyd rode on horseback, their faces etched with intense worry, their gazes scanning every inch of the rugged terrain. Tessa and Jasmine trotted alongside, sensing the tension that gripped their riders.

"In the far distance," Barend's voice broke the heavy silence, his eyes catching a glimpse of something fluttering amidst the bush. His heart skipped a beat as he nudged his horse forward, urging it into a gallop toward the tantalizing clue.

"There!" Barend exclaimed as he reached the spot where a piece of fabric swayed gently in the breeze. It was magenta pink, unmistakably matching Katelyn's dress. Anxiety coiled in Barend's chest as he dismounted and retrieved the cloth from where it had snagged on a gnarled branch.

"This is definitely hers…" Barend muttered grimly, his fingers trembling slightly as he examined the torn material. "She can't be too far away now…"

Vuyo and Lloyd joined him, their faces etched with concern. Tessa whimpered softly, sensing her master's distress. Jasmine pawed at the ground, her ears flicking back and forth as if listening for any clue that might lead them closer to Katelyn.

"We need to move quickly, fellars," Vuyo urged, his voice tense with urgency. "If her dress is torn, she might be injured or…"

Barend held up a hand, cutting Vuyo off. "Let's not speculate, now…" he said firmly, though his own thoughts raced with dread. "Let's follow this trail. I am sure it'll lead us to her."

Lloyd glanced around, scanning the surroundings for any signs of movement. "She's out here somewhere," he muttered, his voice barely audible over the rustle of leaves and the distant call of birds. "We'll find her."

With renewed determination, Barend mounted his horse again, clutching Katelyn's torn piece of dress fabric tightly in his hand. The group pressed on, their hearts heavy with worry yet fueled by hope. They rode deeper into the wilderness, following the faint trail left behind by the fluttering piece of magenta pink, praying it would lead them to Katelyn before it was too late

As Barend approached the scene, his heart sank at the sight of a few drops of blood staining the sand. His mind raced, trying to grasp the implications of what he was seeing.

Just as the tension reached its peak and the hyenas seemed poised to strike, a low, guttural growl reverberated through the night air. The hyenas instantly froze, their predatory instincts momentarily overridden by a primal fear.

In a swift and unexpected turn of events, a mother cheetah pounced onto the scene, her sleek form cutting through the darkness with grace and power. Her arrival was swift and decisive, a blur of spotted fur and lethal grace. With a fierce snarl, she lunged at the nearest hyena, teeth bared and claws slashing through the air.

The hyenas, startled by this new threat, backed away momentarily, their growls now tinged with uncertainty. The mother cheetah, undeterred, positioned herself protectively between Katelyn and the predators, her amber eyes blazing with fierce determination.

Barend and the others arrived just a few moments later, their horses galloping hard across the sandy terrain. They skidded to a halt near Katelyn, who had never been more relieved to see her father.

"Daddy!!!" Katelyn cried out at once, with tears of relief streaming down her dirt-streaked face.

Barend leaped from his horse, his heart pounding with a mix of fear and relief. He rushed to Katelyn's side, pulling her into a tight embrace. "I'm here, sweetheart," he murmured, his voice thick with emotion. "Don't worry... You're safe now..."

Vuyo and Lloyd approached cautiously, their eyes scanning the perimeter for any lingering threats. Tessa and Jasmine circled protectively nearby, their senses keenly attuned to the danger still lurking in the darkness.

"Thank you, Momma Cheetah," Katelyn whispered gratefully, her eyes flickering towards the brave feline who had come to her rescue, almost like an answer to prayer.

The mother cheetah regarded them with a stern, steady gaze, her tearful blue ears flicking back and forth as she remained vigilant. She seemed to understand the gratitude in Katelyn's voice, a silent acknowledgment passing between them.

With the immediate threat quelled, Barend carefully examined Katelyn for injuries, his hands gentle yet thorough. "Are you hurt, my baby girl?" he asked, his voice trembling slightly.

Katelyn shook her head, clutching onto her father and sobbing onto his shoulder, as if afraid he might disappear again. "I-I'm okay, Daddy," she replied shakily. "Just so scared."

Barend kissed the top of her head, relief flooding through him. "You were so brave," he murmured, his voice choked with emotion. "I'm so so proud of you..."

Together, they made their way back to camp, the mother cheetah watching over them until they were safely out of harm's reach. The night air was filled with a sense of gratitude and awe, their ordeal a stark reminder of the dangers that lurked in the wild. Yet, amidst the peril, there was also a profound sense of resilience and the unbreakable bond between father and daughter, strengthened by their harrowing experience under the African sky. It was at this very moment that Barend instinctively knew... he was destined to turn his own story and his daughter's around for good. It was only a matter of time and perseverance.

Town in the Middle of Nowhere

They had left the familiar lands of Bantuland behind days ago, venturing into the vast emptiness of the wilderness. The landscape stretched endlessly, barren and unforgiving under the scorching African sun. Supplies dwindled, and water became a precious commodity. Even the horses, usually stalwart companions, showed signs of weariness, moving ahead more slowly than usual.

Katelyn, usually full of energy and laughter, now looked drained. Her cheeks were flushed with exhaustion, and her sunken eyes, usually bright with curiosity, held a hint of worry. She sat atop Jasmine, her small hands bearing bruises from gripping the reins of the stubborn donkey.

"Just a little bit further, Katelyn," Barend urged gently, his voice tinged with reassurance. He secured a rope between his horse and Jasmine's donkey, ensuring they stayed together as they plodded forward.

Katelyn shook her head weakly, her eyelids almost falling shut, her voice barely above a whisper. "I can't, Daddy. I just can't do this anymore."

Barend's heart sank at the sight of his daughter's fatigue. He knew they were pushing the limits of endurance, but they had absolutely no choice. They needed to find a town of some sorts... a place with water, supplies, and perhaps some resemblance of safety in this harsh wilderness.

"Promise you, we will find a town soon," Barend promised again, his tone firm despite the uncertainty gnawing at him. He cast a worried glance over the desolate landscape, scanning for any signs of civilization.

The journey continued, each step feeling heavier than the last. The sun beat down relentlessly, causing the landscape to blur in the distance and casting long shadows here and there across the arid land. The horses trod wearily, their hooves kicking up clouds of dust with each heavy step.

Hours passed by in silence broken only by the occasional creak of leather and the rhythmic plodding of hooves. Katelyn leaned against Jasmine's back, her eyes drooping with exhaustion. Barend kept a vigilant watch, his mind racing with thoughts of finding refuge before nightfall descended upon them once more.

As the day wore on, hope flickered like a dying flame. Then, in the distance, a faint silhouette emerged. They noticed a cluster of buildings shimmering in the heat haze. Barend's heart raced with renewed determination.

"There, Katelyn," he murmured, a surge of relief flooding through him. "I can see the town now...We're almost there. Hang on just a little longer, my girl..."

Katelyn lifted her head slowly, almost as if she were intoxicated, her eyes suddenly widening as she observed the distant shapes. A spark of hope reignited within her weary frame. "A town?" she asked hopefully.

Barend nodded, a smile tugging at the corners of his lips despite his exhaustion. "Yes, sweetheart. A town."

With newfound determination, they pressed on, guided by the promise of shelter, water, and breathing space from the harsh realities of their journey. The town beckoned like an oasis in the desert. For them it surely was a beacon of hope amidst the vast, taxing wilderness that had tested their endurance and strength to the utmost.

A Town Frozen in Time

As they slowly approached the outskirts of the town, a haunting stillness hung in the air, broken only by the soft shuffle of their horses' hooves against the dry, dusty ground. The forlorn buildings that lined the main street bore the marks of a bygone era... weathered wood and faded paint telling intricate stories of boom and bust during the mining rush.

"One thing I'm sure of is that this town was probably bustling during the mine rush," Barend remarked, his husky voice carrying a hint of nostalgia for a time he had never lived through. "People came from all over, hoping to strike it rich with diamonds and gold."

Katelyn, perched on Jasmine's back, craned her neck to take in the sight. "Whoa, It looks so old," she observed, her eyes wide with curiosity.

Barend smiled at her and nodded in agreement. "Yes, sweetheart. These towns were once vibrant places, filled with dreams and hopes of prosperity. But now..." He trailed off, sighing as the unspoken truth hanging heavy between them.

The streets were eerily dusty and quiet as they entered the heart of the town. As they cautiously entered there, the remnants of a long-forgotten era surrounded them. There were buildings with old faded signs, cobblestone paths inbetween buildings, slightly overgrown with weeds, and the occasional rusted relic of a mining cart left to decay.

Despite its antiquated appearance, signs of life lingered there. Barend stopped them, dismounted and went to turn a rusty tap near a rundown building, and to his relief, clear water flowed into the trough for their horses.

"Guys, we're in luck," Barend remarked, a touch of relief in his voice. "There's still running water."

Their immediate concern, however, was food supplies. They were running very low on essentials, and replenishing their provisions was paramount before they could continue their journey.

"We can't leave without stocking up," Barend said firmly, glancing over at Vuyo and Lloyd, who stood watch at the town's edge. "I'll go into town and see what I can find. You two stay here and keep a watchful eye..."

Vuyo stared at him, then nodded solemnly, his gaze sweeping the empty streets warily. "Be careful, Barend. We really don't know what we might encounter here."

Barend gave a reassuring nod before attempting to leave. Adjusting his hat, he took a deep breath and began walking towards the main street. The buildings loomed over him like silent sentinels, their windows dark and doorways shadowed.

As Barend ventured deeper into the town, the silence became almost oppressive. The footsteps in his leather shoes echoed faintly against the cobblestones, a stark contrast to the bustling memories the town must have once held. He passed boarded-up shops, their blackened windows covered in dust and neglect.

At the end of the main street, Barend spotted a small general store. The wooden sign above the door creaked slightly in the breeze, its paint faded but still half readable. With cautious steps, Barend pushed open the creaking door and stepped inside, hoping to find the supplies they desperately needed and perhaps some clue about the town's abandoned state. He was able to help himself to a few goods, until a rustle behind a door leading to a hidden storeroom startled him. Barend swiftly made his way out the shop's frontdoor while shoving a few essentials in his bag, moving quietly to avoid being caught.

As Barend ventured further into the town, the eeriness intensified. Windows and doors slammed shut at his approach, a strange kind of reception that put him on the edge. It was as if the town itself held its breath, waiting for something ominous to unfold.

Approaching the flickering lights of a bar, Barend's instincts told him to tread very carefully. A faint movement inside caught his attention, drawing him towards the dimly lit entrance. Unbeknownst to him, he was walking straight into the midst of a dire situation... a hold-up by a gang of ruthless hooligans.

Pushing open the creaky door, Barend entered cautiously, only to have the cold muzzle of a gun pressed firmly against his temple. The sight that greeted him was grim: a gang of armed men, faces obscured by shadows and dark accessories, their intent clear and dangerous. Barend raised his hands slowly, knowing any sudden move could spell immediate disaster.

In the tense silence that followed, Barend found himself roughly bound and forced to sit on the floor beside a young woman who worked at the bar. Their captors were aggressively barking orders, their voices laced with menace as they demanded a ransom, their greed palpable in the stale air of the bar.

Time stretched painfully as they waited, each passing minute weighing heavily on Barend's nerves. Outside the bar, Vuyo and Lloyd, stationed at the edge of town, felt a growing unease settle upon them. It had been too long since Barend had left them there, and the absence of any sign or sound from within the bar fueled their apprehension.

Vuyo sternly glanced at Lloyd, their silent communication speaking volumes. They knew their primary objective was to reach the border, to escape the dangers lurking in these forgotten towns. Yet, a solemn oath bound Vuyo. He had made a commitment to his companions, a loyalty that surpassed personal safety.

"We can't leave him here," Vuyo muttered, his voice a low murmur in the cool night air. "I'm telling you… Something's gone wrong in there. We can't just abandon him."

Lloyd's sweaty brow furrowed with concern, his eyes scanning the empty streets nervously. "But Vuyo, we don't know what we're dealing with in there. It could be a major trap."

Vuyo clenched his jaw as he looked down at his old dusty shoes, torn between duty and prudence. He knew the risks full well, he clearly understood the peril they faced by lingering in the town. Yet, leaving Barend to face the unknown alone went against every fiber of his being.

"We have to go in," Vuyo declared firmly, gritting his teeth as his resolve hardened. "We stick together, watch each other's backs. We find Barend and we get out, whatever it takes, mfondini..*(friend)*."

With grim determination, Vuyo took a deep breath and led the way back towards the bar, his heart heavy with concern for his friend and the dangerous game unfolding inside.

"Can I ask you for once to just please keep your eyes fixed on Katelyn?" Vuyo's voice carried a rare urgency, breaking the tense silence that had settled between them.

"Of course," Lloyd replied with a nod that vigorously shook his scruffy long hair through a serious expression. He understood full well the gravity of their situation, the need for sobriety and vigilance in these perilous times.

But before Lloyd could fully grasp the weight of Vuyo's request, Vuyo intervened with a sharp, sudden gesture. He quickly seized an empty beer bottle from behind Lloyd, flung it into the air with practiced ease, and sent a bullet through its heart. Shards of glass scattered like stars in the dim light of their campfire.

"Now that is just not trusting, brother!" Lloyd remarked, his tone laced with a hint of amusement, though his eyes bore a steely resolve.

Vuyo chuckled softly, a hint of resignation in his voice. "No word now... You please just make sure that you're here with the girl when I return, then drinks will be on me at the next stop."

"Well, you better start counting your coins, old man," Lloyd grunted as he teased, though the underlying tension was palpable.

With a stern nod, Vuyo turned away, striding purposefully towards the town ahead. His weighty steps echoed faintly in the quiet of the night, a solitary figure navigating the shadows cast by the flickering streetlights.

As Vuyo slowly approached, he passed by a cluster of prominent businessmen, their voices murmuring in hushed tones that carried on in the cool breeze. Curiosity piqued and Vuyo retarded his pace, listening intently without revealing his presence.

"That fool walked himself straight into it," one of the men remarked with a hint of disdain, his husky voice laced with contempt.

"The ransom they're demanding... It's insane," another added, his tone tinged with terror and disbelief.

From the snippets of conversation he overheard behind the bar's wooden doors, Vuyo pieced together the grim reality unfolding within the town's boundaries. A ransom, a dangerous game orchestrated by ruthless criminals. This was the situation Barend unwittingly found himself embroiled in.

"From the looks of it, he seems to be a cop," the first man continued, his words sinking heavily into Vuyo's consciousness. The implications were clear: Barend had unexpectedly stumbled into a trap, a perilous encounter that threatened to escalate beyond their control and explode into destruction.

"What do we seem to be dealing with, sir?" Vuyo's voice suddenly cut through the tense atmosphere, his uniform marking him as a figure of authority amidst the troubled town.

The man he addressed, Mayor Jamison, turned sharply at the sound of Vuyo's approach. Weariness etched lines on his anxious face, evidence of sleepless nights and the weight of responsibility. "Well, our small town has been terrorized like many others by the Davies gang," Mayor Jamison explained, his voice heavy with resignation. "They've ransacked homes, taken what they could, and now they're holding a few girls hostage. Not much we can do but give in to their demands. Don't want blood on our hands, you know."

Vuyo listened intently, absorbing the gravity of the situation. His jaw tightened slightly, betraying his resolve. "And the fool that walked in?" he inquired and folded his arms, his tone edged with concern.

The mayor sighed heavily, his gaze flickering with concern as he lifted his head. "He was a man, probably in his late twenties, dressed like a cop, I would say," Mayor Jamison replied grimly with a shake of his head. "But he hasn't surfaced again... Horses and money are on the way. Just a matter of minutes now until they arrive..."

Accepting a communication device from the mayor, Vuyo nodded in acknowledgment. "Thank you," he said shortly, nodding with a stern expression before turning away, his mind already racing with plans.

"That's a no-go now!" Mayor Jamison hastily called after him, his voice tinged with urgency. "You'll only get yourself killed, brother!"

Vuyo shook his head, a grim determination settling over him. "Have a little faith now," he retorted calmly, his voice firm as he strode slowly and purposefully towards the bar where danger loomed and lives hung in the balance.

Inside the dimly lit establishment, tension crackled in the air like static electricity. Patrons huddled together in a strenuous fashion, their sweaty faces etched with fear and resignation. The Davies gang, a shadowy presence of menace, held sway over the room, their guns serving as silent reminders of their authority.

Vuyo's gaze swept across the room, his instincts on high alert. He spotted Barend, bound and seated on the floor beside a young woman, their faces drawn with worry but their spirits unbroken. Without hesitation, Vuyo approached, his posture conveying both authority and a readiness to act.

"Easy now..." Vuyo murmured quietly to Barend and the girl as he cautiously knelt beside them, ensuring his voice carried reassurance despite the perilous circumstances. "We're getting you out of here in no time...I guarantee you!"

Barend's weary eyes flickered with relief and gratitude, though his expression remained stoic. "Good to see you, Vuyo," he replied quietly, his voice tinged with exhaustion and gratitude.

"Likewise," Vuyo replied with a momentary half-smile, his gaze assessing their bindings and the position of their captors. His mind raced with possibilities, weighing risks and planning his next power-move.

Outside, the steady sound of approaching hooves signaled the arrival of the ransom. It was now a race against time, a test of nerve and strategy amidst the looming threat of violence.

With a steady hand and a determined spirit, Vuyo prepared to confront the Davies gang, his heart steadfast in its resolve to bring justice and safety to the small town caught in the grip of fear and desperation.

"What's taking them so long?" The bearded man grumbled from his seat at the worn wooden table, his eyes darting impatiently towards the entrance. "We might have to start using some bullets if they don't hurry up, eh!?"

A gang member, a rough-looking man with a moustache and brown hair cascading into a mullet, sauntered closer to where the captive girl sat. His grin was a sinister twist of amusement and malice. "Looks like we'll have to show 'em what happens when they dawdle," he taunted, reaching out to touch the girl's face before crudely unzipping his pants.

In that tense moment, Barend's presence suddenly loomed like an impending cloud of thunder before the leering man. With a swift and decisive motion, Barend's heavy boot lashed out, connecting squarely with the man's groin. A guttural cry of pain erupted from the mullet-haired gang member as he crumpled to the ground, clutching himself in agony.

The bearded man at the table chuckled darkly as he arose and started approaching slowly, his gaze narrowing on Barend with a mixture of recognition and menace. "Well, well, well, if it ain't my old friend.." he drawled, a twisted smile playing on his lips. He stood there with his hands on his hips, looking down at his shoes. For a moment he appeared intimidated until he broke the silence, staring at Barend brazenly "Do I know you?"

Barend's eyes narrowed as he regarded the bearded man with cool disdain. "Let's see," he responded evenly, his voice carrying a hint of gravelly authority. "I remember a stinky sock shoved in my mouth and a preacher man trying to teach me and my brother a lesson. Well, guess what? That didn't work."

The bearded man's smile faltered slightly, a flicker of uncertainty crossing his weathered features. "Well, well," he muttered under his breath, his tone darkening. "Looks like you've found yourself in a bit of a bind now, preacher man."

Barend's jaw tightened as he assessed the situation, his mind secretly racing with strategies to turn the tide in their favor. Around them, tension crackled in the air like static electricity, the stalemate broken only by the occasional rustle of movement or muttered threat.

Outside, the rumble of approaching hooves drew ever nearer, signaling the impending arrival of the ransom and the potential for either rescue or further tyranny. In the dimly lit bar, amidst the shadows, broken glass and the palpable fear, Barend stood firm, his resolve unyielding in the face of danger, determined to protect the innocent and confront the evil that threatened to destroy them all.

The man's boot unapologetically connected solidly with Barend's stomach, knocking the wind right out of him. Barend staggered back, eventually bowing down with his hands resting on his knees, gritting his teeth against the pain that shot through him.

"I don't see your brother now," Barend managed to utter through clenched teeth, his hand pressing against his abdomen to ease the ache.

"Oh, you're a funny guy, eh?" the bearded Davies brother sneered, stepping closer as his cohorts gathered around. "I think I kinda like you. But I must warn you, that badge of yours is the only thing saving your hide right now. Otherwise, we'd carve you up right here and now."

The rest of the gang sneered and glanced at one another, then closed ranks, their faces set in varying degrees of hostility and anticipation. Barend quickly assessed their numbers. He spotted a total of eight men in the bar, including the two keeping watch over the hostages.

"Well, it looks like your counting skills aren't so sharp either," Barend retorted coolly, his eyes flicking over each of the men confronting him. "Only eight of you, right?"

Davies grunted, nodding his head slightly while being planted wide-legged, hands on his hips. "Don't need no maths for this. Enough to deal with the likes of you and your meddling friend."

As severe tension hung thick in the dimly lit bar, the standoff crackled with unspoken threats and palpable danger. Barend's mind raced faster than a Grand Prix car, calculating their only options amid the mounting peril. Outside, the sounds of approaching horses' hooves signaled the imminent arrival of the ransom and the need for swift action.

In the face of overwhelming odds, Barend courageously stood his ground, his resolve unshaken, ready to confront whatever fate had in store.

The four assailants unleashed a barrage of kicks and punches upon Barend, each blow landing with force and intent. Barend staggered under the onslaught, blood dripping from the corners of his mouth onto the gritty floor of the bar. Through the haze of pain and sweat, Barend muttered something unintelligible, prompting Davies to lean in closer, curiosity etched on his face.

Davies bent down, grabbing Barend by the head, demanding, "Speak up now, brave one!"

In a swift and desperate move, Barend headbutted Davies without warning, mustering up all his remaining strength and stunning the gang leader momentarily. Seizing the opportunity, Barend quickly snatched the rope that had bound his arms only moments earlier and looped it around Davies' neck. With a quick twist, he tightened the makeshift noose, using Davies as a shield against the gang members who were now brandishing their guns.

The gang hesitated, anxious and unsure whether to risk shooting their own leader. Barend took advantage of their hesitation, maneuvering behind Davies to maintain cover. As one of the gang members heaved and lunged forward with a knife, intent on freeing Davies, Barend reacted swiftly, delivering a powerful kick of the boot that sent the assailant sprawling across the floor.

With each step towards the door, Barend look back, calculating his chances of escape, his mind racing with anxious thoughts as adrenaline surged through his battered body

A voice thundered from outside, reverberating through the tense air inside the bar. "We have you surrounded! Come out with your hands in the air, and we may spare your life!"

One of the gang members cautiously poked his head out the door, only to have a bullet slice through his hat with a sharp whiz. Startled, he swiftly yanked back inside and peered anxiously through the nearest window, but another shot rang out, knocking his gun from his hand.

"I will count to ten, or we will open fire!" The loud authoritative voice outside declared. Three more shots cracked through the air, striking perilously close to the lookout gang members. Four men bolted outside, brandishing their weapons and scanning frantically for the source of the gunfire.

More shots followed without warning, targeting each man's feet with precision. The gang members cried out in pain as they collapsed to the ground, incapacitated by the disabling shots.

"Now, throw your guns away immediately, or the next shot goes to your head!" The voice commanded. Reluctantly, the wounded men obeyed, casting their firearms onto the ground in front of them with trembling hands, the clattering noises of surrendered weapons concealing their breathlessness.

Good.. Good," the authoritative voice declared from outside. "I will spare the life of only one, the last one who remains standing. You sort it out."

The distraught gang members exchanged bewildered glances, unsure of how to proceed. Before they could react, another sharp crack echoed through the air, prompting them into action. The first punch landed swiftly, setting off a chaotic brawl right outside the bar. Onlookers peered through their windows, curiosity drawing them to the spectacle unfolding in the street.

Amidst the rampant chaos, only one man managed to stay on his feet, lifting his hands in surrender. The creaky bar doors swung open, and Barend charged outside with four men tethered to Davies by a rope around his neck. With decisive force, Barend swung his arm and struck the remaining gang member with a powerful punch to the face.

Lloyd and Katelyn cautiously hurried over to where Barend and Vuyo stood, watching as the dust settled on the scene of their victory. After a long eerie silence that felt like hours, people cautiously began emerging from their houses, observing the aftermath of the intense confrontation.

Barend grinned confidently. "Got it covered," he assured Vuyo and nodded.

"Sure looks like it," Vuyo replied in a feeble tone, sharing in the relief that their ordeal was finally over.

"What kind of preacher are you anyway?" Barend quipped and wiped his brow, his voice edged with both humor and exhaustion. "Castrated a man, made four walk limb…"

Vuyo smiled as he efficiently tied the remaining gang members together, securing them for transport. His steady hands betrayed no hesitation, each knot a silent testament to his resolve. The mayor approached with visible relief, his gratitude palpable as he surveyed the subdued criminals.

In the distance, Lloyd guided the donkey and horses closer to town. Their hoofbeats echoed steadily, mingling with the distant applause of grateful townspeople and drawing the community's attention to the unfolding scene. Suddenly a voice rose above the others, exclaiming, "Thank the Lord! These men took my fine china!" as if to underline the curious mix of chaos and order that had become their town's new rhythm.

"The fine cops," the mayor announced proudly, gesturing towards Barend and Vuyo, "have made our town safe again." His tone was firm yet laced with warmth, a subtle reminder of the town's reliance on unexpected heroes.

Lloyd nudged Barend lightly. "Told you these skills would come in handy," he remarked with a smile, his eyes dancing with satisfaction, acknowledging their unexpected roles in restoring peace to the troubled town.

Barend looked over at Lloyd, a mix of curiosity and caution in his expression as he weighed the events of the day against the uncertain promise of the future. "And our package… well hidden?" he inquired, his voice low yet edged with anticipation.

Lloyd grinned broadly. "You better hope so," he replied.

"Apologies for the delay," Lloyd announced to the gathering crowd, his tone both respectful and commanding. "Let me introduce you to my partners." The murmurs of the crowd started settling, as his voice drew the attention of every listener.

Barend raised an eyebrow, glancing around at the expectant faces. In that brief moment, the collective hope and tension of the crowd seemed to converge in the space between each heartbeat. Lloyd's smile widened as he gestured proudly to his companions.

"Firstly, we have a man whose right hand was anointed and can shoot like no other," Lloyd continued theatrically. "Known only by his call name, The Cowboy Referent." His words floated on the air, mingling with the memories of past exploits and the promise of future deeds.

With a flick of his wrist, Lloyd tossed an apple into the air. Before it could fall, Vuyo's shot rang out, splitting the apple cleanly into two halves that dropped to the ground. Applause erupted from the onlookers, impressed by the sharpshooter's skill and the unspoken precision behind each movement.

"Secondly," Lloyd proclaimed, his voice carrying over the crowd's murmurs, "we have someone who needs little introduction, a man who can make objects disappear into thin air." His tone was both mysterious and inviting, drawing the crowd further into the spectacle.

A skeptical voice interrupted from the back. "Nonsense! Show us!" The challenge hung in the air, a small ripple of doubt amid the swelling excitement.

Lloyd chuckled softly, glancing back at Barend with a mischievous gleam in his eye.

Then he strolled confidently toward the mayor, his swiss-made Zobo pocket watch glinting in the sunlight. "If you may," he began, tapping the watch with a flourish that spoke of practiced showmanship. "Here in my hands, as you can see, we have a one-of-a-kind pocket watch." The crowd's attention sharpened in anticipation.

He held it up for all to see, then swiftly transferred it from his left hand to his right, and finally clasped his hands together in a silent query that begged an answer. "So, where is it?" a child's voice piped up from the crowd, breaking the tension with innocent wonder. "In your sleeve!"

Lloyd tried to avoid bursting out with laughter at the unexpected reply. "My sleeves? No way..." His voice carried both disbelief and amusement, inviting the audience to share in the light-hearted banter.

"Yes, it is!" the child insisted, bounding up to Lloyd with unbridled energy and plunging hands into his sleeves. Out came another watch, much to the astonishment of the onlookers. "Hey, that's my watch!" a man protested from the back of the gathering, his tone revealing his irritation as the magic of the moment took hold.

Lloyd grinned, unfazed by the interruption. "Wow, wow, wow! So, if we've magically transformed this man's watch, then where is the mayor's watch?" He turned to the amused mayor, his tone light yet inquisitive. "What do you say, sir?"

The mayor watched with a bemused expression as Lloyd continued his performance. Lloyd walked confidently toward a little girl in a cute red dress, who stood there staring wide-eyed at him, her expression a mix of wonder and curiosity. "I think this little girl right here is hiding something," he announced playfully.

The girl shook her head, blushing and hiding her arms behind her back. "I sure think you do..." Lloyd persisted, his voice gentle and teasing as he leaned in slightly. "What's in your pocket?"

Hesitantly, the girl slipped her hand into her dress pocket and withdrew the Zobo watch, revealing it with a shy smile that spoke of innocence and surprise.

Lloyd chuckled almost inaudibly before turning to the crowd, swinging his arms with a dramatic flair. "Alright then, how about a joke?" he suggested, inviting everyone to share in the moment.

In his element as the center of attention, Lloyd continued his playful banter with the crowd, turning the atmosphere into a whirlwind of light and engaging chatter. "What do you call a robbery in China?" he began, his voice carrying easily across the gathering, prompting people to exchange amused glances as they anticipated the punchline.

"A Chinese take away!" he announced, and laughter rippled through the crowd like a gentle wave, drawing smiles even from those who had earlier worn serious expressions.

"But wait, wait," Lloyd continued, his eyes twinkling with mischief as he posed another riddle. "What kind of robbery is not dangerous?" He paused on purpose, letting the anticipation build among the listeners.

"A safe robbery!" he declared with a grin, which brought more chuckles and a few playful groans of mockery from the audience.

Nearby, Barend stood there staring at Lloyd with his arms folded, sporting a slight frown. The tied-up criminal gang still sat there passively among the onlookers. Their expressions were a sober reminder of recent events. Some onlookers couldn't resist pulling faces at them, a subtle mix of scorn and relief passing through the crowd.

"Now, without further ado," Lloyd proclaimed, raising his voice slightly to draw everyone's attention. "We have a man who needs little introduction, as we've all seen him take the bull by the horns!" His words blended humor with the gravity of the moment, resonating with both children and adults as giggles and murmurs followed his announcement.

Lloyd then deftly removed a hat from a nearby man, its brim marked by a conspicuous bullet hole. "Now, feel free to throw in whatever you can spare," he announced with a charismatic smile, holding the hat out for donations. His voice carried a subtle mischief amidst genuine goodwill as he added, "Don't worry… every bit of it will go to those in need."

Moments later, an elderly lady, who had been distressed over her stolen fine china, stepped forward and dropped some coins into the hat. One by one, others followed, and soon the hat brimmed with money. Lloyd, with a satisfied smile, tipped the hat onto his own head, leaving coins clattering wildly on the floor, a gesture that brought a light-hearted chuckle from the crowd.

Barend, on the other hand, remained focused on leading the tied-up gang members toward the town's makeshift prison. He glanced over at Lloyd with a mix of amusement, admiring his rare ability to turn a dire situation into a moment of charity and entertainment.

Later, as the townspeople gradually settled back into their routines, the mayor approached Barend and Lloyd for a private conversation. His expression turned serious, hinting at matters of greater importance than the recent lighthearted antics. "Now, I happened to notice that you aren''t really men of the law," the mayor began, his measured tone capturing Barend's full attention. Barend listened intently, fully aware that the conversation might change the course of their immediate future.

"No need to worry now. I have a little proposition for you, hey!" the mayor continued, his steady gaze addressing both Barend and Lloyd. "We are mostly a peaceful town," he explained with a hint of concern. "People settle here for the tranquility, away from the hustle and bustle of larger cities. They're good-hearted folk, simple in their ways. The last thing we need is for fear to grip this town, or worse, for families to pack up and leave. Too many have already left for brighter prospects elsewhere."

Lloyd glanced at Barend and whispered discreetly behind his hand, "Look, we did a good deed, made some money. Let's grab a drink and be on our way." The mayor's proposition hung in the air, heavy with the weight of a decision that might influence not just their lives but also the town's future. Barend felt the gravity of the moment, knowing that their decision at this point would carry consequences for everyone involved.

As Barend listened attentively, the mayor outlined his proposition with an urgency underscored by genuine concern. "Well, you four entertainers can play a certain role—say that of town police," he suggested earnestly. "You already have the people cheering for you…"

Barend considered the proposal carefully. "I am sure you have the best of intentions," he began respectfully, "but we have an important commitment we can't afford to miss, unfortunately."

The mayor's expression shifted, revealing a blend of disappointment and resolve as he reached into his coat and produced a sizable bag of money. He placed it firmly on the table between them. The audible clink of coins served as a tangible reminder of the town's trust and expectations.

"It might not be much," the mayor continued sincerely, "…but the trust of the people in this town is its lifeblood." Barend's gaze quickly moved from the bag to the mayor's eyes, silently acknowledging the weight of the request for help in maintaining the community's stability.

Lloyd's fingers deftly slipped under the stack of money. As he lifted it slightly, his eyes caught a few hastily drawn sketches tucked between the bills… sketches depicting faces, including his own and Vuyo's, rendered in rough lines that conveyed urgency and secrecy. With careful subtlety, Lloyd slid the page out from under the money, keeping his movements discreet to avoid alerting anyone nearby. He absorbed the cryptic message written below the sketches, a directive that spoke of national blockades, the use of force, and a mandate to prevent criminals from crossing borders.

The gravity of the directive settled over him like a heavy fog. This was no ordinary instruction; it hinted at a larger operation that went far beyond their immediate troubles. Lloyd folded the paper carefully and slipped it into his coat pocket, his mind now racing with questions and uncertainties about the true scope of their entanglement.

Outside, as they stepped into the cool evening air, Barend glanced back at the mayor's office with a thoughtful expression. The mayor's promises of safety and peace echoed in his mind, yet Lloyd's uneasy demeanor told a deeper story. Barend noticed him fidgeting and scratching his head, his usual behavior when he finds himself in the midst of an unnerving situation.

Lloyd tapped Barend lightly on the shoulder, drawing him away from the town hall. "What is it?" Barend frowned and asked in a hushed tone, matching Lloyd's cautious demeanor as they strolled down the quiet street.

Glancing around briefly to ensure they were not overheard, Lloyd led Barend into a quieter, more secluded part of town. Lloyd unfolded the mysterious page and showed it to Barend. "Take a look at this... I found it under the money. It's a directive... blockades, using force, and preventing criminals from crossing borders..." he whispered. Barend's eyes narrowed as he read the words, absorbing their implications. The realization that they were now part of a larger, dangerous game settled between them.

"This changes things," Barend muttered and folded his arms. Looking down at the dusty road beneath him. As he looked up again, Lloyd carefully noted his determination and concern. He nodded in solemn agreement. "We need to decide what to do next. This town isn't just about peace and trust anymore. It's part of something bigger."

Barend sighed heavily, and the weight of the decision lay heavily on him. "Let's gather everyone. We need to talk about our next move." With that, Lloyd agreed, shook his hand and they turned and headed back toward their makeshift camp, both aware that the peace they had helped restore might now demand a higher price than they had ever imagined.

As the sun dipped low on the horizon, casting long shadows across the quiet town, the mayor's invitation hung in the air, blending with the fading daylight. As Barend arrived there waiting at the door, a little nervous and uncertain yet intrigued, she opened up and he extended his hand in greeting to the mayor's daughter, Helen. Her presence was a gentle contrast to the weight of their recent revelations.

"Pleased to meet you," Barend said warmly, his hand clasping hers briefly before she could speak. There was a quiet assurance in his greeting that set the tone for this unexpected encounter.

"Please, sir," Helen began with a polite smile, her voice soft and inviting. "My mother has prepared the table. It would mean a great deal if you would stay the night." Her words were warm and clear. Barend glanced at her and noticed the gentle insistence that left little room for refusal.

However, before he could respond, Lloyd interjected, hesitanting slightly as he weighed the implications of their journey. "Uh...It's getting late, and we should keep moving." His remark was matter-of-fact, a reminder of the uncertain road that lay ahead.

Helen's eyes tilted as her gaze shifted toward Lloyd, and a glow of mischief lit up her angelic face. "But my sister would be so disappointed to miss meeting a real magician," she pointedly remarked, gesturing playfully in Lloyd's direction. Her unexpected comment carried an undercurrent of teasing that suddenly broke the tension in the atmosphere, causing Barend to grin and blush.

Lloyd chuckled lightly, acknowledging the playful challenge. "Showbiz never rests, does it?" he replied, his smile genuine as he shared a brief moment of levity with Helen.

Barend glanced at Vuyo, who discreetly concealed papers beneath his shirt... a silent signal of caution amid the hospitality. Meanwhile, Katelyn and Helen had already begun to bond over shared interests. Their conversation, unburdened by the gravity of their situation, flowed with innocent enthusiasm.

Helen, dressed in a charming pink summer dress adorned with small cat prints, awaited their decision with gentle persistence. Barend hesitated for a moment, scratching underneath his chin while exchanging a look with Vuyo that conveyed unspoken concerns. Yet Lloyd, sensing an opportunity or perhaps something deeper in the gesture, took charge.

"It would be rude to refuse such generous hospitality," Lloyd declared with a smile, gently guiding Helen by the arm. His tone was firm and reassuring, leaving little doubt about the path they should take.

Barend, somewhat bewildered by the sudden turn of events, sheepishly followed Lloyd's lead. The mayor, evidently pleased by their acceptance, beamed warmly as they moved toward the inviting glow of his home, leaving behind the dusk-veiled town square.

In the sanctuary of the small town, far removed from the prying eyes of the authorities, Barend, Vuyo, and Lloyd soon found themselves partially settled. The mayor's offer to take over the defunct police station had provided a temporary shield from the looming threat of pursuit. Yet, even in this moment, the weight of their predicament pressed heavily upon them, a constant reminder of the extensive manhunt orchestrated by law enforcement.

What was meant to be a one-night stopover gradually stretched into an unexpected hideout, chosen strategically to buy them time and allow for regrouping. The border, once just a day's journey away, now seemed an elusive goal, with each passing day turning their escape into a waiting game fraught with uncertainty.

Eager to maintain order in his town, the mayor had readily endorsed their temporary role as caretakers of the police station. He assigned them the old cop's quarters—a spacious, though neglected, dwelling echoing with layers of dust and memories of a long-gone era. Townspeople, familiar with their customs, were summoned to help clean the premises; a voluntary act of hospitality.

With no intention of lingering longer than necessary, Barend, Vuyo, and Lloyd settled into the least conspicuous corners of the house. Their presence was quietly noted by the townsfolk as days passed in a blur of cautious routines. They kept a low profile, avoiding any hint of their true identities, and listening keenly for any news or whispers that might aid their escape.

As the house slowly regained a semblance of order, the men remained ever alert, ready to depart at the first sign of danger or opportunity. They had found temporary respite in the town's kindness, yet the constant threat of capture loomed, their minds ever calculating the next move toward the elusive safety of the border.

When the house finally settled into an evening quietude, the weariness of a busy day allowed a moment of introspection. Barend glanced around, taking in the familiar yet weathered surroundings of their temporary haven. It was a reminder of both comfort and impermanence.

In the midst of their strategizing for the journey ahead, Katelyn found solace in a nice warm bath, her thoughts wandering beyond the immediate concerns. Lloyd, ever vigilant, was soon alerted by the clear chime of the doorbell, a sound that cut through the calm.

He jumped up with cautious curiosity and walked toward the door nonchalantly. Upon opening it, he was greeted by a woman whose genuine warmth and sincere manner immediately softened the tension that had settled over them.

"Good evening," Lloyd responded, his tone measured but welcoming.

"We just want to welcome you to our neighborhood and town," the woman introduced herself with a friendly smile. "I'm Sophie Jacobs." Her openness made Lloyd feel momentarily less like an intruder.

His greasy hair shook as he nodded, while a flicker of guarded optimism crossed his face. The unexpected visit brought with it a mix of relief and caution. They were grateful for the hospitality but extremely wary of drawing too much attention. Nevertheless, Sophie's friendly demeanor offered a glimmer of hope that perhaps allies or at least sympathetic neighbors could be found in this unfamiliar place.

"Why, thanks alot, Sophie," Lloyd replied, extending his hand in greeting. "I'm Lloyd, and these are my companions, Barend and Katelyn."

Sophie nodded graciously, her eyes briefly scanning the interior of the house as if to absorb the scene and the subtle whispers among the townsfolk.

"We appreciate the welcome," Lloyd continued sincerely. "It's been... quite an adjustment, finding ourselves here." There was a note of honesty in his admission, a reflection of the unexpected turn their lives had taken.

Lloyd shook Sophie's hand warmly, his smile genuine despite the underlying unease that had become a constant companion. Then, the aroma of food caught his attention, a tantalizing scent that stirred a hint of hunger. Sophie presented a large pan filled with Malva pudding, its sweet fragrance immediately filling the room with comfort.

"Thank you very much, Miss Sophie," Lloyd said politely. Yet Sophie seemed intent on sharing more than just a dessert; she began explaining how the recipe had been passed down through generations, recounting fond memories of learning to bake the dessert as a young girl.

As Sophie spoke, Lloyd closed the door behind her and placed the pan on the table where maps and plans had been spread out. The tempting dish proved irresistible. Katelyn, shrieking with delight, ran to the kitchenette to go and fetch pudding bowls. Immediately their careful planning was placed on hold as Barend, Vuyo, and Katelyn each served themselves generous portions of the warm, comforting pudding.

As they sat there enjoying the soft, sponge-like texture and syrupy sauce, their troubles evaded them. Although this provided a momentary escape from the weight of their troubles, Barend was constantly aware of the looming anxiety gnawing at his stomach. He tried his best to push the ruminating thoughts aside, however.

Around the table, conversation began to flow more freely as they savored the taste of home-cooked comfort in a place far from everything familiar. For a brief hour, the urgency of their mission faded into the background, replaced by the simple pleasure of good food and unexpected kindness.

Katelyn had just finished her bath, and even Tessa, their loyal companion, managed to sneak a taste from the pan Sophie had brought. Barend noticed the little mishap, remnants clinging to Tessa's snout. He chuckled, turning to Katelyn with a gentle command, "Go wash that, Katelyn. Don't want to give Miss Sophie her pan back smelling like... like dog...Sies! (*gross*)"

Katelyn stood up and giggled mischievously in response. "Silly Billy," she said, her tone light and playful.

But their solitude was short-lived. Throughout the night, more neighbors came by, welcoming them to the neighborhood. Their old refrigerator was soon bursting at the seams with an assortment of perishable foods. It was a sure testament to the town's hospitality and the genuine care its people took in offering support.

One neighbor, Old Oom Piet, the town's postman, arrived bearing a bottle of Mampoer, a potent peach-based liquor from his farm. "To keep you warm," he said with a deep voice and an unmatched grin, pouring generous measures for each of them. The first sip of Mampoer hit Lloyd like a jolt as he shook his head; it was like swallowing fire, searing his throat and catching him off guard. He coughed uncontrollably as he tried to recover, while Barend and Vuyo exchanged amused glances. Out of politeness, they each took another sip, the fiery drink warming them from the inside out.

As they sipped and listened, Oom Piet made himself comfortable on the couch and began to regale them with stories of the town's history... anecdotes that captivated the group and drew Katelyn, peeking from the kitchen, into the circle of storytelling. Barend stared at her gravely as she asked about the Mampoer. "Not for children, Katelyn...", he reprimanded, sending her back to the kitchen for a glass of milk.

Despite the pressing need to finalize their escape plans, they found solace for the night and camaraderie in the unexpected warmth of their new neighbors and the lively introduction of Oom Piet's Mampoer.

Oom Piet's storytelling wove a tapestry of intrigue and history around the fiery drink. He told tales that reached back to the days of Pedi chief Mampuru, who had sought justice for his murdered half-brother Sekoekoenie, and went on to describe how General Joubert had once acquired the potent liquor from Mampuru himself. As the group indulged in more shots, the details of the history began to blur into the haze of shared laughter and spirited conversation.

After hearty greetings to Oom Piet, he patted each of the men on the back and Katelyn managed to sneak in a little side-hug, for fear of being excluded. They waved him goodbye and retired for the night with plans to revisit their escape strategy in the morning.

Yet the rhythms of small-town life had their own way of stretching time. What was meant to be a brief stopover gradually extended into days, then weeks. Barend, Katelyn, Vuyo, Lloyd, and their loyal animals slowly formed an odd kind of family. Despite the urgency of their original mission, the charm of small-town life seeped into their days, softening the edges of their constant alertness.

Katelyn, though only of preschool age, joined the local school, offering a good routine amid their clandestine stay. Meanwhile, the others assumed roles as makeshift law enforcers, tackling the quaint mysteries and dramas of the town. It was a stark contrast to the urban crime they had once known. As they settled into these roles, their days filled with community interactions and the simple rituals of small-town existence, the urgency of their mission began to blur. Yet, beneath the calm, the border remained a looming reminder that their comforting break was only temporary.

One midday, as the hot sun beat down on the dusty streets, Barend and Vuyo strolled purposefully toward Old Lady Smith's quaint cottage. A report from Mrs. Jenkins, the town gossip, had mentioned a series of "stolen" goods that had mysteriously vanished from several homes. As they approached the grey picket fence, Barend couldn't help but notice curious glances from neighbors peering through their curtains. "Ugh... bored old people!", he remarked, causing Vuyo to burst out laughing, but Barend quickly hushed him.

Upon entering the garden, they found Old Lady Smith tending to her roses. Startled by the unexpected visit, she turned around, her face softening into a warm smile at the sight of the two uniformed men.

"Good afternoon, gentlemen. What brings you here today?" she asked with genuine curiosity, patting her kempt hairdo carefully with the side of her wrist for fear of soiling it with her garden gloves

Barend took the lead with a serious yet kind expression. "Good afternoon, Mrs. Smith. We've received reports about some missing items around town and thought we should check with you, just to rule out any misunderstandings?" His voice was calm and respectful.

"Missing items? Oh my!" Old Lady Smith exclaimed, her hands flying to her chest in surprise. "Well, you're welcome to look around, though I assure you, I haven't taken anything that doesn't belong to me." Her tone remained friendly despite the unexpected intrusion.

Vuyo nodded politely. "Of course, ma'am. Just a routine check. We'll be very very quick, neh!" he uttered reassuringly, causing her to nod in fearful agreement.

The trio began their search, methodically inspecting each room of the cozy cottage. Despite any initial suspicions, it became clear that Old Lady Smith was meticulous, almost obsessive with her organization skills. Her living room featured antique trinkets arranged on polished wooden shelves and a cupboard full of kitch porcelain teasets. As they continued into the kitchen, its shelves boasted neatly labeled jars of homemade preserves.

In the pantry, Barend noticed a small wooden box tucked away on a high shelf. "Mind if I take a look at this, Mrs. Smith?" he looked at her and asked politely.

"Ofcourse, dear," she replied, amusement in her voice as she allowed him a closer inspection.

Inside the box, Barend found a collection of odds and ends... a small silver pocket watch, a porcelain teacup decorated by colourful flowers, and a pair of spectacles. Each item held a sentimental value, more memories than monetary worth.

"These are just some old keepsakes," Old Lady Smith explained softly, leaning on her walking cane. "Memories from my travels and years gone by. They may seem precious to me, but I assure you, none of them were stolen." Barend nodded in understanding, exchanging a glance with Vuyo that spoke of the simple truth behind the misunderstanding.

"Thank you, Mrs. Smith. We appreciate your cooperation. It seems there has been a slight misunderstanding. We'll inform the others that their missing items might just be misplaced." His tone was respectful and conclusive.

Old Lady Smith chuckled warmly, touching him on the shoulder. "Oh, trust me... I've lived long enough to know how rumors spread in this town. Thank you for making a turn, gentlemen. And if you ever want to hear some stories from the good old days, you know where to find me."

As they bid farewell and walked back toward the town center, Barend reflected on the investigation. What began as a search for stolen goods had evolved into a glimpse of the quaint dynamics of small-town life, where rumors swirled like dust and every face held a story. Amid the occasional hearsay and drama, there was a genuine warmth and sense of community that made their temporary stay feel unexpectedly comforting.

"Seems like another case closed," Vuyo remarked with a grin as they passed by the local bakery, the scent of freshly baked bread wafting in the air, causing him to glance through the windows.

Barend nodded as they strolled, a small smile of satisfaction crossing his face. "Indeed. And just another day in this charming town." Little did they know, their presence was already weaving itself into the ongoing tale of the town ... a story of strangers turned neighbors, slowly blending into the fabric of everyday life.

In the small town of quaint streets and friendly faces, news traveled faster than the wind through open fields. Katelyn quickly found herself embraced by the local children at school, forming bonds that mirrored the inherent warmth of the community. Among her new friends was Helen, the mayor's daughter, and their camaraderie blossomed effortlessly in the shadow of the old town hall.

Meanwhile, as the charm of community life enveloped them, Barend, Vuyo, Lloyd, and Katelyn found that their carefully laid plans to reach the border were being thwarted by an unexpected police presence. Each morning, reports of tightening patrols near the border forced them to remain hidden in their borrowed roles as local law enforcers.

The days settled into a cautious routine. Barend and Vuyo, now known as the town's reliable officers, kept vigilant watch over the narrow streets and outskirts. Lloyd, adept at casually blending into the background, listened intently to the town's gossip, hoping to extract clues on when they might safely slip away. Evenings were spent in the musty confines of the old cop's quarters, where maps and hastily drawn plans covered the dining table like a patchwork quilt of escape routes. They debated their next moves over copious amounts of caffeine in hushed tones, interrupted only by the distant laughter of children or the occasional chime of the town clock echoing through quiet streets.

As the weeks went by, the town's idiosyncrasies began to grow on them. They adapted to the rhythms of small-town life... the morning bustle at the market, the afternoon lull broken by the clang of the blacksmith's hammer, and the evening gatherings at the town square where stories were shared over steaming bowls of hearty stew. Yet beneath this calm exterior lay a restless urge to move on, to break free from the invisible chains binding them to this picturesque sanctuary. Their eyes remained fixed on the distant horizon, where the border promised both freedom and uncertainty. It would be a gateway to a future although still shrouded in the unknown.

For now, they bided their time, navigating the delicate balance between laying low and preparing for the inevitable moment when they would have to vanish into the anonymity of the open road once more.

Under the late afternoon sun, Katelyn stood beside her father, Barend, in a quiet corner of the town square. She fidgeted with the hem of her blue floral dress, the sunlight casting a warm glow on her freckled cheeks. Her eyes, wide with curiosity and a touch of apprehension, remained fixed on Barend as he prepared to impart his wisdom.

"Daddy... what can I do if, say, I was in danger or someone fights with me?" she asked softly, looking up at him whilst pulling her face at the striking glare of the sun. Barend knelt down to her level, looking into those innocent eyes while his weathered hands gently took hers. "Are you in danger, my dear?" he asked, his voice filled with tenderness and concern.

Katelyn shook her head, a small smile gracing her lips. "No, it's just... I want to be ready, like you," she replied earnestly, her eyes meeting his with determination.

Understanding the seriousness beneath her question, Barend nodded. "Alright then, let's start with something simple," he began in a calm, reassuring tone. "Firstly, it's important to know how to block a punch." With patient care, he demonstrated the technique, guiding Katelyn's small hands through the motions until she could mimic the defensive maneuver. At first, her movements were hesitant and awkward, but with each little bit of coaxing and Barend's encouraging words, her confidence grew.

As they practiced, the sounds of children playing nearby and distant market vendors provided a comforting backdrop. Occasional giggles punctuated the lesson, and Barend couldn't help but chuckle softly at her efforts.

"You're doing great, sweetheart," he praised, his eyes twinkling with paternal pride. "Remember, these moves are for emergencies. The best way to stay safe is to avoid trouble altogether."

Katelyn nodded eagerly, her eyes wide with concentration. "I'll remember, Daddy," she promised, sincerity in her voice.

Their lesson continued as the sun began its descent, painting the sky in soft hues of orange and pink. Barend took a moment to reflect on the fleeting innocence of her childhood, grateful for the precious bond they now shared. As they wrapped up, Katelyn cheerfully threw her arms around him in a spontaneous hug, her small frame enveloped in his protective embrace.

"Thank you, Daddy," she whispered gently, her voice muffled against his shoulder.

Barend held her close, feeling a mixture of love, gratitude and sorrow toward this timeless moment etched in his heart, wishing it could last forever. The regret he once felt for missing out on her baby days only intensified his resolve to protect Katelyn and keep her close to him at all costs. He quickly buried his tender emotions under serious contemplation, the strong intention to develop their escape plan as soon as possible. As he headed home and began their supper, Lloyd and Vuyo could hardly distract Barned from his deep thoughts.

The ringing phone shattered the morning calm the next day, its urgent tone setting Barend's nerves on edge. The teacher's distressed voice crackled through the receiver, summoning him swiftly to the school. Entering the familiar smelly corridors, he found a tense scene waiting in the principal's office.

Katelyn sat quietly with hands folded, her eyes cast downward, flanked by Klein Willie and his father. The boy bore a noticeable blue eye which served as sure evidence of the previous day's turmoil.

"What's the matter here?" Barend asked calmly, though concern etched lines on his brow.

Klein Willie's father wasted no time. "How do you justify giving my boy a black eye and kicking him... down there?" His accusation was sharp and immediate, leaving tense silence begging for an answer.

Barend quickly turned to Katelyn, grinding his teeth while staring at her, with arms folded. Kicking her feet together with shame, she slowly looked up and met his gaze, her shoulders lifting in a gesture of resignation.

"Now, I understand she's new here, but ... fighting?" The teacher's voice was stern, disapproval in every word. "Did you teach her this?"

Barend exhaled slowly. "I've only taught her how to defend herself if she's in danger," he defended in a frank manner.

"And it was daddy who said that ..." Katelyn began softly before a stern stare from Barend made her stop mid-sentence,

The atmosphere grew tense. Klein Willie's father shifted uncomfortably. "This is ridiculous. My boy's become the laughingstock of his class because of this!"

Barend turned to face the boy directly. "If I were you, son ... I'd consider apologizing right now," he suggested firmly.

Confusion clouded the father's face as he looked at his son. "What did you do?" he demanded frowning angrily.

"I was just playing, Dad. I promise," Klein Willie replied, his young voice tinged with fear.

"And what exactly did you do?!" the father probed further.

"We were just playing 'wolf wolf,' Dad... and she was running, so I caught her and grabbed her hair," Klein Willie explained, trying to justify his actions.

"Okay, but that's just a normal game," the father dismissed lightly. "A bit of hair-pulling can't be that bad."

Katelyn interjected, her voice laced with upset. "No.. he grabbed my ponytail and... he kissed me," she confessed, her tone clear with disgust.

"You did what?" The father's eyes widened in shock, turning to his son for an explanation.

The teacher intervened, attempting to defuse the escalating tension. "Now, I'm sure this was all just child's play, but these actions will need to be addressed and appropriately punished," she declared firmly, pushing her black-framed glasses back on her nose.

The father's gaze hardened as he turned to his son. "You forcibly kissed her ...?" he asked sternly, the rage evident in his voice.

"I was just playing!" Klein Willie defended himself. "I caught her, so I kissed her..."

Barend shook his head, a mixture of disbelief and resignation in his tone. "I should've been an athlete," he muttered wryly, his irony hanging in the air. "I could've caught plenty of women."

"Klein Willie, we'll discuss this at home!" he barked at his son and turned towards the other adults in the room. "I... uh... I apologize for this," the father conceded in a subdued tone, assuring that he would handle the matter. "Very well, then..." the teacher nodded, acknowledging the need for parental involvement. As the father abruptly led his son out, Klein Willie's protests faded against the stern resolve in his voice.

Barend sighed heavily, watching them depart with a heavy heart. He turned to Katelyn, who had observed the unfolding scene quietly.

"Katelyn, could I have a moment with you?" Barend asked gently, sensing the weight of the situation on her small shoulders.

Katelyn nodded silently, her eyes downcast as she walked out with her father. The echoes of childish games and unintended consequences lingered, leaving Barend to ponder the complexities of parenthood and the fragile innocence of youth.

After a brief awkward discussion about the birds and bees, biys and handling conflict, they rendered to the school office. After an uncomfortable silence that felt like forever to Katelyn, the teacher remarked, "You're new at this...?" her tone mixing understanding with subtle critique.

Barend sat across from her, calm and attentive. "Fighting... no, I've been at it all my life," he replied with a half-smile. "When you're working on some case, you need to..."

"I mean fathering," she gently interjected, her eyes meeting his with a blend of curiosity and concern.

"Must have been difficult on you to raise a girl by yourself," she continued softly.

"Nah... she's very easy," Barend assured her, a trace of pride in his voice.

"She is quite a clever girl from what the class teacher tells me," the teacher remarked thoughtfully, shifting the conversation to Katelyn. "It's a very important part of a child's development, Mr. Barend."

"She has the ability to really go far in life," the teacher continued, her admiration for Katelyn evident.

"So, I have a clever girl then?" Barend asked, paternal pride coloring his tone.

The teacher nodded firmly with a smile. "Very."

"But you will have to give her more attention. A clever mind like hers needs to be trained and disciplined," she advised gently. "We can't have her getting into fights with boys."

Barend sighed, nodding in understanding. "That was well deserved," he conceded, reflecting on the incident.

"Even so, Mr. Barend," the teacher continued with a firm yet compassionate tone, "it is not an appropriate way for a girl to behave."

Barend furrowed his brow in thought. "As punishment, she will need to write a story which is two pages long," the teacher announced, her decision both firm and fair.

Barend nodded in acknowledgment, grateful for her guidance. "About what?" he inquired, curious about the intended lesson.

"About respect," she suggested, her gaze steady. "And how to handle disagreements without resorting to physical means."

Barend nodded again, understanding the importance of the lesson as he prepared to leave, thankful for the teacher's insight in nurturing Katelyn's intellect and character.

Another scorching day dawned over the town of Sandrift, its dusty streets already bustling with daily life. Children hurried off to school under the unrelenting sun, while Barend was jolted awake by a knock on his window, carrying a sense of urgent alarm.

"They're going to kill each other! Come quick!" The man's voice cracked with desperation as he relayed the urgent summons.

Without hesitation, Barend grabbed his gun and hurried out, with Vuyo close behind. Meanwhile, Lloyd still slumbered, snoring blissfully on the couch with his mouth wide open, oblivious to the brewing turmoil.

Racing to the scene, Barend arrived to find an old woman, a man, and a young colored worker locked in a heated confrontation. "It's my money! I found it fair and square!" thundered the man, his eyes blazing with defiance.

"It's my house!" countered the older man, his voice equally vehement.

Vuyo stepped in swiftly, keeping the two adversaries from coming to blows. Barend assessed the situation with calm determination, his voice steady amidst the rising tension. "I'm sure this is a matter for the court to handle, isn't it?" he interjected, his gaze scanning the gathered trio.

The older man shook his head vigorously. "No, sir. Here, we have no need for a court. We have the law for that." His stern tone left no room for further argument.

The old woman, her expression set with resolve, suddenly brandished a garden rake, prompting Vuyo to intervene deftly. "How do we resolve this then?" Barend inquired, his voice a beacon of reason amid the storm of emotions.

The town square seemed to hold its breath as they awaited Barend's decision. The heat of the day bore down upon them all, mirroring the intensity of the dispute. In Sandrift, where the law was as dusty and unyielding as the landscape, Barend knew he had to navigate this conflict with precision.

Barend listened intently as Mr. Aswegen and his worker presented their sides of the story with fervor, each adamant about their claim to the jars and the money found within. Mr. Aswegen declared his ownership of the house and, in his view, the rightful claim to the money discovered during renovations.

"I have bought the house with my own hard-earned money," Mr. Aswegen proclaimed, wiping the sweat from his brow, his tone laced with indignation. "It needed repairs, and upon fixing a leak in the roof, my worker found these jars. One of them contained money, clearly meant for the homeowner, which is me, ofcourse."

His worker, a stout man with a weathered face, rose in support. "Finders are keepers," he asserted boldly, swaying his index finger to signal his disapproval. "The money caused no harm until I discovered it! I should *mos* rightfully keep it!"

Lloyd, ever the opportunist, subtly nodded in agreement, his eyes flickering half with amusement at the worker's speech errors and half with interest at the prospect of gaining from the situation. Barend shot him a reproachful glance, silently urging restraint. He instinctively knew that confiscating the money even temporarily would only inflame tensions further.

"No, that won't do," Barend interjected firmly, shaking his head. "It will only escalate matters."

Turning his attention to a quiet figure seated in the corner, Barend motioned toward the elderly woman. "Please, Anneliene, tell us your side of the story," he invited gently as he raised his hand signaling toward her.

Anneliene's voice, tinged with both nostalgia and determination, filled the room as she began. "My grandmother was a peculiar woman," she started, her words carrying the weight of years gone by. "She didn't trust banks, so she hoarded her savings in 23 jars hidden in the attic for decades. No one knew of this secret stash until her passing, when I inherited the property." As she spoke, it became clear that the jar with her name inscribed held a special significance.

"It seems," Barend summarized thoughtfully, "that the money in the jar rightfully belongs to Anneliene, as it was clearly intended for her by her grandmother."

Mr. Aswegen sighed heavily, recognizing the weight of her claim. After a moment of consideration, he nodded reluctantly, shrugging his shoulders. "Oh, alright then," he conceded, his voice tinged with resignation. "If that's the case, then so be it."

With the matter settled, Barend ensured that Anneliene received the jar and its contents, bringing a sense of closure to the peculiar case of the old jars hidden in the attic. As the participants departed, the town square returned to its usual quietude, the intense heat of the day dissipating with the resolution of the dispute.

Later, as the sun beat down on the quiet street, Barend, Vuyo, and Lloyd followed Mr. van Aswegen back to his house. Their footsteps echoed lightly against the cobblestones, each man lost in thought about the implications of the jars and the money within.

Inside Mr. van Aswegen's modest home, the group gathered around a table covered by a crocheted tablecloth adorned with an assortment of aged glass jars. Their surfaces, dusted and marked with faint smudges resembling copper residue, hinted at the long-hidden wealth they contained. Among them, one jar stood out, its stained marks clearly spelling out the name "Anneliene" in faded ink.

"It's clear whose money this belongs to," Barend remarked, his tone carrying a note of certainty as he held up the jar, inspecting it closely.

Vuyo, ever the thoughtful observer, leaned in with a measured expression as his fingers brushed over his chin. "Mr. van Aswegen, do you believe in the teachings of the Bible?" he asked with a gentle sincerity.

The older man nodded emphatically. "Yes, yes, I do," he affirmed. "I attend church faithfully, pay my tithe..."

Before he could finish, Vuyo interjected gently, recounting the story of David and the stolen lamb. "In the story, David's sin was stealing a lamb that belonged to another," he explained, his gaze steady. "While you may not have stolen a lamb, the principle of rightful ownership applies here, does it not?"

Mr. van Aswegen shifted uncomfortably, grappling with the implications. "But I didn't steal anything," he protested weakly as more sweat droplets started emanating from his forehead.

"Lambs, jars..," Vuyo continued calmly. "Well... in essence, it's about recognizing what rightfully belongs to whom."

Barend intervened before the conversation could escalate further, sensing the rising tension. "Alrighty, gentlemen," he declared in an authoritative yet conciliatory tone, "we'll take a short break to deliberate and reconvene shortly with our decision."

Outside, away from the scrutiny of Mr. van Aswegen's home, Barend, Vuyo, and Lloyd huddled together, their expressions thoughtful. "What do we do about this, Barend?" Lloyd asked, brow furrowed. "It's clear the money belongs to Anneliene, but Mr. van Aswegen might argue he found it on his property."

Barend considered the dilemma as he inhaled deeply from his cigarette, weighing the moral and legal implications. "Legally, the house and its contents belong to Mr. van Aswegen," he mused aloud as he blew out smoke, "but morally, the money in those jars belonged to Anneliene's grandmother, passed down to her. It's a delicate balance."

Vuyo nodded. "Indeed, legality versus morality," he murmured agreeably. "Perhaps a compromise could be reached?"

A moment of silent reflection passed by as they were resting on the fence outside. After inhaling copious drags of the withering cigarette before crushing it under his shoe, Barend straightened his posture, his decision firming in his mind. "We'll uphold the principle of rightful ownership," he declared resolutely. "The money rightfully belongs to Anneliene. We'll find a way to ensure justice is served." Vuyo, coughing from the dying whiff of second-hand smoke, nodded in agreement

With their course of action decided, the trio bravely returned to Mr. van Aswegen's house, ready to deliver their verdict and bring closure to the enigmatic case of the old jars and their hidden fortune.

Barend leaned forward, his expression thoughtful as he considered Anneliene's suggestion. The midday sun poured warmth into the room, casting a golden hue over their discussion. "What do you think your community really needs?" he asked in a measured yet inviting tone, seeking insight that might guide their next steps.

Mr. van Aswegen and the worker exchanged uneasy glances, clearly uncomfortable with the unexpected turn the conversation had taken.

"And, of course," Barend continued, his gaze inclusive as he addressed everyone, "We'll commemorate the generosity of these two gentlemen right here." His voice sought to bring everyone together in a shared vision.

A tentative smile touched Mr. van Aswegen's lips as he considered the idea. "I wouldn't mind being able to cool down every now and then," he admitted, his tone softening with a touch of humor.

Annelien beamed, her face lighting up with satisfaction as she extended her hand. "Let's do it," she said warmly, her words carrying genuine hope.

Barend and Mr. van Aswegen shook hands, sealing the agreement with a gesture of mutual understanding and goodwill.

Outside, the town bustled with its daily rhythm, completely unaware of the quiet resolution reached in Mr. van Aswegen's home. It not only settled the dispute over jars and money but also planted the seeds for community unity and a shared vision for the future.

The Vet

As Barend stepped into the cozy living room, his weary eyes caught sight of little Tessa hobbling towards him. Her legs, wrapped in bandages and supported by a stick, gave her an appearance reminiscent of a pirate on a makeshift voyage. On the table lay an assortment of supplies. There were rolls of toilet paper, bandages, and scissors… a silent trail pointing unmistakably to one culprit.

"Katelyn!" Barend called out, his voice mixing amusement and exasperation as he followed the trail of evidence through the house. Peeking through the window, he spotted Jasmine the donkey standing patiently outside, adorned in layers of toilet paper fashioned into makeshift bandages.

As he slowly walked nearer, Barend found Katelyn sitting next to Jasmine. Her small hands worked deftly to wrap the makeshift bandages around the donkey's leg. Met with the soft sound of cheerful humming, he could clearly see that she was content in her little world of veterinary care.

"Good day, Daddy," Katelyn greeted joyfully, not pausing her task as she acknowledged him with a quick smile before returning her focus to Jasmine.

Barend stood right in the middle of what he now called Katelyn's makeshift veterinary clinic. Outside, Jasmine the donkey remained stoic, her leg now wrapped in bandages that looked more like mummy wrappings than proper medical care.

"Katelyn… What on earth do you think you are doing?" Barend asked with a blend of amusement and mild concern, positioning himself like a statue with hands folded.

Katelyn turned to face him with wide eyes. "Isn't it clear, Daddy? They needed to be treated," she replied earnestly, her small hands never stopping their work on the bandages.

"Treated? Well, it looks more like you're making mummies out of them," Barend chuckled as he carefully unwrapped Tessa's leg. The dog licked his hand and bounced away with fierce energy before Katelyn could react. "Wait… It should stay like that for at least two days, Daddyyyy…"

"Now look what you've done, Dad…" Katelyn exclaimed, a note of dismay in her voice. "Now her leg will never grow straight."

Barend scratched his head, clearly puzzled. "I'm confused. As far as I can remember, she hasn't had any broken legs... and I've been keeping a close eye on that dog. There's no way that..."

"Dad, it's simple," Katelyn interrupted patiently. "If I want to become an animal doctor, I need to study and practice hard. It's difficult being the only woman in the house, you know... I would have to cook... and clean..."

Glancing around at the scattered supplies and the clear evidence of Katelyn's 'studies,' Barend sighed heavily and sank back onto the couch with a cold beer in hand. "You clean up now, my girl" he said with a hint of amusement.

Katelyn grinned mischievously, her eyes sparkling with a secret plan. In her young mind, she was already plotting ways to secure more time for her studies. She believed that in order to pursue her dream of becoming an animal doctor, her father needed someone special in his life, a significant other. It was an idea she had been planting quietly in his thoughts for some time now.

This innocent notion began to set in motion a series of events that would leave a lasting mark on Barend's tranquil life. As a single father, he had managed the challenges of raising Katelyn with determination and care. Yet her recent musings about potential stepmothers had introduced a new, unexpected element into their daily routine. It was a prospect that both intrigued and unsettled him.

The first possible candidate in Katelyn's mind was her teacher. To her, Miss Johnson was kind and knowledgeable. What a perfect fit for their small family, she thought. Katelyn believed that if Miss Johnson could be brought closer into their lives, it might ease some of the burdens on her father.

Later that evening, after Barend had finished reading one of Katelyn's favorite bedtime stories and closed the book, she touched his arm and looked up with a question that caught him off guard.

"Daddy, do you like my teacher?" she asked, her voice mixing innocence with curiosity, her eyes searching his for an answer.

Barend slowly sat down at the edge of her bed, trying to conceal his smile as the mention of her teacher stirred memories and emotions he rarely spoke of. "Daddy... where's mommy?" Katelyn added softly, gaping at him with her mouth hanging open while waiting for an answer, her wide eyes reflecting both curiosity and a hint of longing.

Barend hesitated, his gaze gentle yet guarded. "Well, she is…" He paused, choosing his words carefully to shield Katelyn from the painful complexities of their past. "She's being taken care of," he finally said, careful not to reveal any bitterness.

"But don't you worry now, my girl.." Barend continued, softening his tone as he reached out to brush a stray lock of hair from her forehead. "Where I am taking you, its beautiful, darling. There are long beaches, many fishes, and even dolphins. You like dolphins, right?"

Katelyn's innocent little face brightened with a smile. "Wow! Yes, dolphins are my favorite!"

"That's where we will build a house for ourselves," Barend assured her, his tone warm and full of promise.

"And mommy?" Katelyn asked hopefully.

Barend's heart sank briefly as he searched for the right words. "Well…" He paused again, careful and measured. "We will invite her to come visit sometime," he finally replied, his voice tender yet steady.

Katelyn's smile widened softly, her eyes sparkling with the trust only a child could have. She threw her arms around Barend in a tight embrace. "I love you, Daddy," she whispered happily.

Barend held her close, feeling the weight of responsibility mixed with a surge of hope for their future… one full of challenges and moments of deep joy, anchored by the bond they shared.

Early morning crept over the horizon, casting its gentle copper-toned light upon the sleepy jailhouse. Vuyo, the no-nonsense sheriff, energetically rattled his keys with a purpose as he entered the cellblock.

"Rise and shine, me darlings!" Vuyo announced, placing shovels on the floor and swinging the cell door open with a creak followed by a reverberating clang.

The Davies brothers slothfully stirred from their makeshift beds, squinting against the sudden intrusion of daylight.

"And you even dare to try and escape…?" Vuyo questioned with a half-amused high-pitched tone that clearly challenged them as his spun his gun around casually. "What, the sun isn't even up yet. We have our human rights, you know," the elder Davies brother groaned, protesting against Vuyo's intrusion, shielding his eyes.

"You got to correct your wrongs before you come talking to me about rights now, eish" Vuyo retorted firmly. "Come on, get up! Yiz' apah!"

The clank of heavy chains echoed through the jail as the Davies brothers were led outside onto the cold concrete.

"So where are we going?" the younger Davies brother asked with a tone of great caution.

"You'll see soon enough," Vuyo replied cryptically, trying to disguise his amusement while nudging them forward.

Outside, the morning air was cool and crisp as they were led out to an open field on the outskirts of the village . Vuyo stood still abruptly and gestured toward the expanse of land.

"Start digging, boys," Vuyo commanded.

"Digging!? What the heck are we digging?" the elder Davies brother asked with his hands on his hips, eyes narrowing suspiciously.

"A very big grave for all of you," Vuyo grunted with a smile that did not reach his eyes.

Vuyo's stern gaze scanned the men as they sluggishly wielded their shovels. He paced around them with purpose, his gun twirling deftly in his hand.

"And don't you even think of trying to escape, amadoda!" Vuyo warned, his loud voice carrying a weight of authority. "This town is not big enough to hide."

Sand erupted into the air, making little clouds of dust here and there as the men began digging, their efforts lacking enthusiasm.

"Hayi, You boys dig like girls..." Vuyo taunted, his eyes narrowing with impatience.

A sudden gunshot shattered the stillness, sending echoes through the field. The men swiftly jerked upright, newfound urgency in their movements as they dug deeper into the earth.

"This guy is crazy, my bru..." muttered one of the men to the older Davies brother, casting a wary glance at Vuyo.

"Just wait for the right time," the Davies brother whispered back, his voice tinged with quiet determination. "I'll bury him in this hole with the rest of them coppers."

Meanwhile, at the school, children had gathered earlier than usual for the long awaited market day, excitedly setting up their stalls to sell a variety of sweets and goods. Laughter and chatter filled the air as kids dashed between makeshift booths adorned with cupcakes, chocolates, soda, toffee apples, toys, and all kinds of treats that only a grandmother could bake.

Katelyn stood beside her stall with her hands behind her back, her expression conveying her deep thoughts as she surveyed the bustling scene. Most of the stalls were laden with colorful candies and tempting ice creams, attracting eager buyers. However, Katelyn had opted for a different approach.

"I told you *mos*, Katelyn, sweets *always* sell," Lloyd remarked from his nearby stall, where he proudly displayed his assortment of candies.

Katelyn nodded absently, her attention drawn to Lloyd's neighboring booth. He had taken a daring leap by offering fluffy little chicks for sale, a choice that intrigued and puzzled her.

"Lloyd, selling chicks?" she asked, raising an eyebrow. "Isn't that a bit strange for you?"

Lloyd grinned mischievously, arranging the chicks in a row. "Trust me, Katelyn. When I was a kid, anything cute and small had everyone lining up to buy. It's all about catching their eye."

Katelyn chuckled softly, watching as a group of curious cackling children approached Lloyd's stall, cooing over the fluffy chicks. She glanced at her own stall, quickly considering her next move.

As the day unfolded, Katelyn decided to take the leap as she took Lloyd's unconventional advice to heart. She had acquired a few chicks from a neighboring farm and set up her stall amidst the bustling market. Initially, most children gravitated towards the colorful and enticing candyfloss stall operated by "Spook Asem," the local nickname for a sweet-toothed vendor who always drew a crowd.

However, Katelyn's stall soon began to attract attention. A group of girls, including her friend Zani, first huddled together, then approached with curious smiles.

"I want that one!" Zani exclaimed with a tone of genuine excitement, bouncing up and down while pointing to a fluffy chick nestled in one of the small wooden tomato boxes Katelyn had repurposed for the occasion.

Katelyn grinned widely and gently lifted the chick on the palm of her hand, holding it steady with another, handing it carefully to Zani. "Well, here you go. Make sure to feed them with some dried corn and seeds. They love those."

Zani's eyes lit up with pure child-like delight as she accepted the chick and the bag of feed from Katelyn. After staring at Katelyn with a smile, she quickly dashed off, eager to show her new feathered friend to her friends gathered nearby at the toffee apple stand.

The market continued to bustle with chatter and activity as children milled about, inspecting various stalls and making purchases. Katelyn's stall, now adorned with a few remaining chicks peeping softly in their boxes, became a quaint attraction of its own, drawing some curious glances and smiles from those passing by.

Meanwhile, back at the police station, Barend silently reflected on the relatively calm atmosphere of the town as he finished his last few rounds on horseback. The day had started with the usual routine of returning the Davies gang to their cells after their laborious digging assignment. He sighed and shook his head, recalling the minor ordeal of getting his beard trimmed by the unsteady hand of Mr. Arendse, the local barber known for his coffee breath and shaky demeanor.

"Getting my hair cut on a Friday afternoon was the most excitement I've had since we moved here," Barend mused to himself, brushing his fingers over his trimmed beard from top to bottom. "Old Mr. Arendse nearly had me thinking I'm about to meet my end right there in that chair."

With the Davies gang safely back in custody, Barend and his fellow officers had taken it upon themselves to patrol the town on horseback, ensuring all was quiet and in order as dusk settled over the quaint cobble streets and securely locked little shops.

However, Barend's contemplative peace was suddenly interrupted by a sight in the distance. A gathering crowd had begun to conglomerate, their murmurs and movements bringing him to a sense of alert caution. Instinctively, he nudged his horse forward, curious to investigate what seemed to be stirring up the town on an otherwise ordinary day

As they slowly drew nearer, the commotion in the field resolved into a chaotic scene of men from Barend's town locked in heated scuffles with unfamiliar faces. The reason for the brawl remained murky amid the flurry of fists and flying dust. Barend, intent on understanding the root of the conflict, attempted to engage one of the participants to shed light on the situation. Before he could glean any information, however, a swift blow from the man knocked Barend back.

Reacting swiftly, Barend retaliated with a punch that landed squarely between the man's eyes, sending him sprawling to the ground. The scuffle intensified as more men converged, forming clusters of grappling bodies, flailing arms and kicking boots. Amidst the fray, Lloyd watched from a safe distance with a half-amused anxious grin, clenching his teeth while Vuyo wasted no time as he dismounted and readied his gun, though he refrained from intervening directly.

Dust violently kicked up around them as the skirmish continued, bodies falling and rising in the tumult until the sharp, shrill blast of Grandpa Mario's whistle pierced the air. The sound cut through the chaos, signaling an end to the brawl and bringing everyone to an abrupt halt. Barend stood amidst a scattering of fallen men, the aftermath settling with groans and grunts as participants pulled each other up with outstretched arms, then dusting off their clothes and shaking hands in a show of mutual respect.

"Till next month," one man from Barend's town remarked to another, who nodded in agreement before stumbling away from the scene. Barend, still trying to process the sudden and seemingly senseless fight, turned to Grandpa Mario with a mix of bewilderment and curiosity, scratching his sweaty scalp.

"Next month?" Barend inquired and frowned, still wiping his forehead and trying to catch his breath while seeking clarification from the old man who had overseen the peculiar spectacle.

"Yup," Grandpa Mario smirked, a hint of amusement in his voice. "It's an old tradition which was started by the first mayor of our town. Once a month, men from our town and the neighboring one gather here to settle their differences. No weapons, just fists, and after 30 minutes, they call it quits." He looked chuff with his own response, nodding proudly while positioned towards Barend with his arms folded

Barend nodded slowly with a raised eyebrow, beginning to grasp the odd yet effective practice that kept the peace between the neighboring towns.

"Could have warned me, though," Barend chuckled ruefully, rubbing his knuckles where they had connected with more than one opponent.

Grandpa Mario uttered a high-pitched chuckle in response, his weathered face creasing with a wry smile. "You did just fine, son. Sometimes, a good fight is all they need to keep trouble at bay."

As Barend absorbed this unconventional lesson in local diplomacy, he couldn't help but marvel curiously at the simplicity and effectiveness of the town's peculiar monthly tradition.

Grandpa Mario's words echoed in Barend's mind as he nodded solemnly, helping Vuyo up from the dust-covered patch of ground where the brawl had just subsided. Lloyd, still perched on his horse nearby, was chuckling to himself hysterically while chewing a piece of gum, seemingly amused by the whole affair.

"And what the hell is so funny, hey?" Barend asked, a mix of exhaustion and curiosity in his voice as he brushed dirt from his clothes.

Lloyd's laughter quieted as he wiped the smirk off his face and straightened up in his saddle. "Just watching you, Barend. You handle yourself pretty well out there."

Barend grunted in acknowledgment, concealing a proud smile while still processing the bizarre tradition that had erupted unexpectedly before them. With a shake of his head, he signaled for everyone to mount their horses, so they followed suit and rode back toward town in a dusty procession.

Upon returning home, the weariness from the day's chaotic events clung to Barend like a thick heavy coat. He walked into the modest kitchen where Katelyn sat at the table, engrossed in counting a pile of coins. Her brow furrowed in concentration as she carefully calculated her earnings. She didn't immediately notice her father's presence until he sank down heavily into the chair beside her.

"Long day?" Katelyn asked, looking up with sincere concern as she pushed a few stray coins into neat stacks.

Barend managed a weary smile. "You could say that, I guess… A bit of trouble in town today."

Katelyn's eyes widened with curiosity as she made herself comfortable, resting her chin on her fist. "Oh…Trouble? What happened?"

Barend waved a hand dismissively. "Ah, was just some old tradition between our town and the neighbors. A monthly fighting match to settle differences, apparently."

Katelyn's expression shifted from concern to intrigue. "Fighting… just like that? Every month…? How strange…"

"Yeah…Very," Barend agreed with a sigh, rubbing his tired eyes. "But oh well, it's over now. What about you, eh? How's business?"

Katelyn's face brightened up, gesturing proudly to the coins. "Good! Really good, actually. Those chicks sold like hotcakes at the market today. I made quite a bit."

Barend glanced at the coins, impressed. "That's great, Katelyn. I'm so proud of you, my girl."

She looked down and back at Barend with a shy momentary glance beaming at the praise she received from her father. "Thanks, Dad…"

Barend leaned back in his chair, arms folded, grateful for the peaceful moment with his daughter after the day's chaos. Despite the unusual events that seemed to follow them wherever they went, he found solace in the simple routines of their home… mealtimes, laundry runs and sometimes just giving into Katelyn's requests to play card games over a cup of coffee. Barend appreciates the unwavering support of Katelyn, who always manages to bring a sense of order to their lives, even in the midst of unpredictability.

He chuckled as he stood up and grabbed a cold drink from the fridge, pleased to hear Katelyn's success. "Well done, Katelyn," he praised, a hint of pride in his voice.

Vuyo, sitting on the opposite end of the kitchen table shook his head in amazement. "Sold them all? Wow.. now that's impressive."

Lloyd, who curiously appeared around the corner when he overheard them talking, leaned against the wall and grinned knowingly. "See? I told you, animals always sell."

Katelyn beamed, her eyes sparkling with satisfaction. "I kept this one," she confessed, gesturing to the smallest chick as she placed it on the table. It started tweeting neurotically and darting around on the table. "She's just too cute, isn't she? And Tessa seems to like her too." Sure enough, Tessa, their loyal dog, jumped up against Vuyo's legs to get a bird's view of the little critter. Her smiling jaw with outstretched tongue quickly turned into a serious dog-frown as she wagged her tail enthusiastically and tracked the chick's movements.

Handing a small stack of coins across the table to Lloyd, Katelyn explained, "Your cut."

Lloyd slowly approaching the table raised an eyebrow in surprise and then came to a sudden halt, positioning his hands to lean on the table. He looked Katelyn straight in the eyes and feigned a look of surprise. "My cut? You're actually giving me a share?"

Katelyn nodded firmly and smiled, looking as smug as ever. "It's only fair. You gave me the idea, after all, you know..."

Lloyd chuckled, wiped the coins off the table into one hand without dropping one, and swiftly threw them into his jeans' pockets, clearly chuffed with the outcome of the situation. "Smart businesswoman already, I see."

Barend leaned back in his chair while carefully observing the exchange with a mixture of amusement and admiration. "Looks like you've got a knack for this, Katelyn."

She grinned widely, her cheeks flushed with pride. "Thanks, Dad!"

The warm atmosphere of success filled the room, a welcome respite from the day-to-day challenges they often faced. For Barend, seeing Katelyn's initiative and resourcefulness bloom brought him a sense of reassurance that despite the unpredictability of their lives, they were building something resilient and meaningful together.

Moments after a few more friendly conversations, the doorbell suddenly rang and Lloyd strode over to answer the door with a curious frown etched on his face. Barend watched with a half a smile, anticipating the unexpected visitor.

At the door stood a middle-aged woman with greyish brown bob hair styled meticulously, arms folded and her expression displaying a mix of apology and concern. "Uh, so sorry to bother you, detective," she began tentatively, "but my daughter bought this little chicken from Katelyn." Her little daughter with the piggy tails peeked out from behind her, clutching the wooden box with the chick inside.

Lloyd nodded knowingly as he took his usual stance with hands on the hips. "Ah, yes… Okay, so do you need help with it?"

The woman hesitated for a moment, then shook her head. "No, thank you. I appreciate it, but… You see the things is… well, we have cats, and I'm afraid they won't get along. I'm so sorry." Her daughter look up at her with a frantic expression pleading with her not to return the chick, but reluctantly, the woman handed the box back to Lloyd and turned away, disappearing down the path and trying to hush her daughter who was now wailing hysterically as she protested the return of the chick.

Moments later, another knock sounded at the door. Barend raised an eyebrow as he approached Lloyd, who was now juggling a growing collection of chick-filled boxes.

"You were saying…?" Barend asked wryly.

Lloyd chuckled, his eyes twinkling with amusement despite the situation. "Well, think about the bright side, eh... no one's asked for their money back."

Barend nodded refusing to relent and agree with Lloyd. He folded his arms and stood there staring sternly at the kitchen table now overflowing with chicks. "And the chickens?"

Lloyd shrugged nonchalantly. "Well, we've got a big backyard. Might as well put it to good use, hey!"

Barend's gaze shifted to Tessa, who was circling the table, submissively taking a seat every now and again while her ears perked up as she listened intently to the chirping from the chicks. "And Tessa?"

Lloyd grinned awkwardly, trying to think of an appropriate response. "Ahhh…They'll get along, man. Just give it some time, what do you say? Anyway, this seems like your and Katelyn's project now."

Barend sighed good-naturedly and stared at the ceiling, realizing that their home had suddenly become a makeshift sanctuary for a brood of chicks. He glanced over at Katelyn, who was already doting over the smallest chick with gentle care, stroking it lovingly and cooing, as if blissfully unaware of their reasoning.

Barend glanced into the nearly empty fridge, disappointment flickering across his face as he noted the absence of food and the lack of his favorite cold beer. He closed the fridge door and sighed, shaking his head slightly as he sat down at the kitchen table once more.

Then he suddenly flung up again. "Well... I'm going to the bar," he announced, turning towards Katelyn with a half-hearted smile. "You take care of these chicks. Make some makeshift home for them. Feed them bread or something... whatever you can find in this house..."

Katelyn's expression fell slightly at his sudden decision to go out, a hint of protest on her lips. "But, Dad..."

Barend cut her off gently but firmly. "No 'buts', little miss... You and your friend will need to figure it out. We need to make space for our growing family..."

He paused, giving her a reassuring look before grabbing his hat on the table and heading for the door. Katelyn watched him go, a mixture of determination and concern in her eyes as she turned back to the kitchen table, where the chicks chirped softly in their wooden boxes. She took a deep breath, knowing she had a job to do.

In the dimly lit bar, Vuyo and Lloyd engaged in a heated game of pool against some of the town locals, their competitive banter echoing amidst the clinking of glasses full of brandy and coke and occasional loud cheers. Meanwhile, Barend nursed a cold piece of meat against his bruised eye, seated at the worn bar table with Katelyn beside him. He could hear her stifling laughter, which made him look at her with a faint attempt at a smile.

"What now?" Barend asked, his voice tinged with amusement despite the ache in his eye.

Katelyn pointed at the makeshift ice pack on his face. "Why on earth would you do that?"

"Well... It helps," Barend replied casually, a hint of pain still evident in his voice. "With what, Dad.." Katelyn asks. "To make you stink?"

Barend lowered the meat, revealing the bruised eye, now a deep shade of blue from the day's unexpected scuffle. "Ouch," Katelyn muttered sympathetically through clenched teeth. "You walked into something?"

Barend nodded, reaching for a cigarette and placing it between his lips. Katelyn swiftly grabbed it from him and dropped it to the floor.

"Smoking can kill you, Daddy," she scolded, wrinkling her nose. "Sies. *Gagga*! (gross)"

"Nonsense, man!" Barend retorted, slightly amused by her reaction. "Who told you such rubbish?" He glanced down at the text on the discarded cigarette box that Katelyn pointed to while pouting authoritatively. "Didn't know you could read, eh... You're a clever little girl. Who taught you to read?"

"I played with the older kids at the home, Dad. They showed me. It's really easy," Katelyn explained proudly.

Barend chuckled softly. "So, read the menu then. What can I get you?" he asked, changing the subject as he signaled to the bartender for another double brandy and coke. The bar buzzed with the familiar sounds of laughter and clinking glassesover classic KFM music, a backdrop to their quiet conversation amidst the evening's activities.

Katelyn's eyes scanned over the menu, her brow furrowing slightly as she tried to make sense of the unfamiliar names and symbols. The bar's offerings were clearly geared towards adults, filled with a variety of alcoholic beverages that held no interest for her. She looked up at Barend, as her curiosity piqued.

"What is vodka, Daddy?" she asked innocently, her gaze returning momentarily to the list before her.

Barend chuckled softly, shaking his head. "That's not a drink for you, little one."

She nodded thoughtfully. "What about a 'springbokkie' shot?" she suggested, pronouncing it carefully.

Barend's expression turned amused. "No, definitely not."

"Well..." Katelyn sighed, glancing away from the menu in defeat. "Maybe they serve a pink milky with strawberries on top then."

Barend signaled the bartender over, a gesture that the bartender acknowledged with a nod. "I need a pink milk drink with strawberries on top," Barend requested with a smile.

"We don't do milkshakes, sir," the bartender replied apologetically.

"You have ice cream, right?" Barend persisted.

The bartender nodded cautiously. "Yes, we do."

"Bring her a soda float then," Barend instructed, his tone firm yet gentle. "Add some pink soda and make it look real fancy."

The bartender nodded again respectfully and retreated to the fridge to prepare the drink as requested.

"Mind if I join?" a voice interrupted from behind. The mayor of the town settled onto a stool beside Barend, his presence commanding respect.

Barend grinned at the mayor. "Oh, of course, Mayor."

"First month on the job and you've already rounded up the Davies gang, castrated a man, and took down half the town in a brawl," the mayor remarked with a hearty laugh, slapping him on the back. "Seems my investment is paying off. You're making the headlines weekly now."

Barend flexed his shoulders and feigned a little chuckle, reaching for the newspaper that lay beside him on the bar. The headline read boldly about their recent exploits, using the colorful "stage names" Lloyd had given them. The accompanying photo was a wide shot, obscuring their faces enough to maintain some anonymity, which reassured Barend as he took a sip of his brandy and coke.

"So, how do you like our little town, eh?" the mayor inquired, genuinely curious about Barend's opinion.

Barend considered the question for a mere moment, reflecting on the whirlwind of events since he had arrived. "It's growing on me," he admitted with a half-smile. "Though I could do without the surprise brawls."

The mayor chuckled, clinking his glass against Barend's. "You'll get used to those. They're a part of our town's unique charm."

As the conversation between Barend and the mayor continued, Katelyn's eyes lit up with excitement as the bartender returned with her soda float, adorned with a flourish of pink soda and a few strawberries carefully arranged on top. She giggled with delight, sipping the sweet concoction through a straw as she occasionally gazed at the adults during their conversation, content in the company of her father and the mayor in the lively atmosphere of the bar.

"Well, it's definitely something else, that I can tell you," Barend remarked with a wry smile before taking another sip, his voice cutting through the ambient buzz of voices and music in the bar. The warm faded glow of the evening lights cast shadows that danced on the rustic brick interior of the bar walls and faces of the patrons, creating a lively atmosphere tinged with anticipation and camaraderie.

A trio of young women seated at a nearby table caught Barend's eye, their concealed laughter and animated chatter temporarily hushed as they stole glances in his direction. They exchanged knowing smiles among themselves, their keen interest unmistakable in the rugged figure of Barend, who had become the talk of the town in recent days.

Amidst the subtle flirtations, hushed giggles and curious gazes, a woman approached Barend with a drink in her slender hand, her expression a mixture of gratitude and admiration. "For saving our men today," she offered with a nod towards a group of weathered individuals nursing their drinks at a corner table. "They keep coming back bruised up and losing to our neighbor town."

Barend's eyebrow arched in amusement as he accepted the drink, taking in the genuine warmth of the gesture. "So, who's the lucky man?" he inquired, his voice carrying above the buzz of conversations and the occasional outburst of excitement from the patrons.

The woman followed his gaze and pointed towards a middle-aged man, comfortably settled at the bar with a beer in hand, his attention fixed intently on the sports game flashing across the large flat tv screen. As a triumphant shout erupted from his lips, he jumped up with excitement in response to a scored try. His enthusiasm and fervor painted a picture of a man deeply invested in both the game and the community.

Barend chuckled softly, his eyes crinkling at the corners as he soaked in the scene unfolding before him. The woman smiled back at him with voluptuous lips decorated in maroon, her hazel eyes reflecting a glimmer of admiration and a hint of playful intrigue. Around them, the bar hummed with the energy of camaraderie, where tales of valor and everyday victories mingled with the clinking of glasses and the distant roar of the television.

In that moment, amidst the bustling warmth of the bar and the camaraderie of the town, Barend found himself appreciating the simple pleasures of community and shared moments. To him it was a reminder that in a place where everyone knew your name, even the smallest gestures carried the weight of genuine appreciation and friendship.

Swim in the Dam

T he sun hung high in the sky, casting shimmering ripples across the dam's surface as Barend approached the edge. The metal windpump nearby hummed rhythmically, drawing water from deep within the earth to fill the expansive dam that offered a cool respite from their arid summer heat.

From a distance, Barend spotted little Katelyn in a white cotton dress, her pink rubber floaties bobbing gently in the water as she engaged in conversation with a woman. As he slowly walked closer, curious to lean in on their conversation, their melodic voices carried over the tranquil sounds of splashing and laughter.

"So, how old are you?" Katelyn's voice rang out, filled with curiosity and youthful exuberance as she smiled.

The woman chuckled softly, her weathered hands gently clasping Katelyn's smaller ones. "Well," she began, casting a fond glance at the spirited young girl in front of her, "I'm about level 3, which means I must almost be a hundred years old."

Katelyn's eyes widened with amazement, her imagination taking flight. "Wow," she exclaimed, "that's a lot of years!"

The woman raised her hands playfully in the air, fingers curling slightly, revealing the subtle markings of time spent swimming and living. The gentle wrinkles around her eyes spoke of stories and experiences gathered over decades, etched into her like the lines of a cherished map.

Katelyn's innocent curiosity echoed through the warm afternoon air at the dam, her voice carrying a sense of urgency that only a child could muster. "So, what are you doing tonight?" she asked as she pretended to have a nonchalant attitude while picking a daisy in front of her on the grass.

The woman, her expression softening with a smile, replied gently, "Well, I will be at the agriculture show. My father's horses will be showing."

"Oooh, yay!!! We can go with you!" Katelyn exclaimed eagerly, her eyes bright with anticipation.

Barend hoisted himself onto the edge of the sinkdam, the algae-covered sides and muddy texture offering a familiar yet oddly comforting sensation. Occasionally, he could feel a gentle brush against his legs as he waded in slowly, as lively little fish darted through the clear depths beneath him.

After splashing his sunburnt arms with some water to get used to the temperature, he curiously glanced over at Katelyn and the woman, their conversation carrying on while he lingered in admiration.

As Katelyn chattered on, Barend found his attention drawn irresistibly to the woman beside his daughter. Her long, flowing blonde hair danced like a stallion's mane, framing her features in a way that evoked a sense of timeless beauty. Suddenly a renaissance painting come to life in front of him, captivating and elegant.

"I hope my little princess isn't bothering you too much," Barend called out with a hint of amusement, including himself in the conversation.

The woman turned around in a startled manner and stared at him, her eyes crinkling with warmth. "Oh … no, not at all …" she assured him, "she's just been telling me my age." Her tone was fond, appreciating the innocence and candidness of Katelyn's company.

Barend smiled gently and with gratitude, his heart warmed by the simple joys of the moment shared in the cool waters of the dam. Around them, the vibrant sounds of summer enveloped them—the distant murmur of the windpump, the laughter of children, and the peaceful rhythm of life flowing gently, much like the waters around them

"Daddy, can we go to the agriculture show tonight? Everyone is going, and there will be horses... many of them. Daddy, please, please, please," Katelyn pleaded with infectious enthusiasm, snapping Barend out of his reverie.

Barend pursed his lips, folded his arms as he stiid tall and slowly nodded, as if reluctant, feeling a slight flush of embarrassment. "I know. I saw you in town, quite a display you put on," he admitted, trying to recover his composure.

The woman smiled and blushed as she looked down, brushing off the attention. "Ah, that was nothing. Someone had to do something."

Katelyn, staring at their expressions and sensing the growing connection between her father and the woman, playfully nudged

Barend in the ribs. He jumped away to try and deflect the gesture and chuckled in response, relieved by her light-hearted interruption. "I was glad no one was seriously injured," he confessed, meeting the woman's gaze with a hint of admiration.

Noticing the undeniable spark between them, Katelyn couldn't contain her excitement. "And to think, this woman has horses... sounds like a match to me," she remarked with a knowing smile, and rubbed her hands together with delight.

"Uh...I've got to go; my father will be waiting. Need the horses ready for tonight," the woman announced suddenly, breaking the awkward moment with a hint of regret.What

"So we'll see you tonight at the show," Katelyn piped in, assuming her father was on board. Barend turned to her, caught off guard. "? What's happening tonight again?" Confusion creased his brow as he glanced back towards the dam, catching sight of her gracefully climbing out.

"I didn't even get her name... and what was the show...?" Barend mumbled to himself, suddenly feeling the sting of missed opportunity.

Katelyn sighed, her hand pressed to her forehead in mock exasperation. "Dad, you really need help."

Barend hesitated, torn between his routine game night with the guys and the alluring prospect of reconnecting with her at the show. Her celestial beauty had left an indelible impression, and seeing her silhouette emerge from the dam with such grace was enough to make any man reconsider his plans and find the courage to take a leap into the unknown.

SHOPPING:

Moments later, Barend and Katelyn wandered through the small aisles of the town's general store, a place that served as the hub for all things necessary in their remote community. The shelves were stocked with all manner of practical items, tools, and an array of clothing that largely reflected the town's utilitarian ethos. There were khakis for work, Hawaiian prints for rare festive occasions, and church wear for Sundays.

As they perused the limited selection of attire, Barend couldn't help but feel a sense of monotony settling in. He tried on various pieces, each time emerging from the poky little makeshift dressing area to Katelyn's critique. Her reactions ranged from hearty laughter at some of the more comical outfits to solemn headshakes accompanied by a definitive "no-no."

In a final attempt to find something unique and stately, Barend inquired with the shop owner, a weathered old man with a grey moustache containing more hair than on his head. He nodded sternly as he listened to Barend's request, seeming to know every story and secret in town. "Do you have anything else?" he asked, hoping against hope for a hidden gem.

The shop owner scratched his bearded chin thoughtfully before his eyes brightened with recollection. "Well, uh… I'd say, we do have these," he began, his voice trailing off with a hint of mystery as he made odd movements with his mouth, as if chewing a piece of gum. "They're not exactly in high demand around here."

He recounted the tale of a prospector who had passed through town years ago, in search of elusive diamond grounds but finding only disappointment in the form of red stones. "He left before they even finished building his house," the shop owner continued, gesturing towards a distant hill where a lone structure stood abandoned, a ghost house, as the locals called it.

Barend's interest piqued at the mention of the clothing. "The clothing?" he prompted eagerly.

The shop owner raised a hand, signalling a request to wait for the unveiling of his best option as he ducked behind a stack of boxes, rummaging until he retrieved a dusty, forgotten box from the depths. He blew off the accumulated grime, causing a small cloud to swirl in the air and elicit a cough from Katelyn. "Uh, pass me that red cloth on the table please, young lass", the old man asked Katelyn, ignoring her sudden allergic reaction to the dust. Slightly annoyed, she grabbed it and handed it over to him, wiping her eyes and sniffing to clear her nose. He wiped the box and stood still, awaiting a response from Barned. "Well, go on then..." he presented the box and stood back. With an expectant smile, Barend lifted the lid, revealing an unexpected treasure trove of Italian brands nestled within.

His eyes widened in pleasant surprise as he ran his fingers over the texture of the fabrics. "Italian brands. Well, now that's more like it," he murmured to himself, a grin spreading across his face. Beside him, Katelyn mirrored his joy with an approving nod, her enthusiasm matching his own for this rare find in their quaint, isolated town.

In that moment, surrounded by the lingering dust of forgotten dreams and the promise of newfound style, Barend knew their shopping trip had turned into a type of small adventure. It was a reminder that even in the most unexpected places, treasures awaited those willing to seek them out.

Date Night

Vuyo and Lloyd sat content at the worn wooden table, engaged in their first round of poker for the evening. The clink of chips and the occasional shuffle of cards filled the room, accompanied by the radio's lively tunes in the background along with the rich aroma of rum that awaited Lloyd. Katelyn descended the staircase, dressed in a vibrant new cerise pink dress that shimmered with each step. Lloyd couldn't resist a whistle, his eyes lighting up with admiration.

"Now now, lookie here. All dressed up like that," Lloyd remarked playfully.

Vuyo turned his head to catch a glimpse of Katelyn twirling in her new attire. "Daddy bought it for me," Katelyn announced proudly, her smile wide and infectious, sporting matching pink lipstick. "Daddy!" she called upstairs, "Come! If you take much longer we're going to be late!"

"We?" Vuyo queried, raising an eyebrow in curiosity.

Lloyd casually set down his four cards and collected the chips from the table. "Looks like we're playing poker with the big stakes tonight," he remarked to Vuyo, who glanced back at the cards. "You better not be keeping those cards up your sleeve," Vuyo warned with a grin.

Loud footsteps announced Barend's arrival as he descended the staircase, dressed immaculately in a crisp white shirt adorned with a bow tie and black corduroy pants, his black leather shoes gleaming. Lloyd and Vuyo turned their attention to him, staring at him wide-eyed with a mixture of surprise and amusement.

"Well, well, well, who do we have here?" Lloyd teased before taking out a cigarette. On his way outside, he walked past Barend and lightly touched his freshly shaven cheeks. "You look like a human... I would have never thought."

"That's the problem," Barend retorted dryly, "you never do think, do you?"

Vuyo interjected with a smirk as he brushed over his beard, "You running for town mayor?"

Barend shook his head, smiling as Katelyn approached and took his hands. "We need to go now, Dad," she urged softly, "She'll be waiting."

"She?" Vuyo echoed with curiosity. "Well, well, well... Tell us more..."

"What's the big occasion now?" Lloyd asked, feigning offense. "We can drink to it. We can even drink to this 'girl' if you like," he suggested, nudging a glass closer to Barend, who pushed it aside at Katelyn's insistence.

"No can do," Katelyn interjected firmly and folded her arms assertively. "We've got a date."

"You mean you're leaving us behind for a girl?" Lloyd teased with a mischievous grin. "Tell us her name at least so we can write it on your funeral card..."

Barend shrugged casually. "Don't know yet, but I'll tell you soon enough." With that, he straightened his bowtie, ignoring their smirks. And so Barend and Katelyn made their way out of the room, leaving Vuyo and Lloyd chuckling in their wake.

"A date?" Vuyo mused aloud. "Well, I'll drink to that nonetheless," Lloyd declared as Vuyo dealt another round of cards. "Guess it's just the two of us then, hey brother!"

A sudden shrill bark from under the table interrupted their banter, prompting Vuyo to reach for some chips and offer them to Tessa, who eagerly accepted the treat. "Oh, sorry, and you too, Tessa," Vuyo chuckled, scratching behind the dog's ears affectionately as the game continued in the warm glow of the evening light

The agriculture festival might seem like nothing more than a passing attraction to most city folk, with its red and white merry-go-rounds and small exhibits, easily missed as their fancy cars speed by. Yet, to the town it was the pulse of their community, their pride and joy. It surely was a time-honored tradition that brought together farmers and families from miles around.

As Barend strolled through the bustling fairgrounds, the vibrant displays of livestock caught his eye. As he observed the activity, he could see that each farmer had brought their finest: sleek cows and robust horses with shiny, healthy hides, and sheep with fleece so soft and pure it seemed to have been spun from the clouds. Each animal stood as a testament to the hard work and dedication of its owner, vying for the coveted trophies and the respect of their families and peers.

Little children squealed with delight as they received the opportunity to ride on horse-drawn carriages, their beaming faces painted with smiles brighter than the midday sun. The air was buzzing with the melodies of old *Afrikaans* lyrics accompanied by guitar strums emanating from a nearby beer tent, where a young girl and a man presented their music, their voices soaring over the joyful chatter of the crowd.

The comforting aroma of chicken and vegetable potjiekos simmering in large black cast-iron pots, sweet pancakes sizzling on griddles, and aromatic boerewors sizzling over open flames wafted through the air, tempting passersby with promises of hearty, homemade delights. But amidst the eclectic colorful chaos of the festival, Barend's heart was fixed on finding one specific person.

Eager to connect with her again, he scanned the sea of faces, searching for a glimpse of long wavering blonde hair and a smile that could light up a room. Katelyn had mentioned meeting her there, and Barend couldn't shake the feeling that this festival held more than just agricultural displays and culinary temptations. In his heart he was certain that it held the promise of exciting new beginnings and a meaningful connection.

As they carefully made their way through the labyrinthine rows of horse stalls, Barend couldn't help but marvel at the care and pride each breeder exhibited for their animals. Some horses were treated like royalty, with fans and elaborate watering systems keeping them cool and comfortable amidst the bustling heat of the festival.

Amidst the grandeur and meticulous grooming, a large white banner with red letters caught Barend's eye in the distance: "Shultz Family - Proud Breed Champions." Standing beside a magnificent black stallion, its shiny coat gleaming in the sunlight like satin, was a stately woman in an elegant figure-hugging red sequined evening dress. Her blonde hair cascaded over her shoulders, transforming her into an artwork of glamour amidst the rustic surroundings.

As Barend and Katelyn approached her, the woman swiftly turned around, a large red smile lighting up her face at the sight of them. Despite the lively conversation around her, her attention shifted immediately to Barend as he drew nearer.

Barend extended his arms in a welcoming gesture, and the woman, Marilize, gracefully linked her arm through his. "Why, thanks for giving me a way of escape …" she said with a hint of relief. "Can't stand another evening talking about the secret breed of the Boerperd…"

Barend chuckled fondly. "Mind if we have some fun then, Miss Marilize?"

"You can call me Marilize," she replied warmly, her eyes twinkling with amusement and intrigue. "Marilize Shultz."

Barend nodded appreciatively, maintaining his composure. "Pleasure, Marilize. I'm Barend, and this here is my daughter Katelyn."

Katelyn greeted Marilize with a warm and friendly smile, sensing the easy chemistry between her father and the elegant horse breeder. As they slowly walked away from the bustling stall, the sounds of the festival blending into the background, Barend smiled within himself, as he couldn't shake the feeling that this chance encounter might lead to something more than just a pleasant evening at the agriculture show.

Wherever they turned, the atmosphere at the agriculture festival buzzed with the chatter of excited families and farmers alike. Amidst the hubbub of stalls and the scent of hearty savoury dishes and baked goods alike, Barend found himself standing near a modest booth, facing off against a thin, wiry man. It was clear that he was challenging them to a simple game of skill.

As they strolled over in a leisurely fashion to the carnival-style game stall, Barend couldn't resist smiling at the scene unfolding before him. Marilize was the first to take on the challenge and so she purchased a handful of tokens, counting them in her slender hands with red painted nails. She grabbed a bean bag, aiming it at the pyramid of cans stacked neatly on the table about three meters away. Her first throw sailed high, missing the target completely. Undeterred by the result of her pathetic attempt, she tried again, this time knocking a few tumbling cans off to the side.

"Me, me, me!" Katelyn piped up eagerly, bouncing up and down close by and barely able to see over the table. Barend heaved and lifted her up, positioning her in mid-air towards the direction of the cans while balancing on his one knee "Aim for the middle of the stack, my girl" he advised gently.

With Barend's guidance, Katelyn nodded and carefully aimed, frowning and clenching her teeth, taking her time before a sudden toss of the bean bag. To her dismay it fell short of the table, eliciting a silly giggle from the man behind the counter. He quickly swallowed his laughter at the sight of Barend's stern glance and lovingly gestured toward a selection of sweets they could choose from based on their performance.

Barend chuckled at the whole situation - Katelyn's failure to hit the cans and the man's awkward appearance as he tried to comfort her with sweets and kind words. Marilize turned towards Barend with arms folded, in a stance of a playful challenge. "What? So you think you can do better. eh?"

"Of course," Barend replied confidently, setting down some coins in front of him on the counter. He listened as the skinny man behind the counter explained the rules – the more cans knocked down, the better the prize. Barend's eyes scanned the assortment of toys displayed atop the counter, settling on a large white teddy bear adorned with gold sunglasses and a dress, almost as tall as Katelyn herself.

"I want that one," Katelyn declared, pointing excitedly at the teddy bear.

The man chuckled and patted the teddy bear on the head. "Now, now. Let's not get carried away…That's a very expensive one - only for anyone who can clear out all the cans. Maybe you would fancy one of these smaller ones…" He began to place a few modest, smaller teddy bears in various colours on the table.

Katelyn frowned and shook her head adamantly. "Nope, I only want that one."

The man scoffed and looked at Barend. "Listen son, if you hit all of them…" the stall attendant mockingly began again with a wry grin, gesturing towards the stack of cans perched on the makeshift platform. "Take your best shot, you have one last throw…"

Barend exchanged a swift glance with Marilize, a mixture of pure amusement and determination flickering in his eyes. He picked up another bean bag, tossing it up in the air a few times and catching it again with precision, focused on the pyramid of cans as he took careful aim. The bean bag flew through the air at once, striking the cans dead center. A satisfying crash followed as the entire stack collapsed with a clatter, sending cans rolling across the table.

The man's eyebrows shot up in surprise as the onlookers cheered, and he soon followed suit, clapping heartily. Barend turned to Katelyn with a wide grin. "Looks like you're getting your teddy bear, sweetheart."

Katelyn squealed with delight, jumping excitedly and clapping her hands as the man handed over the coveted prize – the big white teddy bear, complete with its gold sunglasses and dress. She held it tightly, beaming up at Barend and Marilize, who shared in her infectious joy.

As they stood a few meters away from the game stall, enjoying a brief pause over a pancake, Katelyn still beamed with delight as she held her new treasure close. Barend couldn't help but feel extremely grateful for the unexpected moments of happiness that life had now brought – moments that made the challenges and struggles worthwhile, if only for the joy on his daughter's face.

The young man signalled for another round and handed Barend three different bean bags this time, each feeling lighter than expected in his hand. Barend raised an eyebrow skeptically. "You mean I now have to throw with these light feathers?"

The man nodded. "That's it. You know the drill… Knock down one row, and you get to choose from these prizes."

Barend keenly examined the pyramid of cans, calculating his strategy. "And if I knock 'em all down?"

The man chuckled. "Well then you can choose whichever you like, but that ain't happening on my watch, see."

In his peripheral vision, Barend caught sight of Katelyn, her excitement palpable as she squeezed the white teddy bear mercilessly while watching with bated breath.

Barend smirked, feeling the weight of the bean bags in his palm. He tossed the first one with force, aiming high. But to his surprise, it sailed right over the cans, barely grazing them. He glanced at Marilize, who stifled a laugh behind her dainty palm. The man behind the counter grinned, placing his hands in his pockets while looking very chuffed with himself. "You got another two tries, sir."

"It seems these 'feathers' are lighter than what I hoped," Barend muttered to himself. He adjusted his stance and focused, aiming lower this time. The bean bag struck the counter, sending a few cans wobbling but not toppling them over.

"Not quite as easy as it looks, huh?" Marilize teased, tilting her gaze and gently bumping into Barend.

"Not to worry, I'm just warming up," Barend replied confidently. He stretched his shoulders, rolled his neck and clicked his fingers, preparing for his final shot. Marilize leaned closer, whispering softly in his ear.

"If you hit ALL the cans," she murmured, her voice playful yet promising, "I'll give you a kiss."

Barend grinned, turning to face her directly. "Is that a promise?"

Taking a moment, Barend adjusted his stance and casually bent down to tie his shoelace, a small ritual to calm his nerves. Rising slowly and gracefully, he focused on the cans ahead. Closing one eye to improve his aim, he let the bean bag fly with a controlled flick of his wrist.

The bag sailed through the air, finding its mark with satisfying accuracy. With a resounding crash, the cans toppled in a clatter of metal against wood. The man at the counter leaped forward in surprise as the entire platform collapsed under the impact.

Katelyn erupted into gleeful cheers and laughter, her voice ringing above the din, as she was about to be rewarded with another custom teddy. "Pink teddy bear... pink teddy bear..."

Barend grinned broadly, swept up in another moment of victory as he took Katelyn's hand. Together, they twirled in a joyful dance, celebrating their double portion of triumph amidst the festival's vibrant backdrop.

As the excitement settled, Barend turned to Marilize, his cheeks tinged with a mix of bashfulness and triumph. "Uh..." he stammered, clearing his throat awkwardly, looking downward.

"What a show off," Marilize teased, playfully nudging Barend in the ribs. "Now, what was it you were saying? If you knock down ALL the cans..."

The man at the counter fetched a stick with a hook to retrieve the coveted pink teddy bear, which he handed to Katelyn. Holding the previous teddy under her left wing, she grabbed the pink one with her right hand and clutched it tightly to her chest, her eyes sparkling with joy.

Barend glanced at Marilize, a mischievous glint in his eye. "Oh, before I forget," he said with a playful grin. "You mentioned something about a kiss..."

Katelyn giggled, hiding behind her two big teddy bears as Marilize leaned in and planted a soft kiss on Barend's cheek. He feigned disappointment, teasing, "Now come on, that ain't no real kiss..."

Marilize laughed, taking Katelyn's hand. "Gotta knock over more than cans to get one of those," she replied, her voice lighthearted as they strolled towards the billy goats.

Barend turned back towards the booth, gesturing towards the man behind the counter with mock seriousness. "What do you want me to knock down next, then?" he called after Marilize, his expression playful yet earnest.

The sun was slowly beginning its descent, casting a warm, rosegold hue over the bustling agriculture festival grounds. Amidst the colorful stalls and lively chatter of attendees, Barend found himself swept up in a rare moment of pure joy. He watched Katelyn darting between booths, her laughter ringing through the air. She played a few games and made funny faces at the goats nearby, then headed off to a confectionary stall to buy a toffee apple, despite Barend's warning about damaged teeth.

It had been a long time since Barend had allowed himself to simply enjoy a day without the weight of responsibilities pressing on his shoulders. The cares of the farm, the worries of the town... here, amidst the festivities, they all seemed distant and inconsequential. There was a lightness in his step, a genuine relieved smile on his face as he soaked in the sights and sounds of the festival.

He couldn't help but chuckle as Katelyn attempted to imitate the bleating of a goat, her enthusiasm infectious. Nearby, Marilize watched with amusement, her own laughter mingling with Barend's. There was a precious warmth in her eyes as she observed Barend and Katelyn, a flicker of something deeper beneath the surface.

For Barend, this day was a rare gift. It was an opportunity to forget the troubles of the world and simply savor the present moment. He savored every laugh, every shared glance, every spontaneous game played with Katelyn. In that fleeting afternoon light, surrounded by the buzz of the festival, Barend found himself rediscovering a part of himself he had long neglected, the part that knew how to embrace joy and let go of worries, if only for a while.

The morning sun painted soft streaks of yellow light across the farmhouse, filtering through the semi-sheer curtains and gently awakening the sleeping world.

Barend, true to his routine, was up very early as usual. After his bitter morning coffee, he was already outside tending to Jasmine and Tessa, his faithful companions in the quiet hours of dawn. Their soft nuzzles and the rhythmic sounds of their feeding mingled with the stillness of the cool morning.

Inside the farmhouse, Katelyn padded through the hallway toward the kitchen on worn-out socks, rubbing the sleep from her eyes. Her steps were light, but purposeful. As she passed the couch, she noticed Lloyd sprawled out, clutching his beloved bottle. His long drawn-out snoring echoed softly in the room, sounding like a zipper being closed carefully. The sight of his heavy slumbering figure was a sure testament to a night of revelry that had come to a peaceful end.

A mischievous smile played on Katelyn's lips as she decided it was time for a bit of morning humor. She sneaked into the kitchen, as if her footsteps would have startled the sleeping giant on the couch. Swiftly, she gathered a few ingredients from the cupboard and fridge, the clinking of bowls and the soft whirr of a mixer breaking the early morning silence. Eggs cracked open into a bowl, oil poured in, and with deft hands, she whisked everything together until a smooth concoction formed.

Approaching Lloyd with a blend of determination and cautious amusement, Katelyn stifled a giggle behind her arm as she took in the lingering scent of alcohol. Holding her nose delicately with one hand and balancing a glass of the mixture in the other, she gently nudged Lloyd's shoulder.

He stirred slowly, his eyelids fluttering open to find Katelyn standing over him. His brow furrowed for a moment as he peered at her through stuffy eyes, apparently confused by the morning light and the unexpected presence beside him.

"What's this?" he murmured, his voice hoarse with sleep and remnants of last night's festivities.

Katelyn nodded with a grin, holding out the glass. "A little pick-me-up for you."

Lloyd managed a weak half-smile, his eyes crinkling at the corners. "Thank you. You really shouldn't have," he muttered playfully, closing his eyes once more, clearly not fully awake.

Undeterred, Katelyn continued to tap his shoulder gently, her expression a mixture of amusement and determination. It was clear that she was not going to take no for an answer. As Lloyd, took a big gulp, his eyes widened with pure shock and horror. He ran to the kitchen trying to prevent himself from spewing the entire contents of the liquid out on the floor.

This was not just a morning beverage, but a small act of mischief and care wrapped into one, a testament to the camaraderie and family bond that surrounded them in this humble farmhouse.

As the morning unfolded in the farmhouse, Lloyd, still recovering from the unexpected jolt of Katelyn's concoction, stood at the kitchen sink furiously rinsing his mouth, while his unkempt Beetles-style hair was shaking vigorously. His expression oscillated between disbelief and irritation, punctuated occasionally by a groan or a muttered curse that was cut short by Katelyn's playful admonishment.

Katelyn stood nearby, half hiding behind the kitchen entrance to shield herself from any possible backlash. Her laughter rang out like a little neighing pony through the room. "Geez…What was that!? Good lord, you really tried to kill me?" Lloyd managed to sputter between rinses, his eyes watering from the potent mixture.

Barend entered the room just in time to witness Lloyd's frantic attempts at cleansing his nasal cavities and palate. His amused grin widened as he took in the scene before him. "Now, now…what on the world is going on here?" he asked, his voice tinged with curiosity and amusement.

Katelyn giggled, still enjoying the aftermath of her prank. "Oh, nothing serious, Dad. Just giving Uncle Lloyd a wake-up call." she winked at Barend as she said the words.

Barend glanced from Katelyn to Lloyd, who was now frantically scrubbing his tongue with his fingers. "You tried to kill me," Lloyd repeated, his voice muffled as he struggled with the taste.

Barend accepted the glass from Lloyd, eyeing its contents warily before taking a cautious sniff. The pungent aroma hit him immediately, and he recoiled instinctively, his face contorting in disgust. "Wow...you didn't smell it before you drank it?" Barend quipped, handing the glass back to Lloyd.

"It's medicine, Daddy," Katelyn chimed in with a mischievous twinkle in her eye. "To stop the drinking."

"Serves you right then," Barend remarked with a chuckle, tousling Katelyn's hair affectionately as he passed by, whistling a familiar tune.

Lloyd finally managed to regain his composure, though his expression remained one of perplexed amusement mixed with a touch of exasperation. "What's with him?" he asked Katelyn, gesturing toward Barend's retreating figure while still wiping his mouth. "And seriously, what the hell did you put in there?"

Katelyn merely shrugged, a playful smirk playing on her lips. "Not telling... its my little secret," she replied cryptically, before humming the same tune as her father and wandering off, leaving Lloyd to ponder both the taste of the concoction and the whimsical nature of his niece

It was a slow day at work, marked by Barend's distracted demeanor as his thoughts wandered far from the mundane tasks at hand. With Lloyd and Vuyo occupied with overseeing the Davies gang while they were slaving away, digging a swimming pool, Barend found himself driving through town, eventually steering his truck toward the Schultz breeding farm.

Marilize was a portrait of beauty to behold as she gracefully navigated the course on horseback, her skilled handling of the animal revealing her deep connection to the farm. Barend watched her every move from a distance, appreciating her confident manner and her natural elegance.

As Marilize carefully dismounted and handed her horse off to a farm worker, she noticed Barend approaching with a bouquet of stunning white wildflowers in hand. A modest smile graced her lips as she accepted the flowers. "These are considered pest plants around here, you know," she teased him gently.

Barend's awkward frown betrayed his uncertainty. "Well, I'm not exactly a flower expert, you know" he admitted sheepishly, retracting the flowers slightly. But before he could withdraw them completely, Marilize closed the gap between them, her presence causing a palpable tension.

She playfully pressed a finger to his lips. "Just joking," she murmured, her eyes gleaming with amusement as she pulled back slightly.

Barend seized the moment. "Can I see you again, maybe tonight?" he ventured, hoping to prolong their interaction.

Marilize shook her head slightly with reluctance, a small smile playing on her lips. "What, can't stand the thought of losing to a guy?" Barend teased.

Again, she shook her head, her smile widening more than before. "The big man himself wants to meet you."

Barend's brow furrowed in confusion. "The big man? You mean God?" he asked, half-jokingly.

Marilize chuckled softly, shaking her head once more. "No, not God," she clarified. "My father. He has a rule: anyone who takes his only daughter out for a date must first go past him..."

Barend scanned her hand, noting the presence of a ring. "So, you're engaged or married?" he asked, a hint of confusion mixed with disappointment evident in his voice.

"No its not what you think ..." Marilize assured him. "This is just my father's protective streak."

Barend couldn't help but smile at her father's stipulation. "He said it like that, though?" he mused aloud.

Marilize nodded with a hint of seriousness. "Pretty much, yeah" she replied. "In his opinion this would be enough to scare off most guys around here."

"Well, I'm not 'most guys,'" Barend declared confidently, earning a shrill laugh from Marilize. "Certainly not," she agreed, her laughter tinkling like wind chimes.

"Well, I've got to get back to work," Marilize said with a softened tone, started to turn away before looking over her shoulder at him with the charm of a puppy dog. "Will I see you tonight then?"

Barend nodded slowly, a spark of anticipation in his eyes. "Six o'clock, strictly," he confirmed.

"And remember... bring Katelyn with you," Marilize added with a smile.

Barend nodded again, his mind already racing with plans for the evening. "Six it is," he affirmed, standing proudly with his hands in his pockets.

With a final nod and a parting smile, Marilize turned and walked away with a spring in her step, leaving Barend with a sense of intrigue and anticipation for the evening ahead.

Evening had descended upon them, casting a soft amber glow over the countryside as Barend and Katelyn approached the grand white Victorian house with its angular shapes and dark frames. Barend, dressed in his only grand suit, felt a mix of excitement and apprehension ripple through him. Marilize stood there waiting for him by the large window, her shy wave a reassuring gesture amidst the nerves.

As they went up the front porch's steps and walked inside, the grandeur of the house enveloped them. It exuded old wealth, evident in every detail from the Victorian architecture to the antique furnishings and the lineage captured in photographs lining the hallway as they entered. The creaking wooden floors whispered tales of generations past as an eager, hardworking servant guided Barend and Katelyn towards the dining room.

Inside, the table was a spectacle of fine dining, set with an array of fine sterling cutlery that hinted at the meal's formality. Barend and Katelyn took their seats, the tension palpable as they waited for Mr. Leon Shultz to arrive. Barend's eyes darted around the room nervously, as he fidgeted and rubbed his hands together, absorbing the atmosphere thick with anticipation.

Then, with a presence that commanded attention, Mr. Leon Shultz entered the diningroom. Tall and imposing, he carried himself with a natural authority that spoke of years spent managing both land and legacy. His meticulously combed dark hair was streaked with hints of silver, his brown eyes sharp and penetrating.

"Now, now, if it ain't the talk of the town," Mr. Shultz greeted them in a deep, resonant voice that filled the room and commanded silence. His gaze fixed on Barend, assessing him with a mixture of curiosity and scrutiny.

Barend stood up, feeling the weight of the moment. "Logan White," he introduced himself, extending, clearing his vocal chords, and extending his hand swiftly towards Mr. Shultz with a respectful nod and a feigned half-smile.

Mr. Shultz's strong grip enveloped Barend's hand briefly before releasing it. His expression softened slightly, a hint of a smile hardly recognizable on his lips, but evident in the softening of his eyes. "Mmm, pleasure to finally meet you, Logan," he replied respectfully, his voice carrying a subtle warmth that eased some of Barend's nerves.

Katelyn watched the exchange quietly and nervously, although her presence was a comforting reassurance amidst the formalities.

Barend's smile widened as Mr. Shultz swooped in and acknowledged Katelyn with a kiss on her hand, a gesture that spoke volumes of old-world courtesy. He sat down, a sense of warmth settling in the room as conversation flowed naturally.

"And you are?" Mr. Shultz inquired politely, prompting Barend to introduce Katelyn formally.

"Katelyn, sir," she replied with a gracious smile. "What a pleasure to meet you, Mr. Shultz."

Barend, ever mindful of tradition, slid a cake forward that he had brought with him. Mr. Shultz chuckled softly, declining with a courteous gesture. "No, you shouldn't have. We have more than enough here."

"In my hometown, it's considered impolite to visit empty-handed, sir," Barend explained warmly, a touch of pride in his voice.

Mr. Shultz nodded appreciatively and settled into his seat, the rest of the company following suit. The dining table was adorned with exotic wildflower arrangements and wineglasses, each display reflecting the history and refinement of the Shultz family. As the first course arrived, served with precision by the attentive servant, Barend found himself momentarily awed by the elegance of the setting.

As they started conversing, the evening unfolded with interesting stories of the town, anecdotes of farming life, and glimpses into the proud heritage that Mr. Shultz held so close to his heart for many years.

Throughout the evening, Barend found himself captivated not just by Marilize's undeniable beauty, but by the rich tapestry of her family's history woven into every corner and in all of the decor in the house. And as the night progressed, amidst their consumption of dry red wine, hearty laughter and shared moments, Barend began to understand that this evening was more than just a dinner. On the contrary, it was a step towards something deeper. What he was experiencing was something that resonated with the timeless rhythms of the land and the bonds that tied people together in unexpected ways.

"This is like dining with the queen," Barend thought to himself, adjusting seamlessly to the etiquette of fine dining. He noticed Katelyn's surprise but was pleased to see her quickly mirroring his actions with the utensils, a testament to her adaptability and upbringing.

Throughout the meal, conversation ebbed and flowed effortlessly. Mr. Shultz steered the course of most of their conversations, engaging both Barend and Katelyn in lively exchanges that bridged the gap between their worlds. As dishes were served and cleared, Barend found himself not just enjoying the exquisite food but also the company and the stories shared around the table.

In the midst of it all, amidst the clinking of their crystal glasses and the mirth that filled the air, Barend began to sense a much deeper connection forming… a thread of understanding and mutual respect that transcended the differences in their backgrounds.

Barend listened intently as Mr. Schultz spoke with unmistakable passion about his family's legacy of breeding Boerperd horses. Around the finely set table, the air seemed to hold the weight of history as Mr. Schultz recounted tales of courage and resilience intertwined with the lineage of these majestic animals.

"Our family has been breeding some of the best Boerperd horses for generations," Mr. Schultz began, his voice carrying a deep reverence.

He paused briefly to slice into the steak in front of him before continuing, his eyes reflecting the pride of a man deeply connected to his heritage.

"The Boerperd has roots similar to the Basuto pony, but we found the precise breeding combination suited for these lands," Mr. Schultz explained, his words resonating like echoes from a bygone era. "Initially known as the Cape Horse, it was refined with Arabian stallions brought into the breed during the Cape Colony period. Renowned for its sound temperament and sure-footedness."

Barend nodded appreciatively, his gaze steadily flickering between Mr. Schultz's animated face and Marilize's hand gently touching his leg in silent support.

"Our family played a pivotal role during the first Boer War," Mr. Schultz continued, as he cleared his voice, which was now taking on a deeper resonance. "We introduced Flemish stallions from the Netherlands and Norfolk Trotters to refine what became known as the Boerperd. These horses proved invaluable for their stamina, hardiness, and mobility, qualities that were thoroughly tested and refined during the war years."

Barend could sense the weight of history in Mr. Schultz's words, the narrative punctuated by moments of solemn reflection. He glanced at Marilize, who whispered softly, "Here comes his favorite part. I've heard this story countless times."

Mr. Schultz's eyes glinted with absolute pride as he recounted tales of how the Boerperd had enabled the Boers to resist the overwhelming British forces during the war. "Well, the Boers were skilled riders, you know... and it was these horses that allowed them to prevail," Mr. Schultz declared with quiet intensity, gesturing with his hands as he explained. "But unfortunately it came at a high cost for them. Many of our most valiant horses were lost on the battlefield. The British even resorted to killing them to deny us our advantage."

As Mr. Schultz spoke, Barend felt a deep sense of respect for the man and his family's heritage. The table fell silent as they resumed eating their main course, the only sound the occasional clink of cutlery against plates. Marilize's gentle touch on his hand was comforting to Barend, it made him freeze, stare at her beauty and contemplate for a moment, a silent acknowledgment of the emotions stirred by her care as well as her father's words.

Barend knew in that moment that the Boerperd horses were more than just pure animals to the Schultz family. To them they were symbols of resilience, courage, and a legacy that spanned over generations. He returned the gesture and squeezed Marilize's hand gently, silently expressing his admiration for her father's passion and the heritage they shared.

Barend sat submissively at the table with Mr. Schultz, the weight of their conversation lingering in the air like the aroma of the luxurious meal now mostly devoured from their plates. The grand Victorian house seemed to hold its breath, the only sound the steady tick-tock of the grandfather clock marking the passage of time.

"I can understand your sense of pride in these horses," Barend finally remarked, breaking the silence that had settled between them.

Mr. Schultz nodded slowly while twisting the ends of his moustache between the tips of his fingers, his gaze drifting towards the doorway through which Marilize had left moments earlier. "It's a family investment, and my dream is to keep it in the family," he murmured, more to himself than to Barend. His eyes reflected a mixture of determination and concern, his thoughts clearly preoccupied with matters beyond the simple pride in his horses.

Barend considered Mr. Schultz's words carefully, sensing the weight of parental expectations and the complexities that come with family legacies. "So... You're a father yourself, sir..." Barend ventured cautiously. "What would you do?"

Mr. Schultz's expression softened slightly, as the frown creasing his forehead dissipated at the mention of fatherhood. He sighed heavily, as if grappling with a decision that weighed heavily on his heart. "Well, ofcourse I would want her to be happy," he admitted, looking at the tablecloth in front of him, his voice tinged with a hint of resignation.

Mr. Schultz glanced at Barend, his eyes revealing that he was about to shed light on his previous remark. "Happy... well, she has all the reasons in the world to be happy," he remarked, his tone turning wistful. "She doesn't have to worry, or even to work."

Before Barend could respond, Marilize abruptly excused herself again, yet this time her departure was swift and laden with unspoken tension. Katelyn, sensing the moment's intensity, quietly and slowly stood up, following her out of the room, leaving Barend and Mr. Schultz alone at the table.

The atmosphere in the room grew heavy with multiple unspoken emotions. Barend nervously glanced around the elegantly appointed dining room, the polished wooden furniture and antique paintings reflecting the wealth and heritage of the Schultz family. Yet beneath the veneer of opulence, Barend sensed a deeper complexity. He became in touch with a father's hopes and dreams, a daughter's unspoken burdens, and the weight of family expectations.

As the grandfather clock continued its rhythmic ticking, Barend and Mr. Schultz sat in silence staring into space, each lost in his own thoughts. The evening had taken an unexpected turn, revealing layers of emotion and familial dynamics that Barend had only begun to grasp now.

Barend excused himself to go to the bathroom. While in solitude, he knew he had to slip away to go and check on Marilize. As he swiftly slipped through the backdoor, hoping not to be noticed by her father, he noticed Marilize sitting on the steps next to Katelyn, hiding her face behind her hands. Katelyn, who was gently stroking her hair in a comforting manner, looked up at Barend with a concerned expression.

Barend knelt beside Katelyn and Marilize, the soft melody of Katelyn humming her song hanging gently in the air. He glanced at Marilize's tear-streaked face and felt a pang of empathy for her silent distress.

"I'm sure he didn't really mean to upset you," Barend said softly, his voice a calming presence in the room.

Marilize looked up, her eyes shimmering with unshed tears. "He told you the story... it was about London, right?"

Barend nodded slowly, understanding dawning in his expression. "He mentioned it, yes."

Marilize sighed deeply while wiping her face, a mixture of frustration and sorrow evident in her features. "London changed her," she murmured, her voice tinged with a hint of bitterness. "She came back with all these... ideas. Different dreams."

Katelyn paused her gentle brushing and looked at Marilize with concern. "What kind of ideas do you mean?"

Marilize's lips curved into a sad smile. "Big city dreams, Katelyn. A life beyond this farm. She saw things there, experienced things..." Her voice trailed off, the weight of unfulfilled expectations lingering in the room.

Barend listened attentively, sensing the complexity of Marilize's emotions and the delicate nature of the situation. He reached out and softly placed a comforting hand on Marilize's shoulder. "Sometimes experiences change us," he offered gently.

Marilize nodded, trying to swallow the tears, her gaze distant yet filled with introspection. "She wanted more than what we have here," she admitted quietly. "And my father... he couldn't understand it."

Barend's brow furrowed slightly in thought. "He's proud of what he's built here," he observed, recalling Mr. Schultz's impassioned pride in his horses and family legacy.

Marilize nodded again, this time facing Barend, and he noticed a touch of resignation in her expression. "Too proud, sometimes," she murmured. "It's hard for him to see things in a different light."

Katelyn leaned closer to Marilize, her eyes wide with curiosity and compassion. "Do you miss London?" she asked softly.

Marilize's gaze softened as she looked at Katelyn. "Sometimes, yes" she admitted, a faint smile playing on her lips. "But being here has its own beauty, its own kind of peace."

Barend stood up, his hand still resting reassuringly on Marilize's shoulder. "Thank you so much for inviting us tonight," he said sincerely. "It really meant a lot to us."

Marilize nodded gratefully and smiled faintly, her earlier distress easing under Barend's comforting presence. "Thank you for coming through," she replied, her voice steadier now. "It was... nice."

As the three of them returned to the dining room, Barend nodded solemnly, understanding the unspoken tension in the air. Marilize's father, Mr. Schultz, stood nearby, his presence casting a shadow over their brief moment together. Barend reluctantly released his hand from

Marilize's shoulder, sensing the weight of propriety and respect for her father's wishes.

"I understand," Barend said quietly, his gaze flickering briefly to Mr. Schultz, who remained stoic and unreadable.

Marilize managed a small, apologetic smile, her eyes betraying a mix of frustration and resignation. "I'm sorry, Barend" she whispered, her voice barely audible above the rustling of the curtains in the breeze. "He's... protective."

Barend nodded again, his hand lingering where it had rested on Marilize's arm. "It's alright," he assured her softly. "I'll see you soon then?"

Marilize nodded hopefully, her expression softening with gratitude. "Yes," she replied, a hint of warmth returning to her voice. "Thank you for understanding."

With a gentle parting smile, Barend turned to leave, his footsteps echoing down the quiet hallway. Mr. Schultz watched him go and Barend almost felt the stern, assessing gaze piercing into his back like a laser, following his every move. Mr Schultz could not hide the brewing jealousy over his daughter. He stood there staring into the distance as his features etched in shadows cast by the dim hallway lights.

As Barend and Katelyn waved goodbye and made their way home through the quiet town, Barend grew increasingly silent as he was driving. He couldn't shake the image of Marilize's sadness and the weight of Mr. Schultz's unyielding pride. He knew then that the Schultz family's legacy was much more than just horses and heritage. It was a story of dreams, expectations, and the delicate balance between holding on and letting go

Once Barend was out of sight, Marilize sighed softly, her shoulders slumping slightly. She turned to her father, meeting his unwavering gaze with a mixture of defiance and resignation.

"He's different, father" Marilize said quietly, her voice tinged with a touch of defiance. "He understands things differently."

Mr. Schultz, immovable as a statue, regarded his daughter for a long moment before finally nodding, his expression softening imperceptibly. "Perhaps," he conceded gruffly, his tone hinting at a begrudging acknowledgment. "But understanding and approval are two different things."

Marilize nodded, her gaze steady and determined. "I know," she murmured, her voice resolute. "But he's... worth it."

With that, Marilize turned away to retreat to her bedroom, her thoughts lingering on Barend's presence and the warmth of his touch. She knew that navigating her father's expectations would not be easy, but she also knew that Barend had stirred something within her—a sense of hope and possibility that she had not felt in a very long time.

As Marilize brushed her teeth, preparing for bed, the weight of her father's disapproval lingered in the air. Yet, beneath it all, a flicker of anticipation burned quietly in her heart—a hope that perhaps, with time and understanding, her father might come to see Barend as she did: a man worthy of both her affection and her father's respect.

back at home

Barend took a long swig from his long glass beer, contemplating the situation. Vuyo's suggestion lingered in the air, a desperate hope veiled in uncertainty.

"They'll be expecting us to try and change our appearance," Barend reiterated, his voice low and measured. "It's too risky."

Lloyd nodded in agreement, his expression grim. "He's right. They've literally got eyes everywhere. Disguises won't cut it this time."

Katelyn, engrossed in coaxing Tessa to perform tricks with a little tennis ball, glanced up briefly, her brow furrowed with concern. "So what do we do then?"

Barend sighed heavily, setting his beer down on the kitchen counter. "Well... simply lay low, fellars. The only option we have is to keep off their radar until things cool down."

"And for how long will that be, heh?" Vuyo asked, a note of frustration creeping into his voice.

Barend shrugged, his gaze fixed on the floor as he pondered the question, tapping his fingers on the table in front of him "Well, can't say for sure. But one thing is certain … we can't afford any slip-ups right now."

Lloyd leaned against the kitchen island, crossing his arms. "So what then? We just sit here and wait?"

"For now we have to, yes" Barend confirmed, his tone resolute. "Only until we figure out our next move."

Tessa, sensing the tension in the room, whimpered softly and nudged against Katelyn's leg. Katelyn absentmindedly scratched behind Tessa's ears, her thoughts wandering. She glanced at Barend, then at Lloyd and Vuyo, a silent understanding passing between them.

"We'll figure something out," she said quietly, more to reassure herself than anyone else.

Barend nodded and looked at the sight of her and Tessa with endearment, a faint smile tugging at his lips. "We always do, yes."

With that, the kitchen fell into a heavy stone cold silence, the weight of their predicament settling over them like a shroud. Outside, the cool night pressed on, oblivious to their worries and plans. They were in uncharted territory now, navigating the unknown with extreme caution and resilience, bound together by loyalty and the shared determination to see this through, whatever it took.

The decision weighed heavy in the air, thick with the tension of their circumstances. Barend paced up and down in the kitchen, hands clasped behind his back, while Vuyo and Lloyd exchanged solemn glances.

"We can't afford to split up, guys" Barend stated firmly, his voice cutting through the uncertainty. "Now that's just asking for trouble."

Lloyd scoffed softly. "He's right, hey! One slip-up and we're all in hot water."

Vuyo leaned against the kitchen counter, his brow furrowed in thought. "So, what's the plan of action then?"

Barend paused, gathering his thoughts. "We go and find a boat. Somewhere down the coast, then we can slip away unnoticed."

Lloyd nodded slowly, the gravity of their situation sinking in. "That might just be our best shot."

"We'll need to move fast then," Vuyo added, his tone resolute. "Before they tighten the net around us."

Barend looked at each of them in turn, his expression determined to begin their course of action. "Well, let's get to work then. We can't afford any mistakes, oaks."

Vuyo and Lloyd nodded in agreement, their resolve firming as they prepared themselves for the task ahead. The kitchen, once filled with uncertainty, now buzzed with a renewed sense of purpose as they made their next cup of coffee. They had a plan, however risky, and they were ready to see it through. Each knew the stakes were high, but they also understood that their bond and shared determination were their greatest assets in the face of adversity.

NEXT DAY

As they rode through the Schultz farm, the serene countryside unfolded around them. The cool breeze carried whispers of tales from the past, epitomized by the weathered grey gravestone they passed. Barend glanced at the stone marking Persie the sheep, and Marelize narrated the touching story of the elderly couple and their beloved companion.

"Small towns make a man do strange things, it seems," Barend remarked, his gaze lingering on the grave.

Marelize shook her head, a wistful smile playing on her lips. "No... I think it's something more."

Barend arched an eyebrow as he looked at her. "Must be something crazy, right?"

Marelize nodded emphatically. "Yep... definitely love."

Barend chuckled softly. "Love…? What's love got to do with a sheep and a tombstone?"

"Well… Just about everything," Marelize replied, her eyes gleaming with sincerity. "Love sure goes beyond what we can imagine."

Barend pondered her words for a moment, before they playfully decided to race back to the farmstead. The excitement of the challenge spurred them into action, and with a playful countdown, they spurred their horses into a gallop. Barend's steed surged forward, but Marelize quickly closed the gap, her melodic laughter carrying on the wind as she excitedly chased after him.

Later that day, after returning the horses to their stalls, Barend found himself face-to-face with Mr. Schultz. The serious tone in the older man's voice hinted at an important conversation.

"Barend… mind if I talk to you for a moment?" he broke the awkward silence. Mr. Schultz's request was sudden and seemingly affrontational, his utterance laced with a weight that demanded immediate attention.

Barend nodded respectfully after overthinking the sudden request for a brief moment . "Oh.. ofcourse, yes"

Mr. Schultz hesitated briefly before continuing, his expression thoughtful. "I…uh… I actually need your advice, with you being a man of the law and all."

Barend's curiosity piqued. "Oh…? Sure, go ahead."

The air around them seemed to thicken with the weight of unspoken words, signaling that whatever Mr. Schultz had on his mind was not to be taken lightly.

Mr. Schultz's troubled expression mirrored the weight of his words as he spoke of the plight facing their stolen horses. The soft murmur of the wind outside carried the gravity of his concerns through the room.

"We transport our horses from here to the various towns and cities as they are required," Mr. Schultz began, his tone of voice deepened with a mixture of frustration and sorrow. "I was made aware of some of our horses that have been stolen; they have been found in the government pounds in Lesotho. They keep our horses with some strays in these pounds until the court case is finalized."

Barend listened intently, the gravity of the situation settling heavily upon his shoulders. "That's not even the worst thing," Mr. Schultz continued, his voice trembling slightly. "They are living in such harsh conditions. From what I was told, there is not a blade of grass to eat for these horses, no water to drink. Some of them have been injured, they roam around listlessly around the enclosure. They found one of our mares, dead, with her young foal trying to suckle."

Barend's eyes widened as he imagined the horrible scene of these poor starving animals. Mr. Schultz continued at the first glance of Barend's dismay,

"It is too much for any breeder to take, you know - and now we are stuck between paper wars. It is truly difficult to work out who is responsible for these atrocious crimes and to figure out a plan to get those horses back alive."

Barend absorbed the heartbreaking details, his mind racing with possible solutions. "What do you suppose one can do about the situation?" Mr. Schultz asked, his eyes searching Barend's for any semblance of hope.

"Well, you have tried the clean approach and the paper war, so to speak…" Barend replied thoughtfully, considering his words carefully.

Mr. Schultz nodded solemnly, uttering a feeble "Yes… yes…" as he acknowledged the truth in Barend's assessment.

"What happens to the strays?" Barend inquired, a glimmer of an idea forming in his mind.

"Well, a man can come and claim the horses as the owner and then take them," Mr. Schultz explained.

Barend smiled wryly. "If you can give me some money, I am sure I have a way around it. That is if you don't mind your horses being written on the papers there as strays, and a bit of bribing."

Mr. Schultz hesitated, wiped over his beard and looked away, his discomfort evident. "I really would want to avoid bribing; it just doesn't seem right."

Barend met Mr. Schultz's gaze firmly. "There are times when the law is protecting the lawless, Mr. Schultz. And then you have to make use of lawless ways to do what is right. You don't want to have more of your horses die over there, am I right?"

The man's expression swiftly softened with understanding, torn between his desire to uphold principles and the urgency of rescuing his beloved horses from their dire circumstances.

Barend walked into the midst of Katelyn and Lloyd's escalating banter, a smile playing on his lips as he observed their playful bickering.

"Well, what do you know, you are just a little girl," Lloyd teased, his tone light but mischievous.

Katelyn's face scrunched up in mock offense. "Well, you are a stinky coconut with long hair!"

Lloyd chuckled. "Whooo... then you are elephant ears not washed for a hundred years!"

Katelyn recoiled in exaggerated disgust. "You are stinky... like sour milk and wet dog mixed on a carpet left in a dark room!"

Barend, looking ever amused as he came nearer, couldn't resist joining in, moving closer with a grin. "Ahhhh," Katelyn exclaimed, pointing at him and laughing.

"Well, at least I ain't in love... that is one disease I sure don't want," Lloyd grunted with a playful glint in his eye.

Vuyo interjected from his seat, trying to calm the situation. "That isn't so bad! What are you on about!?"

"Sorry, old man, didn't know you could still hear," Lloyd teased, turning his attention to Vuyo.

"Who are you calling old man?" Vuyo shot back, his tone laced with mock offense. "What, you blind also?"

Lloyd stood up, his playful demeanor shifting slightly. "Come on, you two, before stinky here gets hurt."

"Lloyd, me? I might just break the old fort," Vuyo quipped back, his stance challenging.

Without warning, Vuyo swung his fist towards Lloyd, who deftly blocked the blow. However, Vuyo seized the opportunity, swiftly wrapping his hand around Lloyd's throat, applying pressure.

Lloyd's eyes widened in surprise and then narrowed in determination as he struggled against Vuyo's grip, trying to pry the larger man's fingers from his throat. The air seemed charged with tension as Barend watched, ready to intervene if necessary.

"Daddy, daddy... he's going to kill him," Katelyn's urgent voice echoed through the kitchen, pulling Barend from his thoughts.

Barend shook his head with a faint smile. "No, they're just playing, sweetheart."

"But, Daddy!" Katelyn persisted.

"Okay, princess," Barend relented, stepping forward to gently pull Vuyo and Lloyd apart.

Vuyo, ever the older brother figure, tried to impart a lesson. "What, I forgot you still need to learn, young man."

Lloyd, always quick with a retort, mimicked Vuyo sarcastically. "Okay, Noah... you can teach me how to build an ark another day, alright?"

Barend chuckled softly, looking over at Katelyn. "I think it's time to go to bed before these two boys get a hiding."

As the others filed out of the room, Lloyd opened the fridge, spotted a bottle of his favourite liquor and grabbed it, intending to take a drink. However, as he brought it to his lips, he caught a whiff of something sour and off waiting on the inside. "Katelyn...!" he muttered to himself, tossing the bottle into the dustbin.

From her room, Katelyn peeked out and flashed a naughty smile before escaping quickly behind a closed door.

"Vuyo, Lloyd, come here," Barend called from the living room, his tone serious.

They entered, looking both concerned and curious about what he had to say.

"I've got an opportunity for us to fetch some horses from an impound not too far from here," Barend explained, his voice low and measured. "It's a good chance to go scouting, see what's happening around town."

Vuyo and Lloyd exchanged nods, intrigued by the prospect.

"It's an easy job," Barend continued, leaning back in his chair. "You two will be back long before anyone notices anything."

Lloyd raised an eyebrow. "The two of us?"

Barend nodded firmly. "Well, of course. Someone needs to look after our treasure here," he said, a hint of a smile playing on his lips, "and it sure ain't going to be you"

In a tense moment, Barend pointed an accusatory finger at Lloyd.

"Bribe money," Barend declared sharply, throwing the bag onto the table. "You bring them back, and you get another bag just like that."

Lloyd smirked, his tone dripping with sarcasm. "Petty cash, just what a millionaire needs to entertain himself."

Barend shook his head ruefully. "Well, if I had any idea what was to follow, I would have gone myself."

The next morning, they set out early on horseback. By the time they reached the town, they were ready to negotiate. It didn't take long for them to sway an official to their side. The bag of money was placed strategically on the table, and soon enough, they had convinced the official that the horses were rightfully theirs…or at least, they were willing to pay handsomely to make it so.

Katelyn returned from school that afternoon with her usual joyful enthusiasm dampened by a sense of worry. In her hands, she carried a tray of food portions for all the animals, including her beloved little chick. Caring for them demanded constant attention and effort, a responsibility she took very seriously.

Approaching the cardboard box in the corner of the laundry room where her chick usually greeted her with shrill chirps and frantic pecking, Katelyn's heart sank heavily. The chick lay still, its usual vigor replaced by a subdued silence. Its fluffy gown seemed dulled, and it didn't stir at her approach.

Noticing the chick's lack of appetite, Katelyn's usual cheerful demeanor gave way to a pang of concern that brewed deep within her spirit. This wasn't just a pet; it was a companion, a tiny life she had nurtured from the moment it hatched. Her emotions surged at once, caught between hope and fear, love and grief.

She tried everything she could possibly think of to coax the chick into eating, spraying formula milk into its beak through a syringe, as she had seen Barend do before, She hoped that would revive its appetite. Barend, too, had stepped in with advice from their neighbor, offering electrolyte water to try and boost the chick's energy.

Under the warm yellow glow of the bulb they had installed for comfort, the chick seemed to muster up some strength. It moved ever so slightly, seeking the solace of the light, but its droppings apparently watery and abnormal, told a tale of illness.

For Katelyn, each moment spent watching over the little chick felt like an eternity. The tiny creature's struggle mirrored her own inner turmoil, as she willed it to recover, pouring all her love and hope into the fragile life before her.

Lloyd and Vuyo rode back with the horses, the animals trotting along steadily under the afternoon sun. As they neared the town, Lloyd's sharp eyes caught a glint of something shiny in the distance. Curious to see what was hiding there in the sand, he reined in his horse and dismounted to investigate. As he approached the shiny object and crouched down to inspect, he found that it was an old silver coin half-buried in the dirt. While briskly brushing it off, he marveled at its age, the likeness of Jan van Riebeeck still visible despite centuries of wear and tear.

"This might fetch a pretty penny," Lloyd mused aloud to himself, imagining the possibilities of wealth and luxury that a rare coin like this could afford him. "Enough for a few good bottles of brandy and maybe a night or two with the ladies."

With that hopeful thought in mind, Lloyd made a detour to a nearby second-hand dealer, hoping to turn his find into a windfall. The dealer greeted him warmly but frowned and pouted upon examining the coin, offering only a handful of notes in return.

"What's this?" Lloyd scoffed, disappointment coloring his voice as his mouth hung open. "This coin's ancient! It's got history...Jan van Riebeeck, the trek boers, battles with the Khoi Khoi..."

The dealer shrugged indifferently, flicking the coin back to Lloyd and folding his arms relentlessly. "Not much demand for old coins these days. Now, if you had stumbled upon some gold on the other hand..."

Lloyd's ears perked up at the mention of gold. "Gold? What if someone found gold in these parts?"

The dealer chuckled knowingly. "There's some gold around, sure. But not the kind you stumble upon. Most of it's deep underground, mined out ages ago. If you did find some, we'd melt it down, keep it off the books."

"Off the books," Lloyd repeated, grinning at the idea of hidden treasures and secretive dealings. "I'll hang onto this coin then. Might just be my lucky charm, eh?"

He flipped the coin in the air, catching it deftly before heading out to join Vuyo and the horses waiting outside.

"Well?" Vuyo asked as Lloyd approached.

Lloyd shook his head and pursed his lips, pocketing the coin. "Nope. Not much luck with the coin, but let's get going. It'll be dark soon..." Vuyo shrugged and nodded, keeping his thoughts about the coin to himself.

With that, they mounted their horses and rode off, leaving the town and its fleeting dreams of wealth behind them in the dust.

That night, as Barend read Katelyn her bedtime story, he couldn't shake the sense that her thoughts were elsewhere, preoccupied with worry for her ailing chick. The little bird now stayed close to her, nestled in a makeshift nest in her room, while Tessa, ever vigilant, yet submissive, lay there nearby on the carpet.

"Aren't you going to say your prayers, Dad?" Katelyn asked, breaking the silence.

"Well, yes... later, in my room," Barend replied, momentarily distracted.

"Can you pray for the little one?" Katelyn pleaded, her voice tinged with concern.

Barend nodded solemnly. "I haven't prayed in many, many years," he confessed quietly.

"You pray for the little one," Barend suggested to Katelyn, who closed her eyes, knelt beside her bed, and looked expectantly at him. Moved by her innocence and faith, Barend joined her on his knees. Katelyn's prayer was soft and earnest, her words barely audible to him, but he caught the heartfelt "Amen" that marked the end before she jumped up and climbed back into bed.

"Afterward, I cradled Katelyn in my arms until she fell asleep," Barend reflected, his thoughts drifting. "Vuyo and Lloyd had returned to town just after sunset, and Lloyd was out celebrating his success with the town's girls, as usual."

Minutes later, Barend heard the soft patter of Katelyn walking on her socks on the creaking wooden floor. This time, she didn't head for his room. Tessa's claws clicked behind her, following faithfully. She made her way to Vuyo's bed, where he lay deeply asleep. Standing by his side, she gently patted his arm, rousing him from his slumber.

"Huh...? Everything okay?" Vuyo asked, blinking in confusion, his mind groggy from sleep.

"Can God help her?" Katelyn asked, her feeble voice trembling with emotion. She held out the little chick wrapped snugly in a small fleece blanket.

Vuyo sat up, the moonlight casting a soft glow into the room, illuminating Katelyn's tear-streaked face. He peered into her eyes, seeing the worry and care etched deeply within them.

"Help whom?" Vuyo queried while rubbing his eyes, still trying to make sense of the situation. His gaze followed Katelyn's gesture toward the tiny bird nestled in her hands.

A sense of compassion and understanding dawned on Vuyo as he realized the depth of Katelyn's concern for the chick. Without another word, he gently took the small creature from her, cradling it in his scruffy palm.

"We'll do what we can," Vuyo reassured her softly, his voice calm and soothing. "Let's see what we can do for this little one."

"Well, ofcourse He can. It's just a matter of... how can I explain it...?" Vuyo beckoned Katelyn to come and sit beside him on the bed, patting next to him on the mattress. As she approached, his voice was gentle, yet thoughtful, as he tried to find the right words.

"These things aren't always simple," Vuyo continued, his brow furrowing slightly. "Sometimes God helps directly. Other times, He wants us to take action, to do something about the situation ourselves."

"But... can we ask Him?" Katelyn's voice was soft, filled with hope and innocence.

"Ofcourse you can," Vuyo assured her warmly, his eyes reflecting understanding. "Anytime, anywhere you are, my dear..."

"Will you pray with me?" Katelyn asked, her innocent eyes wide and earnest as she looked up at Vuyo. Without hesitation, Vuyo joined her on his knees beside the bed.

Katelyn closed her eyes, folding her hands together in prayer. "Dear God, if you can hear me, please listen to me tonight..." she began, her voice sincere and clear. "I know you are very busy, but the little one is weak. She doesn't eat. Please help her to eat and get better again. Amen."

The room fell silent after Katelyn's prayer, the evening calm enveloping them both.

"Now please go to sleep. Get some rest for tommorow..." Vuyo gently urged, a flicker of concern in his eyes as he tucked Katelyn into bed.

The next morning brought a glimmer of hope. The little chicken, though still weak, was up and about, pecking at its food a bit. Katelyn, ever resilient and full of cheer, bounded off to school with her usual enthusiasm.

In the quiet of the room, Vuyo stood there in amazement. He couldn't help but wonder if their prayers had been heard. He watched over the little chick with renewed hope, knowing that sometimes, even the smallest prayers could bring about the greatest miracles.

Katelyn went to school that morning, her thoughts preoccupied with her ailing little chick. She couldn't concentrate on her lessons, her mind drifting to the fragile creature she had left at home. When the final bell rang, she rushed back home as fast as she could, despite the heavy backpack she was carrying, her heart racing with anxiety.

Upon arriving home, Katelyn expected to find her chick in its usual spot. Instead, she was greeted by an eerie silence. She dropped her bag like a pile of heavy bricks and ran to the laundry room. The box, which usually held her beloved pet, was empty. Panic started to rise within her as she searched the room, her breath quickening.

"Where is she?" Katelyn called out frantically, her voice trembling.

Barend stepped into the room, his expression somber. "Katelyn, we need to talk."

"What happened to her, Daddy? Where is my little chicky?" Her voice cracked with fear and confusion.

Barend knelt down to her level, taking her hands in his. "I took her to the vet this morning. She was very very sick, Katelyn."

Katelyn's eyes widened with a mixture of hope and dread. "Is she okay? Did the doctor make her better?"

Barend took a deep breath, sighed, looked down, and back into her anxious eyes, his heart aching at the sight of his daughter's distress. "The vet did everything he could, but... she was just too weak. Sometimes, animals are born with problems that we can't see, and they don't always make it..."

Tears welled up like pools of water in Katelyn's eyes as she processed his words. "But she was getting better! She was eating yesterday..?!"

Barend pulled her into his embrace, trying to soothe her as she sobbed into his shoulder. "I know, sweetheart. I know... But we did everything we could."

Katelyn pulled away, her face streaked with dust and tears, and her little chin quivering. "Where is she now? What did you do with her?"

Barend knelt down beside Katelyn holding her chin up and looking straight into her eyes, his voice gentle but firm. "Katelyn, just listen for a moment," he said, his eyes searching her tear-streaked face. "We got you a new chick, a healthy, strong one. The doctor guaranteed me that this one is good."

Katelyn shook her head, her small frame trembling with sorrow and frustration. "She was good, Daddy," she whispered through snorts of tears, her voice cracking. "She was..."

Before Barend could even respond, Katelyn turned and stormed out of the room, her heartbreaking sobs echoing through the hallway. Barend watched her go, his heart heavy with a mixture of helplessness and hope. He knew how much she had loved the little chick, how much it had meant to her.

In the kitchen, the new chick stood there in its box, chirping softly. Its bright eyes and lively movements were a stark contrast to the stillness of the one they had just buried. Barend sighed and reached for a handful of chicken feed in the large straw bag beside him, sprinkling it liberally into the box. The chick pecked eagerly at the food, its tiny beak tapping against the cardboard.

Barend stood there for a moment, observing the new chick. He knew it certainly wasn't a replacement for the one Katelyn had lost, but he hoped it would help heal her broken heart. He hoped it would remove her focus from the loss she had experienced and bring a little joy back into her life.

The sun was slowly setting over the town, casting long shadows and a sombre atmosphere over everything. Each person seemed lost in their own thoughts, the weight of the day heavy on their shoulders. Marelize had come over to visit them, and now sat with Katelyn on the steps in the old dusty garage. Newspapers were spread out all over the floor to protect it from being soiled as Katelyn had started painting, her brush strokes uncertain. It was hard to tell whether she was crying or painting, as she was crouched over her art project hiding her face behind her long blonde hair. Although the box in front of her displayed bright, vibrant colors with a little chick painted on it, Marelize noticed a teardrop falling on the newspaper beside Katelyn.

Barend lovingly watched the two of them from the doorway, arms folded. Marelize caught his eye and gave a gentle smile. Barend nodded in acknowledgement and came nearer. He took the brush she handed him and joined them, adding his own strokes to the colorful box. Tessa, their loyal dog, was constantly running around, almost seemingly unaware of the melancholy atmosphere as her fur was now speckled with paint. However, it was clear that she tried to comfort Katelyn with gentle licks whenever she noticed her crying. There wasn't much more anyone could do to ease this painful moment for Katelyn. After a while, Barend and Marelize went inside for a cup of tea while Katelyn completed her project

As Barend turned to leave the kitchen, he heard the door creak open. He paused, listening to Katelyn's heavy footsteps as she walked back in with her white sports takkies. She stood at the back entrance to the kitchen, her eyes red from crying, her face streaked with tears. She looked at the new chick, shaking with sadness, then at her father.

"Daddy," Katelyn said, her voice barely above a whisper, "Can we bury the little one under the old tree, in this box?"

Barend nodded slowly, unable to speak past the lump in his throat. The three of them went outside in the cold backyard and Barend started digging a hole next to the old yellowwood tree, a silent witness to many of their family's moments. As he dug, he thought about the stories this tree could tell, and the fact that it was about to gain another chapter at this present moment.

No words were exchanged, and no music played. The only sound that broke through the heavy silence was Katelyn's crying. Marelize gently stroked her hair in an attempt to console her. With the hole in the ground ready, Barend gathered everyone together to say goodbye. Vuyo fetched the cold, lifeless body of the chick. Katelyn's eyes burned with anger and pain as she stared at him, almost unwilling to face the reality of it all. The group stood there quietly, but again the only sound interrupting the silence was Katelyn's relentless sobs arising like waves of the ocean every few seconds. Marelize held her even closer, trying to offer comfort as Barend gently placed the colorful box into the ground and began to cover it with soil. Each scoop of dirt felt like a weight pressing down on his heart.

When the ground was level again, Katelyn turned to Vuyo, her eyes filled with a seriousness that belied her age. "Promise me you will never do it again," she said, her voice trembling but firm.

Vuyo sighed deeply. "I did not mean to, Katelyn. It had to be done..."

"Be quiet...! Promise me," she insisted, her voice rising with a hint of hysteria. "Promise me you will never kill again. Or I will never forgive you!"

Barend shook his head slightly, urging Katelyn to understand. Vuyo's voice, filled with regret, echoed in the quiet. "I promise," he said.

"Then shake hands on it," Katelyn demanded, stretching her hand forward.

Vuyo took her small hand in his, and they shook. Marelize gently broke the two hands apart after they held, her eyes full of understanding.

In that moment, Barend realized the depth of a child's promise. It was not just words, but a binding vow that carried the weight of forgiveness and trust. For now, it brought a small measure of peace to Katelyn's heart, and that was enough

The new chick chirped joyfully from its box in the kitchen, a small reminder that there was still life and hope, even in the midst of loss. Barend watched Katelyn as she carefully tended to the new chick, uttering a faint smile as her young heart was already beginning to heal. The cycle of life was hard, but it also held the promise of new beginnings, and for Katelyn, the love she had for her little chick would always be a part of her.

Next Day at Work

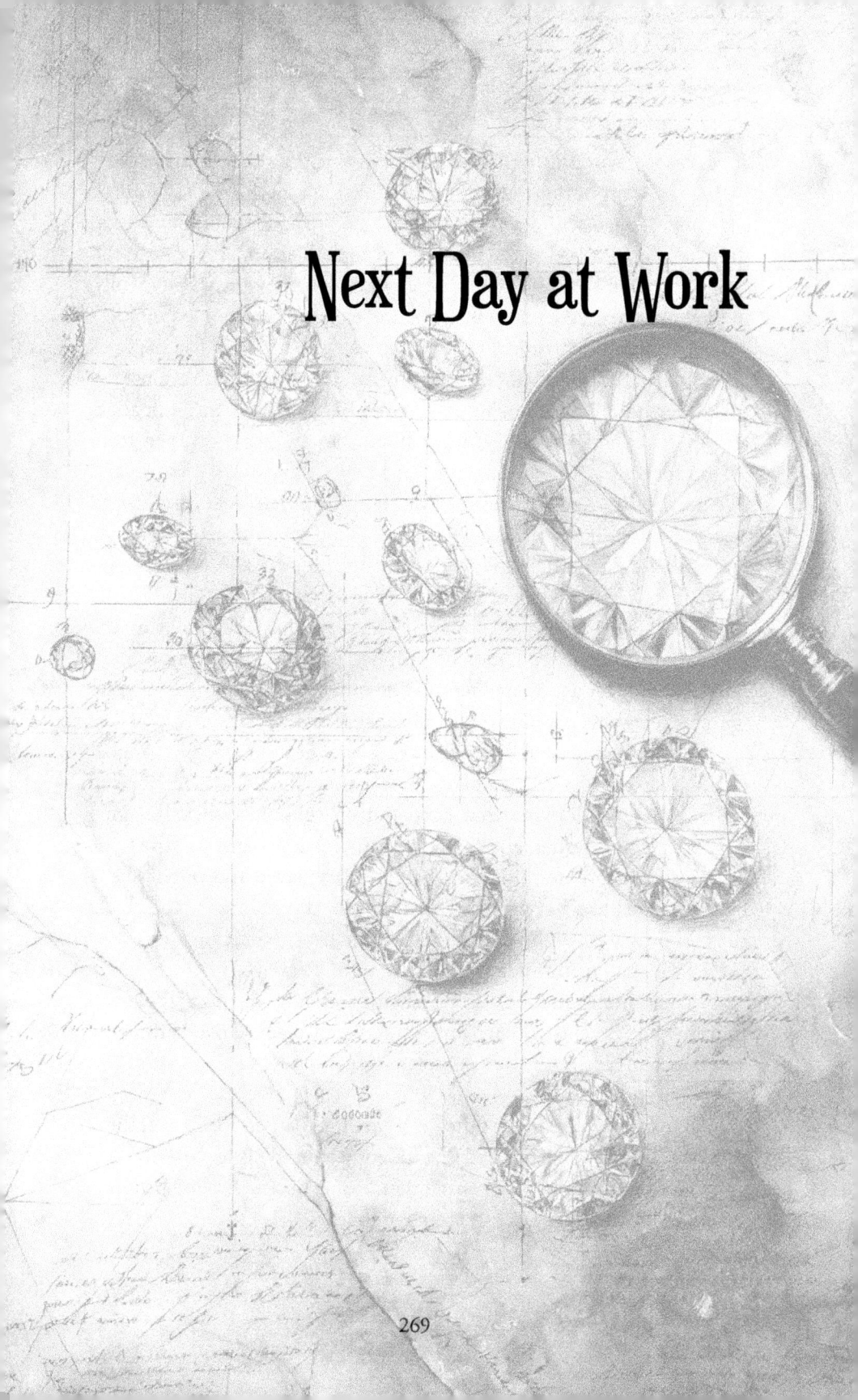

uyo was working harder than ever, wiping the sweat from his brow as he was pouring his energy into finishing the swimming pool. If anyone had witnessed the Davies gang labor before, they would have been astonished at the intensity of today's efforts. It was as if the weight of yesterday's events drove Vuyo to exhaust himself physically, in the hopes of easing his conscience and clearing his troubled mind.

The hot midday sun beat down relentlessly, casting sharp shadows across the half-finished pool. The sound of shovels scraping against the dirt, the rhythmic thud of wheelbarrows being loaded and unloaded, and the occasional grunt of effort filled the air. Sweat dripped from Vuyo's forehead, stinging his eyes, but he hardly gave it any thought. His muscles burned with fatigue, but he gladly welcomed the pain. It was a distraction, a way to push away the lingering image of Katelyn's tear-streaked face and her piercing, accusing blue eyes.

Vuyo's coworkers noticed the sudden change in him. Usually quick with a joke or a smile, today he was silent, his focus solely on the task at hand. He moved with a determined precision, every movement purposeful, every action deliberate. The others worked hard to keep up with his relentless pace, driven by his unspoken intensity.

The sun climbed higher, causing the heat to become almost unbearable, but Vuyo didn't allow this to slow him down. He attacked the work with a ferocity that bordered on self-punishment, digging deeper, pushing harder. His hands, raw and blistered, gripped the tools with a vice-like determination. His mind replayed the burial scene over and over, like an unforgettable drama... the stillness of the chick, the vibrant colors of the box, and Katelyn's heart-wrenching plea for a promise he had made in desperation.

The phone suddenly rang sharply, slicing through the mid-morning lull. Barend frowned and immediately reached over, lifting the receiver to his ear.

"Barend speaking," he said.

A hurried voice on the other end gave him pause. "I'll be over there right away," Barend responded, the urgency clear in his tone.

"Hey...! What about our lunch?" one of the Davies brothers asked, visibly upset as Barend prepared to leave.

Barend glanced at the steaming pot of mieliepap and the pack of bread he had brought for the crew. "Here we go," he said, thrusting the entire pot and the bread into the Davies brother's hands. "It's your lucky day. You divide it yourself."

Davies grinned, his eyes lighting up as he took a big spoonful, not even thinking of sharing with the others. However, he soon felt the shadows of the rest of his gang looming over him. Uncomfortably, he smiled. "I was going to give you guys some, I just checked if it was good enough..." he started, but they clearly would not accept his excuses as they began to protest.

Barend left before the situation could escalate even further, his mind preoccupied with Katelyn. The phone call had been from her school, and it wasn't the first time he'd been called away for her.

It was not until he received this latest call that he truly realized the seriousness of her situation. As he arrived, he found Katelyn sitting in pain at the nurse's office, a sight that instantly filled him with worry. Lloyd was conspicuously absent, and without his usual antics to lighten the mood, the gravity of the situation hit Barend even harder.

At first, he thought it might be another incident involving a boy or lingering grief over her little chick, but this was something different entirely, something that caused his stomach to turn with angst. Katelyn sat hunched over, her face pale and contorted with pain. The nurse recommended seeing Dr. van Poens, the town doctor, as her pain seemed to be increasing as the minutes went by. Barend had hoped it was something minor, possibly curable with cranberry juice as one of the older ladies in town had suggested. But this was clearly beyond "old wives" remedies.

Dr. van Poens was a peculiar old man, known not only for his medical expertise but also for his interest in old Afrikaans treatments. His office was a curious blend of modern medicine and ancient herbology, resembling a scientist's laboratory with plants and roots preserved in various jars of different shapes and sizes.

Barend and Katelyn sat anxiously in the waiting room, the air thick with the mingling scents of antiseptic and herbs. Katelyn clutched her side, her eyes glistening with unshed tears.

"I'm sorry, Dad," Katelyn said softly, her voice trembling with weakness. "I didn't mean to call you away from work."

Barend's heart ached at her apology. "Don't be sorry at all, sweetheart," he replied, trying to keep his voice steady.

"Shhh," Barend gently soothed her, his voice barely above a whisper. "The doctor will have a look at this and get you better in no time... promise!" Katelyn attempted a brave smile but couldn't disguise the pain, her hand pressed firmly against her side.

Dr. van Poens made an abrupt entrance into the waiting room, then stood still with an air of calm authority, securing his ballpoint pen in his shirt's pocket, as he called their names. Nervously Barend and Katelyn followed him into the consultation room, where they settled into the two rounded chairs in front of his desk. The doctor took out his black notepad, his eyes scrutinizing them with a mix of curiosity and concern.

"So... how can I help you today, sir? How do you feel?" he began, looking directly at Katelyn with a stern expression.

Barend spoke up, his voice steady but anxious. "I'm perfectly fine, it's just my daughter. She's been having cramps, well... pains in her side."

The doctor turned his attention to Katelyn. "For how long have these pains been continuing?"

Katelyn shook her head slowly and sighed with exhaustion. "Not sure, doctor. A long time ago already..."

Barend added, "She's had them repeatedly, but they've been more consistent the last few weeks. It was the school nurse who insisted we bring her to you this time."

"Very well then," the doctor replied, motioning for Katelyn to climb onto the step leader in order to launch herself onto the examination bed, its brown covering cracked and well-worn. He took out his stethoscope and other instruments from a trolley with neatly organised buckets nearby, his movements precise and practiced.

Katelyn shivered as the cold metal of the stethoscope suddenly touched her chest. "Deep breaths in and out," Dr. van Poens instructed, and Katelyn complied, her breaths shaky but even.

The doctor pressed at various points on her abdomen, his fingers probing with gentle but firm pressure. Katelyn winced noticeably when he touched her left side and near her bladder, her face paling with discomfort.

He then stood back, placed his hands on his hips and sighed, shaking his head, which stirred up a considerable amount of anxiety amongst them. "I will need to ask for some blood samples as well as scans, just to confirm," he said finally, his tone even more serious this time.

"Confirm what?" Barend asked, fear slowly creeping into his voice.

"Well, it is early to say, so let's wait for the results before we chase up a storm, but I suspect renal failure."

"Renal failure?" Barend echoed, his confusion evident. "I'm sorry, I don't understand these terminologies at all."

Dr. van Poens offered a reassuring half-smile. "Let's wait for the results, then I will explain everything in detail."

Barend stood up awkwardly, his intense frown exposing his worried, racing mind.

"Please ... she must not eat anything tonight so we can have a clear scan tomorrow," the doctor added.

Barend nodded, feeling the weight of the doctor's words settle heavily on his shoulders. "Alright," he said, his voice thick with concern.

As they left the clinical consultation room, the gravity of the situation hung over them like a dark heavy cloud. The sun was setting outside, casting long shadows that mirrored their growing fears. Katelyn clung to Barend's hand fiercely, her facial expression tightened with pain and anxiety. As they walked back to their car, the silence between them grew heavy with unspoken dread.

It was already quite late, and the night seemed to stretch endlessly. Barend sat next to Katelyn on her bed holding a big colourful book, his voice soft as he read her a bedtime story. He hoped the familiar tales would take her mind off the pain that twisted her small face in discomfort. She wasn't allowed to eat anything, and her stomach's hollow emptiness only further added to her misery. Lloyd, always the joker, tried his usual tricks to lighten the mood, but every time Katelyn laughed, her face contorted as her insides hurt even more.

Eventually, Katelyn clung to her big fluffy teddy bear and, holding her side, drifted into a peaceful sleep. Barend stood there staring at her for a moment longer, the sight of her fragile form stirring a deep ache within him.

Wandering through the quiet Schultz house, Barend's mind raced with worrisome thoughts. The shadows cast by the dim lights seemed darker and more intimidating tonight, mirroring his troubled thoughts. He found himself pacing up and down in the hallway, unsure of what to do next. The soft creak of the floorboards under his feet was the only sound in the stillness.

In her room, Marelize was already in her fleecy nightwear, preparing for bed, when she heard a soft knock on her window. Startled, grabbed her gown and walked over, her heart pounding with a mix of curiosity and fear. As she opened the curtain, she saw Barend standing there, his face etched with worry.

"Something wrong?" she asked, her voice barely above a whisper as she secured her gown's tie around her waist.

Barend nodded, dropped his head with dismay, then glanced at her once more, his eyes heavy with concern.

Marelize grabbed a warm coat for extra insulation and climbed out of her window cautiously. "If my father gets just as much of a whiff that you here..."

"I am sure I can deal with your father," Barend interjected, his voice firm but low.

"It's Katelyn," he continued, his voice cracking slightly. "She's in a lot of pain. I took her to Dr. van Poens, and they're going to take some scans tomorrow. He said it might be renal failure."

Marelize's face softened with empathy framed by a comforting half-smile. "He's a very good doctor, one of the best in town. You really have nothing to worry about. I'm sure he'll find what's wrong and be able to help her."

"I'm not too sure..." Barend admitted, his voice a rough whisper.

Marelize wrapped her arms around him, her touch gentle and warm. She felt the coldness of his hands, a testament to how long he had been outside in the biting night air. "Sometimes you need to trust in Him," she said softly.

Barend briefly locked eyes with her, then shook his head, his eyes downcast. "It's not so easy."

"Of course it is. Even a child can do that," she replied, as her smile playfully widened.

"Well, I haven't been a child for a very long time," he said and pursed his lips, his voice heavy with years of unspoken burdens.

They stood in silence, the night enveloping them in its quiet embrace. Marelize's touch was a small solace, a brief respite from the storm of worry raging within him.

"Do you need me to come with you tomorrow?" Marelize asked after a moment, her voice steady and reassuring.

Barend nodded, wiped his nose and looked at her with desperation, a silent plea for support. She gently squeezed his hand, her presence a beacon of warmth and hope in the cold night. As they stood there, the world around them seemed to hold its breath, waiting for the dawn to bring answers

Upon returning home, Barend found Vuyo and Lloyd huddled together in the dimly lit room, their voices carrying a sense of urgency that matched the tension etched on their faces. Katelyn lay fast asleep under thick warm blankets on a couch nearby, her innocence a stark contrast to the weighty conversation unfolding.

"I'm tired of sitting around here, playing cop," Lloyd muttered, frustration evident in his tone. "I must be the richest fool in the world … living like a poor man."

Vuyo's response was pragmatic, tinged with a touch of sarcasm as he scoffed. "That's 'cause you spend all your income on them booze, my friend.."

Lloyd's frown deepened as he stood there, folding his arms arrogantly. "What do you mean, 'that bit of money'?"

"I say we make way for the border," Lloyd continued, ignoring Vuyo's remark. "It makes no sense to sit around here."

Barend, weary but alert, interjected with caution. "Well, have you found a way through? Or someone who will help us with a boat? I can't take any silly risks just because you've got an itch."

"Itch?" Lloyd scoffed, shaking his head, clearly impatient and annoyed by Barned's remark.

"Well, on my last trip with the horses, I went scouting," Lloyd explained. "From here, we're less than a day to the closest harbor by car, and we can skip any big towns with ease."

"We need to save up some cash for petrol and the boat, then," Barend mused, considering the logistics.

Lloyd's impulsive nature reared its head again. "Why not just point a gun and take the boat? We'll be over the border long before anyone can report it."

Barend shook his head firmly. "We'll need a fast getaway car to start with, nothing too flashy but fast enough if we need it."

"You saying what I think you're saying," Lloyd pressed, his gaze intense.

"I'm really tired, Lloyd... can't think straight right now," Barend admitted wearily.

Lloyd persisted, his tone urgent. "Come on. We can't keep hiding here forever. What's the use of having all those riches and not being able to use any of it? If not for me, then do it for her... for your daughter. You can take her to a proper hospital, buy her a golden pony if you want..."

Barend raised an eyebrow at Vuyo, who seemed caught between disbelief and cautious agreement. "Golden pony?" Barend repeated, bemused.

"All I'm saying is, sooner or later, your little girlfriend and these lousy small-town people are going to sniff something they don't like or something shiny they really like," Lloyd continued passionately. "And I'm sure as heck not gonna lam around here waiting for that to happen."

Vuyo interjected calmly, trying to assuage their fears. "We've got it covered, fellars. It's well hidden. No one has been at that barn for ages. People believe someone died in there from what I heard."

Lloyd shook his head in resignation, his voice a mix of exasperation and disbelief. "I seriously can't believe you guys. You're the richest fools I've ever met."

"Daddy..." Katelyn's soft voice cut through the heated discussion, her presence a poignant reminder of their greater responsibility.

Barend turned immediately, his expression softening at the sight of his daughter standing there, vulnerable and pale yet determined.

"I'm coming, sweetie," Barend assured her, sweeping her up into his arms and carrying her back to bed.

Lloyd glanced at Vuyo, a mixture of confusion and concern evident on his face. "What?"

Vuyo simply shook his head and sighed deeply, his eyes reflecting the weight of their choices and the uncertainty of their future.

Inside the stifling confines of the cold prison visitation room, tension crackled like static electricity. Barend sat across from Samantha, the reporter whose patience was visibly waning. Her frustration was palpable as she scribbled something in her notebook, then leaning forward, determination etched into her every feature.

"Barend," Samantha began, her voice edged with urgency. "I've been chasing this story for weeks now. I've followed every lead you gave me, but I can't find a single reference to this town. No records, no maps, absolutely nothing. It's almost as if it never existed."

Barend's eyes remained still and guarded, his face a mask of calm despite the undercurrent of anxiety. "I told you, Samantha. We were off the grid. We wanted to stay hidden."

Samantha's fingers drummed impatiently on the table, her frustration bubbling over. "Off the grid is one thing, but completely non-existent? Come on, Barend. Either you're lying to me, or you're still hiding something..."

Barend's jaw tightened in a square, a flicker of defiance in his eyes. "I have no reason to lie to you."

"Then give me something substantial!" Samantha's voice rose, her desperation spilling out. "I need to have a story for the press. I need the truth, Barend. Where is this town? What are you hiding?"

Barend leaned back in his chair, arms folded and exhaling slowly. The weight of his secrets pressed heavily on him. "You have to understand, Samantha. There are reasons why we kept to ourselves. Reasons why we wanted to disappear."

Samantha's eyes narrowed, a mix of skepticism and frustration. "Oh...? Reasons like what? What could be so important that you'd erase an entire town from existence?"

Barend remained silent for a long moment, the tension in the room thickening with every passing second. Finally, he leaned forward, his voice barely above a whisper. "There were things in that town..."

Samantha's eyes widened, sensing she was finally getting somewhere. "Like what, Barend? What things?" she probed as she leaned forward.

Barend shook his head, his expression one of haunted resignation. "Just trust me when I say, some mysteries are better left unsolved."

Samantha's patience snapped. She instantly slammed her hand on the table, startling Barend. "Damn it, Barend! I didn't come here for riddles. I came here for the truth. You owe me that much."

Barend's gaze met hers, and for a mere moment, there was a flicker of something... fear, regret, perhaps even guilt. "The truth," he echoed, his voice hollow. "The truth is that town was a sanctuary for people running from their pasts. People like me, like my family. We didn't want to be found."

Samantha's eyes softened slightly, as she leaned back in her chair, but her resolve remained firm. "I understand the need for privacy, but this is a much bigger issue than that. People have a right to learn what happened, you know. What happened in that town, Barend? Why did you all just go and disappear?"

Barend swallowed hard, his folded hands trembling slightly on the table in front of him. But it seems that the shadow falls on us all at some point in time.

Samantha drove back to her hotel in Kimberley, the sun setting behind her, casting long shadows across the barren landscape. The long frustrating conversation with Barend weighed heavily on her mind, a swirl of half-truths and haunting confessions. As she pulled into the half-full hotel parking lot, she could still hear his words echoing in her ears.

Inside her room, she tossed her luxury Polo bag onto the bed and sank into the vintage leather chair by the window. The view of Kimberley's old mining town was a stark reminder of the history she was up against... one filled with insidious secrets, greed, and the lure of diamonds. She pulled out her notebook and began scribbling down everything she remembered from her talk with Barend.

"Experiments... dangerous... hidden town..." she muttered to herself, flipping through her notes anxiosuly. "But what does this have to do with the missing diamonds? And the bodies?"

She opened her bag and started cross-referencing her notes with the scant information she had on the missing diamonds, the police files, newpaper reports and the mysterious deaths that had followed before it all disappeared.

Many hours passed, the room growing ever darker as the night settled in. Samantha looks at her notes and scribbles under the dim light of the bedlamp, as she dug deeper into the history of the area. She found old newspaper clippings, police reports, and eyewitness accounts. Each piece was a fragment of a larger, more sinister puzzle it seemed.

The town Barend spoke of, though seemingly erased from maps, had to be somewhere. She searched for any reference, any hint that might reveal its location. She remembered Barend's haunted eyes and cryptic warnings.

Her heart began to race as she pieced together the clues. The missing diamonds, the hidden town, the dangerous experiments... it was all connected somehow. The people who had fled there were all trying to escape something, but they couldn't outrun their pasts.

Just then, her phone rang with a shrill tone, startling her from her thoughts. It was her editor, checking in on her progress. She took a deep breath and answered.

"Hey, Steve," she said, trying to keep her voice steady so as to not reveal her frustration.

"Samantha, how's it going? Got anything for the story yet?" Steve's voice was impatient, the deadline looming over them.

"I think I'm onto something," she replied, her eyes scanning her notes. "I spoke to Barend. He's in prison, but his story... Steve, it's more than I ever imagined. There's a hidden town, missing diamonds, and people dead because of it. It's a tangled mess, but I think I can untangle it."

"Good, because we need a headline. Keep digging, but please be careful. This sounds rather dangerous."

"I will, don't you worry…" she promised. "I'll keep you updated then."

After a brief hang-up, Samantha stared at the map she had stuck onto the wall with pieces of cellotape. Kimberley, the old mining community, the hidden town somewhere between Lesotho and Mozambique, each location marked with a red dot. She was so close to uncovering the truth, but she was well aware of the danger that lay ahead of her. Barend's warnings echoed in her mind, but she couldn't stop digging now. Too much was at stake here.

She leaned back in the comfy leather chair beside her bed, the weight of the story pressing down on her heavily. She had to get to the bottom of this, not just for the headline, but for the people who had suffered, for the lives lost along the way. The truth was out there, buried beneath layers of secrets and lies. And she was determined to uncover it, no matter the cost.

With renewed determination, Samantha began to plot her next move. The truth was within reach, and she wouldn't rest until she had it all. The mysterious town, the missing diamonds, and the dead left in its wake, was all connected in some way, and she simply knew that this whole matter depended on her dedication to bring it to light.

Early the Next Morning
– Small Town Hospital

arend found a little sticky note left by Lloyd on the kitchen table. Lloyd had been sent out on an assignment by Mr. Schultz to fetch some horses from another pound. Tensions between them had been rising, but Barend had bigger worries to deal with at that present moment.

At the small town hospital, the shatp sterile smell of antiseptics filled the air. The waiting room was eerily quiet, with Barend and Katelyn the only ones having been present there. Barend approached the stern nurse at the front desk, who surprisingly smiled politely and handed him a thick stack of forms to fill out. He sighed heavily, the weight of his responsibilities pressing down on him.

As he sat down with the paperwork, Marelize gracefully walked into the hospital, a small wrapped present in her hand. She handed it to Katelyn, displaying a loving smile. "This is for afterwards, my girl" she said softly.

Katelyn nodded, her eyes wide with a mix of curiosity and anxiety. "So be a big girl now... the doctors won't hurt you, okay?"

Marelize leaned in and kissed Barend gently on the lips. Katelyn closed her eyes and frowned, trying to process the strange mix of comfort and worry in the air.

"I really can't stay long today," Marelize said, her voice tinged with regret. "We have a few very big clients coming in from Arabia. They're looking for horses for rough terrain for falconry, to hunt with their hawks."

Barend looked up at her, his eyes distant. "Sorry, my mind is not at all here today..."

Marelize placed a comforting hand on his back. "It's going to be fine, Barend. You just need to believe."

Barend stared down at the forms and nervously rustled through the pages. "Believe me, this here is enough to make anyone feel sick."

Marelize smiled and kissed him on the head. "I'll see you later today, okay?" She turned to Katelyn. "Be a strong girl now..." She gestured, flexing her muscles, and Katelyn mimicked the gesture, managing a weak smile. Marelize walked out with her stately leather boots, leaving Barend to the daunting task of completing the forms.

Barend made up details, filling in the blanks with fabricated information. He couldn't risk putting down anything too close to the truth. When he finished, he abruptly handed the forms back to the nurse and hurried to sit down again, his mind racing with anxious muddled thoughts.

Moments later, a nurse approached Katelyn with a blue plastic dress. "Come with me, sweetie," she said gently, leading Katelyn to the dressing room. Barend stood up, wanting to follow, but the nurse at the front desk stopped him. "She's in good hands. No need to worry. We treat these kids as if they're our own."

Katelyn returned shortly, dressed in the oversized plastic gown, shivering slightly from the cold. Barend took off his top and wrapped it around her. "You make even this little plastic look like a fashion gown," he said, trying to lighten the mood.

Katelyn laughed and shook her head while shivering incessantly. "They should at least have it in pink," she said, managing a hint of cheerfulness through a small smile.

Barend smiled back at her, grateful for the brief moment of levity. "Call me if you need me, anytime, and I'll come as soon as possible, okay honey!"

As they waited for the doctor, Barend couldn't shake the feeling of dread that had settled in his stomach. He hoped Marelize was right, that everything would indeed be fine. But the uncertainty constantly gnawed at him, and he couldn't help but fear the worst.

The large X-ray machine was positioned with meticulous care onto Katelyn's abdomen. Its metallic surface was cold, pressing uncomfortably against her skin. From the doorway, Barend could see the frown of sheer discomfort etched on her face as the side of the X-ray machine was closed tight. The doctor, observing from another room through a glass window, gently instructed Katelyn to hold still. The machine began to rotate around her middle as she stood there, rigid and tense.

Barend's heart ached seeing his daughter endure this, but he knew it was necessary. The doctor came out and directed Katelyn to lay down. Several different X-rays were taken, each one adding to the tension in the room.

The wait for the X-rays to develop felt interminable. In the meantime, the nurses took Katelyn to draw blood and a urine sample. Blood was no stranger to Barend, but witnessing Katelyn's reaction to the needle was an entirely different experience.

"You will barely feel it," Barend said, a feeble attempt at comforting her.

"It's all okay," he repeated, his voice gentle. Katelyn turned her head as the nurse placed a cold cotton pad onto her arm.

"You won't feel a thing," the nurse reassured. "I do this all the time." She opened a sealed package, extracting a long, thin needle attached to the front of a tube. Katelyn's wide eyes darted to Barend.

"It's all okay, my baby. Just look at me…" Barend said, his voice steady. The nurse palpated Katelyn's outstretched arm, searching for the right vein. Katelyn cringed as she saw the needle approach.

Barend grasped Katelyn's left hand. "Daddy, it hurts…!" she whimpered.

"It will be over in a moment, don't look there," Barend said, squeezing her hand gently.

Katelyn tried to focus on Barend but couldn't help glancing at the needle every now and then as the tube slowly filled with dark red blood from her veins. Her arm tightened each time she instinctively pulled away from the pain. The nurse held her arm steady and eventually withdrew the needle.

The nurse pressed cotton over the puncture site, preventing any further blood from escaping. "Now, that's my brave girl," Barend said, his voice full of pride.

Katelyn's eyes were teary and her face flushed, but she managed a small, brave nod. The nurse smiled calmly and walked away, returning with a large lollipop. "These we only keep for the brave ones," she said smiling cheerfully, handing it to Katelyn.

Katelyn's face lit up like a sunbeam, a small reward for her bravery in a day filled with too much pain and fear. Barend felt a mix of pride and helplessness. He knew they were doing everything they could, but the uncertainty of what lay ahead was almost too much to much for him to bear.

Katelyn's face brightened as she saw the big red and white lollipop. The small comfort helped, but the waiting that followed was unbearable. They had to wait a full day for the doctor to return with the results, and every moment felt like an eternity. It was like walking on eggshells around Barend, who was consatntly tense and distracted. However, Marelize's presence was a blessing; she kept Katelyn smiling and distracted despite the waves of pain that came and went unpredictably, making it hard to gauge the extent of the seriousness of her condition.

Barend tried to focus on their daily routine, but every little noise made his heart race. Sitting in the kitchen for lunch, the tense silence was interrupted by the distant sound of a car approaching. Barend's senses instantly went on high alert. Vuyo was out with the Davies gang, and Lloyd was supposed to be fetching horses. He wasn't expecting anyone else to pitch up there.

He moved closer to the window, peeking through the white lace curtains with suspicion. His hand instinctively went to his side, where his gun was holstered. Marelize, nervously noticing his tension, quietly led Katelyn to her room, leaving Barend to handle whatever was coming.

Through the window, Barend saw a sleek emerald green Jaguar XJS pulling up. Such a car was a rare sight in their small town. The laughter of two girls reached his ears before he saw Lloyd climb out, swinging his keys around his finger with a casual confidence.

Barend stepped outside, his eyes narrowing as he took in the luxurious vehicle. Lloyd walked over confidently with a smug smile on his face.

"Car ticked," Lloyd said softly.

Barend raised an eyebrow and put his hands on his hips. "Not too flashy perhaps?"

"You mean the Jag?" Lloyd chuckled. "Nah... Did you hear those purring V12 engines? Full independent suspension, floats over bumps, dances around corners with ease, and its four-wheel disc brakes are plenty powerful for this cruiser. Even pulled a trailer with the horses with this baby. Now that's real horsepower. And the ladies... they dig it, I tell you."

Barend glanced at the girls, who smiled back, looked at one another and giggled flirtatiously, clearly enjoying the ride.

"No need to worry," Lloyd continued. "I paid the deposit on this one, got a good deal too. Just came to say I'm back." He turned and climbed back into the car. "Time to go, ladies."

The car's engine roared like a feisty animal, and Lloyd spun off, the Jaguar's powerful sound fading into the distance. Barend stood there frozen, watching them leave, a mix of frustration and admiration bubbling inside him. He couldn't deny Lloyd's resourcefulness, but the flashiness of it all made him really uneasy.

Returning to the kitchen, he found Marelize and Katelyn waiting at the table over a cup of tea. Marelize was trying to draw Katelyn away to a more serene situation than what Barend had just encountered. He forced a half-smile, trying to shake off the unease. They had bigger worries now, starting with Katelyn's health. The day dragged on, even though Marelize tried her utmost to distract them with light conversation and jokes. Barend could not shake off the anxiety though, and it felt as though his expectation to receive the doctor's call was stretching every second. Not even the delightful curry that Marelize had prepared for lunch could ease his nerves.

A Walk in the Moonlight

T he next few days felt like months. Lloyd's new-found freedom, coupled with his flashy car and constant parade of girls, contrasted sharply with Barend's growing confinement. Troubled and exhausted, he found it increasingly hard to keep up the facade. Vuyo noticed the strain and offered to look after Katelyn, insisting Barend take the night off and enjoy some time with Marelize.

The night air was still warm, even though the sun had long set. The small town looked almost romantic under the soft glow of the streetlights. The shops' rustic windows cast a cozy light onto the sidewalks, and various people strolled down the main road, their conversations a gentle hum against the backdrop of the night. The moon hung low and ghostlike, casting an ominous, soft yellow light across the town.

As they strolled down the street side by side, Marelize looked up at Barend. "Do you believe in true love?"

Barend hesitated as he stood still before leaning in and kissing her gently on the cheek. "I'd like to," he said, his voice carrying a hint of melancholy.

"You can't be serious," Marelize said, with slight laughter in her voice. "Everybody believes, or at least wants to."

Barend shook his head slowly, pursing his lips. "Take that guy, for example." He nodded after pointing toward a couple looking at rings in a jewelry store window. "They look in love, right?"

Marelize nodded, smiling. "Very much. So the logical next step is marriage, babies, the whole cycle, right?"

Barend sighed. "That ain't so bad now."

"No, not at all."

"Only thing is, he's already thinking elsewhere." Marelize looked at him with surprise. "Oh … ?" Barend pointed discreetly at a girl in a short dress walking past. The man's eyes followed her, then snapped back to his girlfriend, who remained engrossed in her conversation.

"We all want to believe this fairy tale, of a man on a horse and a beauty. But when I look around, I see it is all one big lie."

"Surely you can't say that," Marelize protested.

"How can anyone really be devoted, true, unconditional? We're all conditionally programmed. As long as we benefit, we stick around. We're selfish to the bone."

"And what about people who give and help those in need?"

"Even they are looking out for their own interests. Why do most of them go around boasting about how they help the poor, put their banners on Feed the Homeless Day? No... Ultimately, we are selfish. We just pretend to be better. We look out for our own interests."

They continued to walk in silence, the only sound their footsteps echoing on the deserted street. The old cop house where Barend stayed came into view, its dark outline a stark reminder of the past.

Marelize broke the silence. "Why did you become a cop then?"

"It served a purpose," Barend replied tersely.

"And what about us?" Marelize asked, her voice soft but insistent.

Barend stopped walking and turned to face her, the moonlight casting deep shadows on his face. He looked into her eyes, searching for words he couldn't find.

"Marelize," he began, his voice breaking slightly. "You and Katelyn mean everything to me. But... everything feels so fragile, like it could all shatter any moment. This town, this life... it's a house of cards."

She reached out and touched his cheek gently. "Barend, we'll get through this. Together. But you have to believe in something."

He took a deep breath, nodding slightly and looking down at his worn-in leather shoes. "Maybe you're right," he said, his voice barely above a whisper. "Maybe."

As they stood there, wrapped in each other's presence, the future seemed uncertain and the past weighed heavily. But for a brief moment, under the ghostly light of the moon, they found a sliver of hope to cling to.

Barend sighed and held Marelize's hand. "It's not so simple. I want to believe in this beautiful world you see... but I just can't. I did not grow up with servants and being able to choose the life I wanted. Whatever you could dream of, you could get."

Marelize turned her head away, her voice shaking with emotion. "No, you are wrong. You are dead wrong."

A sightly awkward silence grew between them as they entered the gate and walked on the pathway towards his frontdoor. Barend opened the door to the house and it creaked heavily. The silence inside was palpable; Katelyn and Vuyo had already gone to bed. He poured a glass of red wine and handed it to Marelize.

"It is easy to declare love when things are easy, comfortable," Barend said, his voice low and heavy. "But what about when it hurts... when things are tough? I doubt someone can even then remain true."

Marelize looked into his eyes and spoke softly, "I will."

Her long hair flowed freely over her shoulders, and the soft moonlight shining through the kitchen window illuminated her eyes, giving them an ethereal glow. Barend could see that her eyes were welling up and looked down at his feet, trying to hide his discomfort.

"Can you believe me when I say so, Barend?" she asked, a tear rolling down her cheek.

Barend put his wine glass down and held her, gently wiping the tear from her face. He rested her head against his chest, right where his heart beat steadily, and wrapped his arms around her. There was something in that moment that offered Barend a sense of surety, a fleeting yet profound connection.

Their eyes locked onto each other as Barend touched her shoulder softly. He could feel her breathing, calm and steady, as his head moved closer to hers. Their lips met, and the world outside seemed to disappear, leaving only the two of them in a shared moment of vulnerability and hope.

That night, Marelize did not return to her father's house. Instead, she stayed over, her presence a comforting anchor for Barend. The house, usually filled with the echoes of uncertainty and fear, felt different. For the first time in a long while, it felt like a home.

As they lay together, Marelize nestled in his arms, Barend stared at the ceiling with a blank expression, yet deep in thought. His mind was racing but his heart feeling a newfound peace. He still had doubts, fears that he couldn't entirely shake off. But in Marelize's arms, with her soft breathing lulling him into a fragile sense of security, he allowed himself to hope, if only for the night.

The moonlight filtered through the curtains, casting gentle shadows that danced across the room. Barend held Marelize close, her warmth seeping into him, and for the first time, he dared to believe that maybe, just maybe, there was a chance for a future where love and truth could coexist, even in a world as harsh as his. They fell asleep in each other's arms, momentarily forgetting the challenges and inner turmoil they have been experiencing. Little did they know that the worst was yet to come.

The
Betrayal

That night. the house was enveloped in an eery stillness that felt almost sacred. The silence was broken only by the occasional creak of the old wooden floors and the soft, rhythmic breathing of those inside. Vuyo, Katelyn, and the others were fast asleep, seemingly lost in their dreams and blissfully unaware of the tension simmering just beneath the surface.

But not everyone was sleeping....

Lloyd lay there in his bed, his eyes wide open, fixated on the ghostly glow of the moon. Its cold light spilled through the thin curtains, casting long shadows that seemed to dance with every subtle movement of the house. He could feel the weight of the night pressing down on him, suffocating in its quiet intensity.

With a slow, deliberate motion, Lloyd pushed the blanket off him. He stood up, his movements careful and measured, not wanting to disturb the fragile peace. His hand reached out for his gun, fingers curling around the familiar grip with a sense of purpose.

Lloyd moved to the door, pausing for a moment to snatch his jacket cautiously from where it was laying on the edge of the couch. He took one last look at his companions, their faces serene and untroubled in their sleep. There was a fleeting pang of something... guilt, regret, perhaps even sadness... but it was quickly smothered by a steely resolve.

Without a sound, he slipped out of the room, the door closing behind him with a barely audible click. The hallway was dark, but Lloyd navigated it with ease, his steps silent on the worn floorboards. He reached the front door, the cool night air rushing in as he opened it, bringing with it the faint scent of impending rain.

Stepping outside onto the front porch, Lloyd felt a strange mix of liberation and dread. The night was alive with the subtle sounds of nature. Outside he could hear the rustle of leaves, the distant hoot of an owl, the whisper of the wind. He walked out by the gate and glanced back at the house, a stark silhouette against the moonlit sky, and for a brief moment, he hesitated.

But the moment passed, and Lloyd turned away, his path set. He had a mission, a purpose that transcended the bonds of camaraderie and loyalty that had tied him to the others. There was absolutely no way that he could risk holding himself back now. The night seemed to swallow him as he moved forward, each step taking him further away from the house and from the life he had known and deeper into the unknown.

Back inside the house where they were blissfully unaware of Lloyd's exit, the silence remained unbroken. But for those who might wake in the coming hours, his absence would be a harbinger of the betrayal that had already begun to unfold.

Soon enough Lloyd reached the abandoned old barn house, where he was scheduled to meet with the dealer. The forlorn building stood silent and forsaken, with no owners nor animals in sight, its remains of old make-shift furniture scattered across the floor like the remnants of a forgotten past. The shadows danced in the moonlight streaming through broken windows, casting eerie patterns on the walls. Lloyd walked into the building, a bag slung over his shoulder, his steps extra cautious as his eyes darted to and fro nervously. The old dealer was waiting there, leaning on a dusty round table, his eyes flickering with a mix of fear and anticipation.

Lloyd came and stood right oin front of him, placed the bag on the counter, and smiled confidently at him. However, as he began to open the bag, a voice echoed from the shadows, sending a chill down his spine.

"Beautiful gold you have there, I say... such coins are sure to be marked by blood?"

Lloyd swiftly spun around, his heart pounding so loud that it was almost audible. "I have no idea what you're talking about. These were all coins I inherited from my grandmother."

A loud, mocking laughter erupted, bouncing off the walls. Lloyd's eyes darted around, trying to locate the source, but he could only see shifting shadows. The dealer stepped back, his face pale.

"You set me up, old man," Lloyd growled, grabbing the dealer by his bloodstained hands, the marks of a knife clear on his trembling skin.

"I had no choice," the dealer stammered, fear evident in his eyes.

A tall man emerged from the darkness, followed by six men in cop gear. Lloyd's heart sank and a feeling of cold sweat surfaced in his body.

"Cops... Ah... Oh, my goodness... I am so glad. For a moment, I thought I was dealing with some lunatic criminal," Lloyd said, trying to keep his voice steady in order to sound relieved.

The tall man, Greef, sneered. "You gonna spill the juice, son...? Or would you rather have us spill your guts? We're running a little late on a planned robbery, one that your friends seem to have gotten away with."

Lloyd gaped and struggled to find a suitable response. "I honestly have no idea what you're talking about. As you can see, sir... all I have here are a few gold coins, enough to keep a man adrift for a little while. This ain't no bank robbery loot, man," Lloyd replied.

Greef shook his head as he looked at the other men. "Ain't that sad, boys? Maybe even tragic. I kind of started liking you. After all these months, I'm even getting emotional about the whole thing," Greef taunted.

"If you want the coins, be my guest. Trace them if you like. They are as clean as gold," Lloyd replied, trying to maintain his composure.

"And so are we!" Greef shouted and signaled to one of his men, who then quickly proceeded to kick Lloyd to the ground. The others joined in, their boots violently thudding against Lloyd's ribs. He gasped and struggled to speak, his face covered and blood and sweat.

One of the cops dragged him to the counter where Greef, now fully visible, stepped into the light and plangted himself like a statue before pulling out a gun.

He crouched over Lloyd and sneered, almost breathing in his face. "Why do you folks have a habit of lying to me, eh? Why ain't you telling me where the rest are?" Greef demanded, pressing the gun violently against Lloyd's head.

"I... I have no idea what you're talking about. And even if I did, do I look stupid to you? What's in it for me, huh? I tell you, then you kill me. I don't tell you, you kill me anyway," Lloyd spat, blood dripping from his mouth.

"Well, for one thing... I can clean your record, give you a second chance at life, maybe even give you a position in our special units. I could put a man like you to good use," Greef offered with a smug expression.

"Huh...? That's waaayyyy too easy for you. There are no guarantees now. I give you all of that for a lousy job? Minimal I want is my share," Lloyd said, defiantly.

Greef moved even closer, picking Looyd up by his collar amd pressing him against the cold steel gate, the gun hard against his head. He stared him straight in the eyes, breathing vehemently. Lloyd frowned and pulled his face to the side, trying to avoid Greef's brandy-laced breath.

"You sure won't be doing yourself any favors if you fire that thing before I tell you now, will you?" Lloyd challenged him.

Greef's eyes widened as he felt a sharp point against his throat. Lloyd had a knife, the blade just piercing his skin, causing blood to drip.

"A quick one we have here. Sure didn't see that coming," Greef muttered, trying to maintain the bravery in his voice.

Lloyd pushed the knife a little deeper. "I'd lower it if I were you, or we can take this discussion further in hell. This is a 14cm sharp point blade, straight to burst your heart... that is, if you have one now."

Greef managed a faint, fake smile and let his gun drop.

"To the floor, I said... all of you and kick the guns away," Lloyd ordered. The men hesitated, but Lloyd pressed the knife harder. "I said... Kick them away now!"

"Well, well... I don't think we can stand for such demands now..." Greef began.

"You want the gold and your neck, right? I want safe passage to the border, a clean record, and my cut. You can take the rest of the loot for all I care," Lloyd said.

"But of course... You have my word for it, that is, if you deliver the goods. And believe me... I ain't a man to wait long," Greef replied.

Lloyd swiftly pulled away the knife and started at him in a skeptical fashion while keeping his distance.

"So... now tell me the whereabouts," Greef demanded after a brief awkward silence.

Lloyd nodded, looking irritated. "Just give me a week or so, and I can bring you your share."

"Fine... One week only...!!! Or you're going down, buster!" Greef threatened.

Lloyd saluted him sarcastically, then managed to pick up one or two of the guns near to his feet. Then he darted for the barn's door like a flash of lightning, making his escape from the vindictive Greef.

He ran as fast as his legs could carry him, his heart racing anxiously as he constantly looked over his shoulder to see if anyone was following. The betrayal hung heavy in the air, each heavy step taking him further into the night and deeper into the perilous web of deceit and survival.

The Departure

Barend stood there in the doorway, the morning light cutting a narrow through the opening of the curtain creating a striking line across the floor like a blade. Behind him, Marelize hummed as she laid the breakfast table, still unaware of the storm gathering around their quiet life. The eggs sizzled. The kettle clicked off. Somewhere down the street, a dog barked twice and fell silent.

(Expand here the concept of wanting time to stand still. Holding her in his arms.)

Barend stood in the doorway, unmoving, one hand on the frame as though it alone could anchor him to this place, this fleeting peace. The morning light spilled in through the curtain from the east, cutting a narrow line across the kitchen floor like a blade—sharp, golden, precise. Dust floated gently in the beam, suspended, as though even gravity had paused to admire the quiet.

Behind him, Marelize moved through the kitchen, humming softly to herself. A tune he couldn't place, old and sweet and wordless. Her hips swayed slightly as she laid the breakfast table, one plate, two mugs, three spoons though they'd only need two. The scent of eggs browning in the pan drifted up, warm and comforting. The kettle clicked off. Somewhere, down the sleepy street, a dog barked twice, then fell quiet again. Everything was too perfect.

Barend felt it…that ache.The knowing that this moment would not last long, although he yearned for it to be like this forever.

That cruel, aching sensation of something being too good, too fragile to last. Like holding a soap bubble in your palm, and knowing it'll vanish at the first breath of wind. Time, at that present moment seemed thinner, as if it were like glass that could crack beneath a word or a footstep. He wanted to step backward, to return to bed, to pour the coffee, to say something small and meaningless just to keep the moment going.

But he didn't move. Because he knew.

He was standing on the edge of something that couldn't be undone. The fire was already building behind the hills. Lloyd was out checking for tails. The diamonds were stacked in a crate under a tarp. And Greef was out there, circling like a hawk, just waiting for the shadows to shift.

Still, for this one breath, Barend let himself pretend like everything was gong to be okay.

He turned from the door and walked slowly across the kitchen. Marelize looked up, startled by the distant look in his eyes, her hands still holding a spoon and a napkin.

"Everything okay, love?" she asked.

He didn't answer right away. Just wrapped his arms around her waist and pulled her in. She smelled like citrus and morning… something soft and grounding. Her body folded into his frame like it belonged there, like it always had. As if this was the way it was meant to be.

Her hands instinctively came to rest gently on his back.

He closed his eyes, breathed deeply and sighed.

And in that moment, he imagined, vivid and aching, what it would be like if life stayed just like this. If there were no bloodstained diamonds, no corrupt cops, no secrets stuffed in barns or plans etched in desperation. If the worst thing they had to worry about was a burnt toast or the power cutting out again. How simple yet blissful it would be.

He pressed his face into her hair, smelling the fresh scent of her shampoo. Her hair felt warm, soft and comforting amidst the morning cool.

Just one more second, he begged time, as he watch the steam rise from the kettle.. Just one more breath like this, unhindered by the lies of the past

But he could hear the clock ticking forward anyway, as the seconds passed by.

Outside, the wind picked up, rustling the trees just enough to remind him the world was still turning. A door slammed somewhere down the block. A car engine ignited. Reality was already folding itself back into place.

It's time," Lloyd suddenly muttered behind him, breaking the quietude of their precious moment. His voice was low, edged with tension. "Back at the old barn. Everything's set. But if they're close… I'll give the signal."

"What signal?" Katelyn asked sharply. She clutched her backpack's strap like it was a lifeline.

"You'll know," Lloyd said, eyes shadowed and unreadable, trying to avoid further discussion with her around the matter.

Barend nodded slowly, his heart sinking heavily.

Barend took a deep breath and stepped into the kitchen. Marelize looked up, instantly noticing that something was wrong purely by the solemn look in his eyes.

"What is it?" she threw the dishcloth over her shoulder and paused.

He didn't answer at first. Just stood there, torn. Then the words that would shatter her entire dream came...

"We're leaving... Now."

Her smile vanished. "Leaving? What do you mean? Where to..?"

"I'll explain later. I just... I really need you to trust me on this one..."

"But Barend..." she started, the emotion evident in her voice. "You said we were done with this," she whispered.

"I know..."

"Are we in danger?"

He hesitated. His silence alone was enough of an answer.

She shook her head, eyes welling up. "So that's it then? Just like that? You're gone?"

Barend reached out to put his hand on her shoulder, but she took a step back. His hand hovered in the air for a second, then fell.

"I... I'm sorry," he murmured.

He instantly pulled her closer, but this time she didn't resist. He then kissed her forehead, lips lingering for a second longer than he meant to. Then he turned, clenched his jaw before looking back at her once more, and left the kitchen. Katelyn was already waiting by the door with a bag stuffed full of clothing, a blanket, a few toys and snacks. Her eyes were glistening with a mixture of concern and anticipation, as she stood there holding Vuyo's hand. The old man gave Marelize a nod of regret.

"Just... believe," Vuyo said quietly before ushering them out.oce

Marelize sank to the floor, the kettle's whistle echoing in the silence as tears slid down her cheeks. Her world, once calm and sunlit, was unraveling thread by thread.

Chapter:
Burn the Trail

The burnt umber sunset hung low as Lloyd suavely approached the barn, carrying a small canvas bag with two bottles of his prized stash. Not diamonds, not cash. But something carrying the potential to create fire inside. He smirked, quietly thinking of how these little bottles could burn more than a hole in their enemy's foolproof plan.

Barend had already cleared their trail. Or so they thought...

Lloyd suddenly crouched behind a broken wall, eyes scanning the tree line.

And then... a rustling through the bushes. Too sha
rp, too synchronized and definitely too loud to be an animal.

They had followed him.

He should've known better.

The inevitable took place as he found himself stuck in the midst of the dangerous dimly lit old barn just a few nerve racking moments later. The air felt thick with tension and the smell of aging wood and dust.

Greef's sudden appearance caused Lloyd to be struck with fear and he could feel the sweat droplets starting to surface on his skin like watery beads. Greef's eyes blazed with unrelenting fury as he closed in on him and pressed the gun against Lloyd's trembling hand.

"Where are my diamonds, hey?!" Greef's voice boomed through the quiet barn, echoing off the walls.

Lloyd winced as the pressure of the gun against his hand intensified. Fear gripped him, but he managed to stammer, "I... I really don't know what you're talking about..."

With a sudden jolt, Greef mercilessly pulled the trigger. The gunshot cracked through the stillness of the barn, the recoil forcing Greef's hand back as a bullet tore right through the middle of Lloyd's hand. With a painstaking grunt Lloyd collapsed to the ground, clutching his bleeding hand and crying out in agony.

"He was about to speak, Bear..." The lead cop's voice cut through the tense silence, addressing Greef.

"Well, If I had followed your method, he'd be gone by now, wouldn't he?!" Greef retorted, his eyes never leaving Lloyd's writhing form on the floor.

Lloyd's hand continued to bleed profusely, staining the hay-covered ground beneath him. He crawled desperately, his eyes darting around in panic.

"Bring me the boxes now!" Greef commanded, his voice loud, cold and dictatorial. He gestured with the gun towards the crates of fine brandy stacked nearby.

Lloyd heaved and nodded weakly, more beads of sweat forming on his forehead. He knew the consequences of disobedience full well.

"You could learn something from this, Bear," Greef continued, his tone laced with menace. "My way is effective. People surely don't talk without motivation. Soon, we'll have what we came for, and we can all be on our way."

Cop 2 interjected nervously, "But boss, we'll have a lot of explaining to do..."

Greef cut him off with a shove against the barn wall. "If you don't want your share, you are welcome to take off your badge and leave now. But beware... don't close your eyes, or you might not open them again."

"That's not what I meant at all..." Cop 2 protested weakly before Greef silenced him with a devious glare.

"Time's up, fellar..." Greef declared, pulling Lloyd forcefully by the arm and yanking him closer, causing Lloyd to stagger like a drunkard.

As Lloyd appeared to be struggling to regain his balance and strength, Greef caught sight of a flicker of movement in Lloyd's hand, a slick movement on his part. He noticed a small flame and a bottle of alcohol. Before he could react, Lloyd dropped the bottle, and flames erupted with a whiff of air across the barn floor.

Greef cursed like a pirate and fired his gun towards the spreading fire. But Lloyd had already thrown another bottle of alcohol into the growing inferno, fueling the blaze further. The barn quickly became engulfed in circles of orange-yellow flames, the crackling fire licking at the wooden beams and sending billowing smoke into the air.

Chaos erupted.

"Get out! GET OUT!" one of the cops shouted frantically.

Lloyd, already burning at the sleeves, backed into the shadows. Pain screamed up his arm,

Before Greef could react, Lloyd flung the bottle of moonshine into the air and struck a match. The explosion wasn't cinematic, but it was enough to set the whole place on fire.

Flames roared up the dry walls like hell itself had opened its jaws.

The men panicked and broke out in sweat. Screams echoed as the fire spread faster than anyone expected. Bear stumbled as the edge of his coat caught fire, and he vanished into the smoke with a shriek. Some of the cops didn't make it out at all.

Lloyd coughing heavily, forced himself toward the back exit

Smoke and Silver

The flames erupted faster than anyone expected.

One second the barn stood in quiet decay; the next, it was an inferno clawing into the night sky. Flames licked through the timber rafters and swallowed the old roof whole, the dry wood feeding it like an altar sacrifice.

Barend saw it first.

He braked hard, dust whipping up around the stolen bakkie as he turned onto a ridge road.

The rearview mirror vibrated from the engine's idle growl.

In the back seat, Katelyn stirred. "Wha…what's that, Daddy?"

She rubbed her eyes, then sat bolt upright. The glow on the horizon was unmistakable. Fire. Big. Spreading fast.

"It's the barn," Barend muttered.

Vuyo leaned forward in his seat, squinting at the blaze. "That's it. That's the signal."

Barend's stomach turned anxiously. "But where's Lloyd then?"

The fire roared in the distance, but no silhouette came running out. No figure darting from the shadows. Just flame devouring wood, and a silence too loud to ignore.

"He should've been out by now," Barend said, scanning the dark.

Vuyo didn't reply. His face was unreadable. Then… Crack!

The rear window exploded, shards of glass showering the truck's interior. Katelyn screamed and dropped down low while little splinters of glass glided down her smooth blonde hair.

A bullet had punched through the cab's frame and sunk somewhere into the loot in the back.

Barend slammed the accelerator.

"Go, go!" Vuyo barked.

Headlights blazed to life behind them, swerving up from a side road. A black SUV… probably two of them. Greef's men had regrouped.

"Hang on!" Barend shouted, throwing the wheel hard to the left as the bakkie screeched onto a narrow gravel trail flanked by dying corn stalks and rusted wire fencing. The vehicle fishtailed wildly, but he held control.

Gunfire snapped behind them. Another bullet smacked into the tailgate, punching through with a clean metallic clang. The diamonds in the back clinked together like warning bells.

Katelyn sobbed softly, her head down in her lap. "They're right behind us!"

Stay low, Katelyn!" Vuyo growled. His hand clutched the side of the door tightly... a little too tightly. Barend glanced, noting the way he leaned stiffly, but kept driving relentlessly.

The SUV was gaining again, bouncing wildly over the uneven ground, its headlights bouncing with each dip. Barend swerved down a ditch, through a rotted wooden fence, and barreled across a dry field.

"We're losing them!" he shouted, his voice almost containing a hint of glee.

The tall grass swept over the undercarriage, with dry shrubs and twigs causing occasional snaps and clicks. The bakkie leapt over a shallow ditch, the suspension shrieking in protest, but the SUV clipped something and slowed. One headlight went dark. The other veered off course. They were pulling away.

"Barend! Look!" Vuyo pointed forward. A narrow service road cut through a line of trees.

He took it.

A minute later, the road fell silent behind them. No engine. No gunshots. Just the wind, the sound of crickets and the ragged breathing of three people barely alive.

Barend finally eased off the gas. They coasted onto an old gravel turnoff beside a dried-up irrigation dam. Eucalyptus trees loomed tall around them like skeletal guards.

He killed the engine. They there sat in silence, only the ticking of the hot engine filling the cab.

"Everyone okay?" Barend asked, his chest still heaving.

Katelyn nodded, pale but alive. "Yeah..."

Vuyo just gave a thumbs up and reached for the door handle.

Barend stepped out—and immediately spotted the problem.

The rear tire was shredded. A bullet must've clipped it during the chase. The rim sagged, chewing the rubber, and the entire truck listed to one side.

"Shit," he muttered to himself.

"Can you fix it, Dad?" Katelyn asked, as she stepped out behind him.

"I'll swap it with the spare. Won't take long."

Barend opened the back and yanked the jack out. As he moved, he kept glancing at Vuyo, who hadn't left his seat yet. The old man looked stiff. Something was wrong.

His hand was resting on his side under his coat. The other gripped the doorframe like he needed it to stand.

"Vuyo?"

"I'm fine," Vuyo said quickly, too quickly.

Barend narrowed his eyes.

He crouched beside the truck, slid the jack under, and began cranking it up. That's when he noticed it on the ground where Vuyo had stepped: dark droplets staining the gravel. Not oil. Not water.

Blood.

Barend stood slowly. "Let me see."

"I said I'm fine."

"Cut the crap."

Barend slowly walked toward him. Vuyo's body tensed for a second, then he sighed and unzipped the jacket. His shirt was soaked down one side, blood still oozing sluggishly from a wound low on his ribs.

"It must've been when the bullet hit the car," Vuyo muttered, almost apologetically. "I didn't feel it... at first."

Barend cursed and grabbed an old cloth from the cubby hole to press against the wound.

"We need to get you to a clinic."

A pause hung between them, thick, heavy, impossible to ignore.

Then Barend looked past Vuyo. His eyes narrowed.

Down the road, far off, a flicker of movement. Headlights. A faint engine hum. Dust curling into the air behind it.

"They're back," he whispered in a low eerie tone.

Vuyo took the cloth, pressed it to his side, and straightened up with every ounce of strength he had left.

You make way for the border," Vuyo heaved and said with a strained expression, his voice barely above a whisper.

"Get in the car, old man," Barend urged, his voice tight with urgency.

But Vuyo shook his head slowly, his gaze steady despite the pain etched across his features. With a grim determination, he lifted his hand, revealing the blood-soaked bandage where another bullet had found its mark.

"Not this time, my friend," Vuyo said, his voice wavering slightly. "I guess my cards have been drawn."

Katelyn, her eyes wide with fear and tears streaming down her cheeks, stepped closer to Vuyo, gripping his wounded hand.

"Daddy, he's hurt!" Katelyn cried out, her voice filled with anguish.

Barend looked at Vuyo anxiously, and then at Katelyn, his heart heavy with dread. He knew the time was running out fast.

"I will try to keep them back as long as I possibly can when they come. And they will come soon…," Vuyo assured Barend, his voice soft but resolute. "You… just take care of your daughter. That's one very rare diamond you have right there."

"Get in the car right now, Katelyn!" Barend's voice cracked with desperation. "We have to go."

But Katelyn refused to let go of Vuyo's hand, her grip tightening as she stared up at him with pleading eyes filled with tears.

"No, Daddy! Please come with us! I forgive you, I'm not mad anymore!" Katelyn's voice trembled with raw emotion.

Vuyo, tears glistening in his eyes, straightened himself and picked up his gun from the ground. His resolve hardened as he looked towards the approaching danger.

"Go," he said firmly to Barend, his voice a quiet command. "Before I change my mind."

Barend hesitated for a moment longer, torn between his duty to protect Katelyn and his loyalty to his friend. With a very heavy heart, he turned and lifted Katelyn into the truck, gently closing the door behind her.

"Daddy!" Katelyn cried out, her voice filled with anguish as she pounded on the window. "Please!"

Barend's jaw tightened as he started the engine and drove off, kicking up a cloud of dust in his wake. He stole one last glance at Vuyo, standing resolute amidst the swirling chaos, before disappearing into the night.

He squared his shoulders and lifted his gun in a deftly manner, aiming towards Greef's men, who had quickly jumped out of the large 4x4 and were approaching with increasing speed. With each shot, he aimed carefully, hitting them in non-lethal areas as promised.

But their numbers were more than what he had expected, and soon Greef himself emerged from the shadows with his men in tow.

"Why did I have to go and make such a silly promise..." Vuyo muttered to himself, the weight of his choices heavy on his heart.

As the police officers closed in around him, Vuyo knew his time was up. He glanced around, meeting Greef's cold gaze with defiance.

"You speak an awful lot with all your henchmen," Vuyo taunted, his voice rough with pain. "Surely you're worth shit on your own."

Greef's expression darkened, but he quickly composed himself, turning to his men with a nod.

"Let's keep this off the record," Greef ordered, his voice cutting through the tension.

The officers nodded at him in agreement, their eyes fixed on Vuyo with a mix of respect and apprehension.

"So, you want to go out in style, old man," Greef grunted, a smirk playing on his lips.

Vuyo straightened even though his breathing was affected by he pain, his cowboy hat cocked defiantly on his head as he accepted the gun handed to him by a police officer. He momentarily took of the hat and glanced at it with sadness. With melancholy he remembered the day he received it as a gift from Katelyn, and felt a pang of regret. This wasn't how he had imagined it would end.

"This was not what I wanted the end of the road to look like," Vuyo thought to himself, his mind racing with memories of better times.

Greef and Vuyo stood back to back, each taking carefully calculated steps, their weapons at the ready. But just as they were about to face off, Greef abruptly turned and fired. The shot hit Vuyo square in the chest, knocking him to the ground.

"You devil," Vuyo gasped, clutching his wound as pain shot through his body. "God will not let you get away with this…"

Greef stepped forward, towering over Vuyo with an evil sneer of triumph.

"You're wrong, old man," Greef retorted coldly. "I've already got a bag with diamonds with my name on it. You and your friends just borrowed them for a while, with a hefty rent."

Vuyo's breathing was labored, but he managed a defiant glare as Greef raised his gun once more.

"You're not half the man he is," Vuyo spat, his voice a rasp of defiance. "There's no way in hell you will catch him."

With a final, brutal motion, Greef pulled the trigger. The shot echoed through the night, mingling with Vuyo's pained cry. Blood sprayed across the dry ground as Vuyo slumped, his strength ebbing away.

Greef kicked the gun from Vuyo's grasp, a cruel smile twisting his features.

"Let him bleed dry," Greef ordered, his voice cold and merciless. "He likes it old school."

With coarse jesting and evil laughter over what might happen to the body next after they leave, Greef and his gang turned away without mercy, leaving Vuyo to his fate amidst the destroyed barn house and fading light. But as Greef climbed into his car, a sudden shot rang out, shattering the silence. The bullet pierced through the car window, striking Greef in the shoulder.

Greef cried out in pain and shock, clutching his wounded shoulder as blood seeped through his fingers. He turned to see Vuyo, his face pale but defiant, a small smile playing on his lips.

"I kept my promise," Vuyo whispered hoarsely, his voice barely audible above the chaos.

With that final act of defiance, Vuyo closed his eyes and breathed out a slow final breath, his weary body finally at rest amidst the turmoil he had faced.

The
Road Splits

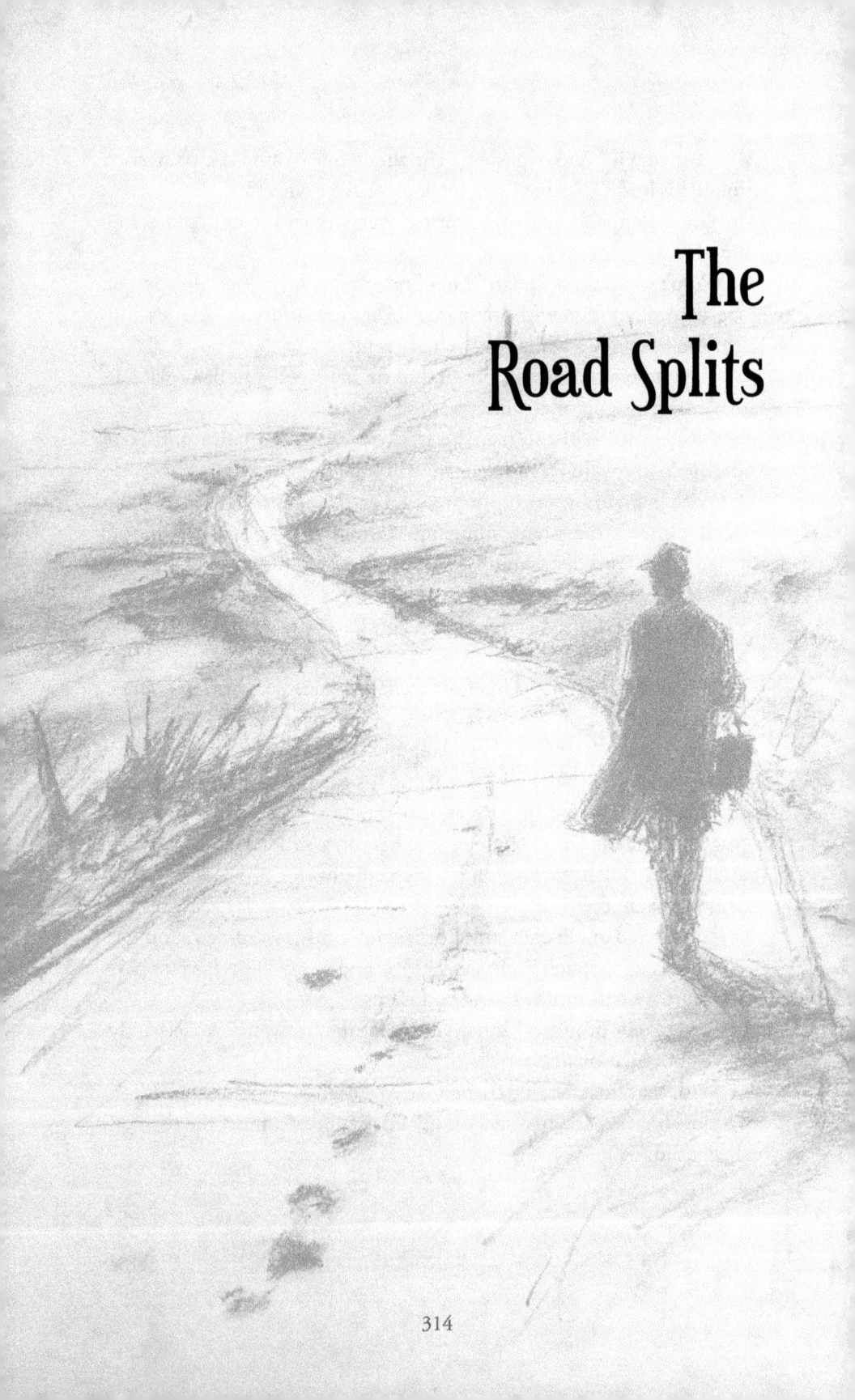

The road stretched out in front of them, sun-scorched and silent, vanishing into a wavering heat mirage in the distance. The bakkie rattled beneath Barend's grip, the engine straining under the load and the urgency pressing down on it like a second weight. Every bump in the road jarred his bones, but he didn't dare slow down at this point.

He stole a glance at Katelyn.

She was slumped in the passenger seat, head tilted against the window, her light hair appearing dull with sweat. Her lips were pale, cracked. Her breathing was shallow and uneven, a soft, raspy drag of air in and out like a wounded animal. One arm hung limp in her lap, her fingers twitching slightly.

"Katie," he said, his voice low, cracked. "Hey! Wake up!"

She stirred faintly, eyelids fluttering open just long enough for her to look at him with that same exhausted gaze he remembered from the clinic visits—except now there was something else behind it: a growing vacancy. That faraway stare that terrified him. The kind that said *I'm slipping away.*

Barend clenched the steering wheel harder, knuckles white with tension.

The road sign came up fast… **Border - 80 miles.**

So close. So goddamn close.

He did the math in his head. Less than two hours. If they could cross before the checkpoints got swamped. If no one recognized the truck. If the papers Lloyd gave them still held up.

If only they could disappear into the next country like shadows.

Then maybe… just *maybe*, they could buy some time. Buy help. Buy a life.

But Katelyn wouldn't make it another two hours.

He could see it in the way her body sagged. The way her jaw had gone slack. He remembered what the doctor said last year: *"Her kidneys are failing, Mr. Smit. She's living on a clock now. You'll know when the time starts to run out."*

This was it. The ticking had begun.

Barend looked down. Her hand had found his on the gearshift, barely clasping it. Weak, cold, like paper.

"I'm so tired, Papa…" she whispered.

His throat locked. He blinked hard and wiped a tear with the back of his arm.

"I know, baby. Just hold on. Just a little bit longer."

Then he saw another sign.

Edenveld – 2 km

Small town. One clinic. It would be a great risk. There could be cops. Could be someone who recognized them. But it also meant doctors. Machines. Sterile rooms and saline and perhaps a chance to stop her slipping further.

He cursed under his breath.

The bakkie shuddered as he slammed the brakes, gravel crunching beneath the tires. Katelyn stirred, eyes fluttering open once again.

Barend's hands hovered on the wheel like he didn't trust them to stay on course.

She looked at him with a faint smile, barely there. "You're thinking too loud."

That broke something in him.

He laughed once, a sound more like a sob, and then turned hard into the dirt road.

The bakkie fishtailed, the engine roaring to life again as he sped toward Edenveld.

"I'm sorry, baby girl" he muttered. "I should've taken you sooner."

Katelyn didn't answer. Her head rested against the seat now, breathing faint but steady.

He reached over, touching her wrist. "You hear me? You stay with me now.

Arriving at the hospital, Barend burst through the doors, Katelyn cradled in his arms. His voice cracked as he shouted for help, his heart pounding so loudly in his chest that it drowned out everything else.

"HELP!!! I need a doctor, please! Can someone help my daughter?!" Barend pleaded frantically, his voice echoing through the sterile corridors.

A dark-haired nurse with glasses and an earnest facial expression quickly guided Barend to a chair, gently taking Katelyn from his arms to check her pulse. Moments later, Katelyn was whisked away on a hospital bed, disappearing through the doors of the emergency room. Barend tried to follow, but another nurse stopped him.

"Sir, if you can please fill in this form with your medical aid number…" the nurse began, holding out a brown clipboard with a stack of papers.

"There's no time! This is an emergency! My daughter is very sick, I need a doctor right now!" Barend exclaimed, raising his voice in the thick of desperation. Other people in the emergency room, some looking ill and half asleep suddenly looked up and stared, startled by his utterance.

A doctor hurried past, clearly on his way to surgery. Barend grabbed his arm, his grip tight with urgency.

"Doctor, please help! My daughter is in incredible pain," Barend implored, his eyes pleading for assistance.

"I would like to help, but I am on my way to surgery," the doctor replied apologetically, trying to extricate himself from Barend's grasp.

Barend held on, his voice shaking. "Please…!! I will pay you, whatever it takes. Just help my daughter, please!"

The doctor hesitated, looking conflicted, then glanced at the file Barend held out – a detailed record of Katelyn's tests and diagnoses. His expression softened slightly as he skimmed through the documents.

"Children with acute kidney failure need immediate and ongoing treatment. Finding the right match for a transplant can be challenging," the doctor explained, his voice calm yet grave. "However, we will monitor your daughter closely."

"But doctor, I am her father. I could be a match, couldn't I?" Barend interjected, his voice cracking with emotion. "Please, you can't let her suffer like this when there's a chance to help."

The doctor exchanged a few discreet words with the nurse, who nodded in understanding. She approached Barend cautiously.

"Sir, do you have medical aid?" she inquired gently.

Barend shook his head, his heart sinking. "No, I have none."

"I'm sorry, sir. Without medical aid or cash upfront, we can't proceed here," the nurse informed him softly.

Barend's mind raced. He hurried out of the hospital to his car, returning moments later with a large bag of money. He placed it on the table with a determined thud, eager to gain the nurse's attention before she could walk away.

"Here we are! This will cover all of our bills and more," Barend declared, his voice tight with resolve. "It was my investment money."

The nurse opened the bag, her eyes widening at the sight of the cash within. She nodded curtly.

"Very well then," she said in a corporate tone. Another nurse appeared through the doors and she quickly pulled her aside, instructing her on what to do next. To Barend's relief, the assistant nurse then escorted Katelyn through the doors to begin treatment.

Alone in the waiting area, Barend pulled out his phone with trembling hands. He dialed a number, his thoughts scattered and frantic.

"I had only one person left to turn to...," Barend murmured to himself as the call connected.

"Barend here," he said when Marelize answered. "Listen...I realized one cannot dwell on the past. What's done is done, and the future is uncertain. All I can see is her pain-filled eyes, and nothing else matters now."

As their heartfelt conversation continued, Marelize began to feel uneasy. She could not explain it, but her gut was telling her that things would soon take a turn for the worst... and she was right. That night when they hung up the phone, she could not get herself to sleep peacefully.

It was only 7 hours later that Barend felt himself slip further away from reality while driving during the early morning hours. He had left Katelyn in hospital, entrusting her to the nurses and Marelize's care.

As his hands rested on the steering wheel, he glided on the highway as if he didn't care what happened to him next. His heart felt torn, but he knew he had to race back to find Vuyo. Lttle did he know it was too late and he would soon have to face the inevitable...

Barend lay there on the ground beside the overturned car, dazed and disoriented, blood trickling down his face from a wound on his forehead. The chaos around him seemed distant, muffled by the ringing in his ears and the haze of pain. Through the swirling dust, he glimpsed the police officers cautiously approaching, their faces etched with determination and caution.

In the back of the wrecked vehicle lay the beloved treasure they had sought... the bags of gleaming gold, diamonds winking in the sunlight, and stacks of cash bundled tightly. Barend's chest heaved with exertion as he struggled to sit up, his dusty hands bound tightly behind his back.

"Here, take it all," he managed to rasp out, his voice strained and raw. "Go on ... Arrest me!"

The officers exchanged uneasy glances, their hands twitching near their holsters. Barend's surrender was unexpected, even unsettling. Yet before they could react at all, a sudden shot rang out, echoing sharply in the tense air. One of the officers dropped to the ground, clutching his chest, a look of disbelief frozen on his face.

"Man down! Man down!" another officer shouted, his voice cracking with frantic urgency. Greef, his eyes narrowed in ruthless determination, swiftly turned his gun, firing at his own subordinate without hesitation. The betrayal unfolded in stark clarity, the air thick with the acrid smell of gunpowder and fear.

Barend, still on the ground, watched in stunned silence as Greef's men fell, victims of their leader's merciless resolve. The chaos around him escalated, the shouts and commands blending into a cacophony of violence and desperation. Blood mingled with the dust, staining the gravel beneath Barend's trembling hands.

Greef strode forward, his expression grim and unyielding, his gaze fixed on Barend with a stark, chilling intensity. "We got him, sir. We got Barend Visagie," one of the officers reported, his voice tinged with both triumph and uncertainty.

Greef nodded slowly as he came closer, his eyes never leaving Barend's. "You got him good, all right," he replied evenly, his voice carrying a cold finality. "Cuff him."

The remaining officer moved to secure Barend, his hands trembling as he reached for the handcuffs. Before he could complete the task, another shot echoed through the air. The officer crumpled to the ground, a growing pool of blood spreading beneath him.

Greef's eyes narrowed into slits as he scanned the chaotic scene, his mind racing with calculated fury. Without any hesitation, he aimed his gun once more, eliminating another of his own men who had faltered in the face of this unexpected turn.

Barend, bloodied and battered, lay helpless on the ground, the weight of his actions and the consequences pressing down heavily upon him. The world spun around him, a whirlwind of violence and betrayal, leaving him stranded in the center of a storm he could no longer control.

As Greef came ever closer, his footsteps heavy with purpose, Barend's gaze met his with a mixture of defiance and resignation. The sun beat down mercilessly, casting stark shadows across the desolate landscape. In that fleeting moment, amidst the chaos and carnage, Barend found himself forced to confront the harsh reality of his choices and their irrevocable consequences.

"I kept my promise," Barend whispered hoarsely, his voice barely audible above the turmoil.

(Back to the present reality - at the cell)

Barend sat alone in his cell, surrounded by the cold concrete walls that had become his new reality. The prison was a labyrinth of cold, lifeless echoes, each sound magnified by the heavy silence that hung in the air. Memories swirled in his mind like a tempest, fragments of a life shattered by one fateful decision.

"What I remembered from there was all just a blur," Barend muttered to himself gravely, his voice barely audible in the stillness. His gaze fell on the crumpled newspaper in his hands, the inked words blurring before his eyes. "Lots of reporters, questioning... I kept Katelyn out of all of it, to give her a chance, to ensure she will be safe from him."

He remembered the trial vividly, the harsh glare of the courtroom, the weight of judgment hanging heavy in the air. "I pleaded guilty to the robbery but not guilty on account of murder," Barend recounted bitterly as he clenched his jaw. "The Bear came out a hero, while I was convicted for life... or rather, death."

He glanced up at Samantha, the only connection to the outside world that he dared trust. Her eyes met his, filled with curiosity and a trace of gentle sympathy. "And the money..." Barend hesitated, his voice trailing off along with his glance, as he momentarily looked away at the wall beside him to avoid Samantha's piercing eyes. She leaned forward with her chin resting on fist, her expression expectant.

"If you want to follow the diamonds, you need to find the Bear," Barend said quietly, inscribing the name "Greef" on the table with deliberate care, ensuring the guards remained oblivious to their conversation.

Samantha nodded knowingly, pulled out a newspaper from her tote bag, unrolled it and placed it on the table in front of him. "You might like this," she said, turning away just as a man approached the prison guard nearby. Barend tensed, a flicker of concern crossing his face.

"Watch your back," Barend warned Samantha quietly. "I think we might have woken the bear from hibernation…"

The prison guard interrupted their exchange, his presence a stark reminder of the walls closing in around them. "Sorry to interrupt, but you have been called," he informed Samantha, his tone clipped and professional.

As Samantha left under escort, Barend retreated to the solitude of his cell, the newspaper clutched tightly in his hands. He unfolded it carefully, scanning the pages until he came upon an article that caught his eye. It was a story about a girl named Katherine who ran a sanctuary for animals, both abused and hunted. It was a place of refuge, a haven of peace amidst the chaos of the world.

His heart skipped a beat as he read on, realizing the significance of the farm and its caretaker. Medical notes indicated that this girl, Katherine, was in fact Katelyn, her name changed by Barend's old girlfriend to protect her identity.

Barend tucked the newspaper into his shirt as he heard footsteps approaching his cell. "Your lunch is here," the guard announced, his voice indifferent to the tumultuous thoughts racing through Barend's mind.

Silently, Barend returned the guard's nod and sat down on his cot, his mind racing with newfound hope and determination. The threads of fate had woven a fragile path, leading him back to Katelyn, to a chance at redemption amidst the darkness that surrounded him.

Barend's senses quickly sharpened as he sensed the new guard's watchful eyes through the small window of his cell. The faint clatter of keys and the subtle shift in shadows hinted at the guard's approach. Years behind bars had taught Barend one crucial lesson: trust was a luxury he couldn't afford.

With a practiced glance over his shoulder, Barend confirmed it was indeed a new face on duty. His mind raced through scenarios, assessing risks and opportunities like pieces on a chessboard. He knew he had to act, and act fast.

In the dim light of his cold cell, Barend's gaze softened momentarily as he suddenly noticed a tiny grey field mouse scurrying along the edge of the wall. It was a welcome sight, a reminder of the small joys and unlikely allies in the harsh confines of prison life. He had befriended the creatures over time, testing food for poison with their instinctual caution.

This particular evening Barend's routine took on an urgency. He discreetly slid a portion of his meal under the table, eyes fixed on the mouse's movements. Minutes passed in tense silence until the mouse emerged cautiously, sniffing at the offering. When it refused to touch the food, Barend's heart sank, as this served as a silent warning that danger lurked.

The scrape of metal on metal echoed through the cell as Barend swiftly withdrew a piece of cutlery, his senses on high alert. The guard entered, his demeanor relaxed, a smirk playing on his lips at the scattered plate on the floor. It was a trap, and Barend was the unsuspecting prey.

Before the guard could react, Barend lunged forward with lightning speed, arms wrapping around the man's neck in a vice-like grip. Surprise flickered across the guard's face before consciousness slipped away, replaced by the stillness of unconsciousness.

With practiced efficiency, Barend swiftly relieved the guard of his cellphone and uniform, exchanging it for his own prison garb in a frantic bid for freedom. In a flurry he discarded his old frumpled clothes in the most hidden corner of the cell. Every second counted now, the risk of discovery a constant shadow over his escape.

As he moved through the labyrinthine corridors of the prison, Barend kept his head low, hat shielding his eyes from the scrutiny of surveillance cameras. His heart pounded in his chest, adrenaline fueling his determination to reach the exit as fast as possible without being detected.

Steady rhythmic footsteps echoed in the distance, each sound magnified in Barend's ears as he navigated the maze of concrete and steel. The weight of uncertainty hung heavy in the air, a reminder of the precariousness of his escape. But Barend Visagie was a man driven by desperation and determination, his resolve unyielding in the face of overwhelming odds.

With each step closer to freedom, Barend left behind the confines of his cell and the ghosts of his past. The world outside awaited him, fraught with danger and opportunity, a landscape where survival meant staying one step ahead of those who sought to drag him back into darkness.

In the depths of his heart, Barend knew this was just the beginning. The journey ahead was uncertain, a testament to his resilience and the unwavering hope of redemption that burned within him.

Barend's heart pounded like a racehorse as he signed out using the name on the access card, aware that every single second counted now. He glanced up and saw Samantha briskly approaching the car where the Indian man's driver stood, talking on his phone. The tension in the air was palpable, heightened by the sense that danger lurked just beneath the surface.

Samantha moved with purpose, checking that her handbag with all of its content was in tact before attempting to enter the vehicle, unaware of the imminent threat. Barend, sensing trouble, surged forward at a rapid pace, closing the distance between them within seconds. Just as Samantha was about to reach for the car door with her dainty hand, Barend's hand gripped her arm with force, yanking her back with great urgency.

Then, in a deafening explosion, the car erupted into a cloud of furious flames. Shards of metal and glass flew in all directions, the force of the blast throwing Barend and Samantha meters away on the tar. Scorching heat washed over them as they shielded themselves against the burning wreckage.

Amid the chaos, the Indian driver appeared with his usual strange sense of dialogue and humor. He rushed towards them, his demeanor oddly calm given the circumstances. "Well, well, well, look like someone did order the special barbecue tonight," he quipped, his thick accent adding an unexpected levity to the grim situation.

Barend, still reeling from the explosion, managed a nod of gratitude as the driver motioned urgently for them to follow. "Quickly now, before they send the fire brigade. We don't want any more drama," he said with a wry grin, his eyes darting around for any signs of pursuit.

Samantha, shaken but grateful for their unexpected savior, scrambled to her feet and followed Barend and the driver into the cover of nearby bushes. They moved swiftly, staying low and out of sight, until they were safely away from the blazing car and the chaos it had caused.

As they regrouped in the shadows, the driver's usual nonchalance returned. "Well, that was quite the fireworks display, don't you think so?" he remarked casually, though his eyes betrayed a hint of concern. "You two seem to attract trouble like bees to honeycomb. Maybe next time we try a quieter exit, eh?"

Barend managed a faint smile while panting heavily, appreciating the driver's unique blend of humor and practicality in the face of danger. "Thanks for the save," he said earnestly, his voice still tinged with adrenaline. "We owe you one."

The driver waved off Barend's gratitude with a dismissive gesture. "Think nothing of it. Consider it a service charge for all the trouble you've brought to my doorstep," he replied with a wink, before turning serious. "Now, let's get moving, what do you say?".

Together, they slipped into the night, leaving behind the burning wreckage and multiple questions hanging in the air. For Barend and Samantha, the danger was far from over, but with their unexpected ally at their side, they faced the uncertain road ahead with newfound determination.

Their Indian friend soon brought Barend and Samantha to a village nearby where they could find temporal safety. Here they had found an unexpected refuge within the close-knit Indian community on the outskirts of the bustling city. As they drove into the streets, they felt both excited and relieved as the busy atmosphere brought a complete change of scenery than what they had experienced before. The community bustled with life, a vibrant tapestry of colors, sounds, and smells that spoke of tradition and unity. Children were playing hopscotch on the sidewalk, their lively shrieks audible from meters away. Narrow streets lined with shops selling spices, colorful textiles, and fragrant foods wove through the tightly packed homes, each adorned with intricate patterns and vibrant hues.

Barend stood at the threshold of a modest yet welcoming home, his eyes scanning the bustling street where the children were playing and women in bright sarees were conversing animatedly. The Indian man, whom Barend had come to rely on as a protector and guide, stood beside him, a reassuring presence amidst the swirl of activity.

"Listen … they're like family here," the Indian man assured Barend in a hushed tone, sensing the tension that radiated from him. "No one will betray you."

Barend nodded, though his unease lingered beneath the surface. The news of his daring escape and the subsequent manhunt had spread like wildfire, painting him as a criminal mastermind in the eyes of the media and law enforcement alike. His face now adorned wanted posters plastered on every street corner, a stark reminder of the perilous position they now found themselves in.

Inside the bustling home, Samantha sat on a threadbare sofa with her cup of ceylon tea, her gaze fixed on a television screen that blared breaking news updates. The headline flashed in bold letters, "Manhunt for Escaped Criminal Barend Visagie Intensifies!" Images of the charred remains of the car engulfed in flames filled the screen, followed by speculations about Barend's whereabouts and the urgency of his capture.

"They're calling you a menace," Samantha murmured, her voice tinged with worry as she turned to Barend. "Every police officer in the country is looking for you, Barend"

Barend looked at her with a stern expression and exhaled slowly, the weight of their predicament pressing down upon him. "I never wanted any of this," he admitted quietly, his eyes flickering with regret and resolve. "Just wanted to keep her safe...more than anything else"

The Indian man nodded understandingly, his eyes reflecting empathy and determination. "Don't worry, we'll protect you," he said firmly, gesturing to the bustling community outside. "Here, you are family. No one will betray us."

As the day wore on, tension hung heavy in the air, mingling with the aromas of various types of curry and the sounds of laughter and conversation that drifted through the open windows. Barend paced up and down restlessly, his mind racing with thoughts of the uncertain future that lay ahead. Voices echoed in the narrow streets outside, a mixture of curiosity and concern that followed in the wake of their arrival.

"We can't stay hidden forever," Samantha said softly, breaking the uneasy silence that enveloped them. "Sooner or later, they'll find us."

Barend glanced out the window, his gaze lingering on the bustling street below where life carried on, seemingly unaffected by their presence. "We need a plan," he murmured, more to himself than to Samantha. "To clear my name."

After stirring his tea in the kitchen, the Indian man approached them, his expression grave yet determined. "We've been discussing our options," he said quietly, his voice barely above a whisper. "For now, you're safe here. But we need to be cautious."

Barend nodded, gratitude and apprehension warring within him. "Thank you," he said sincerely and sat on the couch next to Samantha, his voice tinged with relief and uncertainty. "No really... for everything."

As dusk descended and the bustling community began to settle into a tranquil rhythm, Barend and Samantha knew that their respite was temporary. The shadows of uncertainty loomed large, casting doubt on their future and the dangers that awaited them beyond the safety of their newfound comfortable haven. With each passing moment, they braced themselves for the inevitable clash with fate, their path uncertain yet intertwined with the bonds of trust and solidarity forged amidst the Indian community's unwavering embrace.

Within this bustling neighborhood on the outskirts of the city, Samantha huddled with Barend and the Indian family, their hideout providing a fragile sense of safety amidst the turmoil. The apartment hummed with activity, the smell of aromatic spices lingering in the air from morning until sunset as the housewives prepared lunch and supper for their families. Their children played nearby, unaware of the danger lurking just beyond their doorstep.

Samantha's fingers trembled as she typed furiously on her laptop, finalizing the explosive exposé that could bring down Greef and his criminal empire. With each keystroke, she poured her fear, determination, and hope into the document, detailing every illicit deal, every corrupt alliance, and every nefarious scheme orchestrated by the elusive figure known as "The Bear."

Beside her, Barend watched with a mixture of concern and admiration, his own battle-hardened instincts telling him they were still far from safe. The Indian man, Mr. Patel, stood nearby running his fingers over his beard, his weathered face a mask of stoicism as Samantha finished her work.

"It's done," Samantha murmured, her voice barely above a whisper. She attached the document to an email addressed to her publisher, along with detailed instructions for its release and a plea for her husband's involvement. Tears welled in her eyes as she stared out the window, trying to find the words to write on a separate note to her husband, urging him to ensure the article's publication if anything happened to her.

"Mr. Patel," Samantha said, turning to the Indian man with urgency. "Please, this needs to get out without anyone noticing. It's crucial."

Mr. Patel nodded solemnly, his eyes reflecting a deep understanding of the gravity of their situation. "You can count on me," he replied quietly, taking the laptop from Samantha's trembling hands.

As Mr. Patel made arrangements to discreetly send the email and a hardcopy to Samantha's husband, Greef was alive and well, and far from idle. In a darkened room across town, he huddled with a handful of corrupt cops, their faces obscured by shadows as they plotted their next move.

"We need to find them," Greef hissed, his voice laced with venomous determination. "No more mistakes. I want them brought straight to me."

The corrupt cops nodded obediently, their loyalty bought with promises of wealth and power. They knew the stakes were high – failure was not an option when dealing with Greef. With the resources at their disposal, they set out to track down Barend and Samantha, their methods ruthless and their pursuit relentless.

Greef, a man of formidable wealth and influence, had built an empire on the bones of the desperate and the corrupt. His opulence was hidden beneath layers of deceit, a fortress of ill-gotten gains. From the outside, his headquarters appeared as an unassuming office building, but beneath its mundane exterior lay a network of underground chambers, filled with stolen treasures and secrets.

The basement, lit by the cold glow of fluorescent lights, housed a vault that could rival any bank. Gold bars stacked neatly, rare jewels glittering in the dim light, and wads of cash filling every available space. His digital real estate consisted of stolen assets, preying on the gullible, innocent and foolish members of society. All of this was also securely hidden within multiple files on a secret computer stationed inside the vault, containing a private network. Greef's fortune was a testament to his ruthless ambition and selfishness, each item a piece of his dark legacy.

As Greef surveyed his wealth, a predatory smile played on his lips. He thrived in the shadows, manipulating the strings of power with a deft hand. His network of influence extended to the highest echelons of society – politicians, reputable businessmen, individuals in the medical & pharmaceutical field with access to schedule seven medications and other illegal subtances. Even those in security and law enforcement fell under his sway.

In the dimly lit room, the corrupt cops awaited his instructions, their eyes betraying a mixture of fear and greed. They had seen what happened to those who failed Greef. His punishments were as legendary as his rewards.

"I don't care what it takes," Greef continued, his voice a low growl. "Use every resource, every contact, everything... I want Barend and Samantha brought to me. Alive."

One of the cops, a burly man with a scar running down his right cheek, stepped forward boldly. "We have eyes on the airport and the docks. If they try to leave the country, we'll know for certain."

Greef nodded, grimly yet satisfied. "Good. And the safe houses?"

"We've got men watching all known locations. They won't get far."

Greef's gaze hardened. "Well, you better make sure that they don't. I want them here, in this room, by the end of the week."

As the meeting broke up, the shady cops dispersed into the night, their mission clear. Greef's influence was vast, but it was built on a foundation of fear and coercion. He knew that maintaining control meant crushing any threats swiftly and decisively.

Across town, Samantha and Barend moved with extreme caution, aware that every step they took was being watched. The weight of Greef's empire bore down on them, an invisible force that dictated their every move. They had allies, but even those connections were fraught with danger.

Back at the apartment, tension hung thick in the air as Samantha, Barend, and the Indian family sat there waiting anxiously for news. Mr Patel's sister would check in every few hours with refreshments as an attempt to try and calm the nerves. However, even her famous homemade ceylon tea was no consolation for the trouble they were facing. Every passing moment felt like an eternity, the threat of discovery looming over them like a thick, dark cloud.

But amidst the uncertainty and fear, Samantha held onto a silver lining of hope - that her message would reach the world, exposing Greef's crimes and ensuring that justice prevailed, no matter what the cost.

The Next Morning

The sun rose over Maputo, casting a warm glow on the city that contrasted sharply with the cold, ruthless plans being enacted within its streets. The morning newspapers hit the stands, the headlines screaming the latest developments in Jennifer O'Nelly's murder. Samantha's latest article detailed the mysterious diamond found on Jennifer and hinted at the possibility of a connection to the infamous Barend Visagie.

The article didn't name Greef directly, but the implications were clear to those who knew the underworld. Greef's phone buzzed incessantly as calls came in from various corrupt officials and business associates. His empire, so meticulously hidden, was being exposed bit by bit.

Greef picked up his phone, his expression darkening as he recognized the caller. It was a high-ranking official in the Mozambican government, someone who had benefited greatly from Greef's financial contributions.

"You need to handle this, Greef," the official said, his voice tense. "The press is poking around too much. If they connect the diamonds to you, we're all screwed."

"I'm already handling it," Greef snapped. "Barend and that journalist will be dealt with soon. They won't have time to spill any more secrets."

"You'd better be right, darn it! Our arrangement depends on discretion. If this blows up, you're on your own."

Greef hung up with a frustrated motion, seething. He turned to his second-in-command, a lean man with calculating eyes. "We need to move faster. Double the efforts to find Barend and Samantha. And find out if they've shared anything else with the press."

As Greef's men scoured the city, he reviewed the latest newspaper article again, anger boiling beneath his calm exterior. Then a name caught his eye, buried within the article's speculations: Katelyn, Jennifer's daughter. The article suggested she might know more about her mother's connections and hinted at a potential link to the missing diamonds.

Greef's mind raced with anxious thoughts. He had believed he'd eliminated all witnesses when he orchestrated the heist that brought him his fortune. But Katelyn was an unknown variable, a potential threat that needed to be neutralized.

"Find this girl," Greef ordered, shoving the folded newspaper at his second-in-command. "She could be the key to tying up loose ends. I want her brought to me, alive."

In Greef's Headquarters

reef paced up and down in his opulent office, walking to and fro over the luxurious rugs and kicking the frayed edges of it every now and then with sheer anger and frustration. His empire, built on fear and corruption, was now under threat from a journalist and a fugitive. He couldn't allow his carefully constructed world to crumble in such a manner.

His phone buzzed again, this time with a message from his second-in-command. "We've located the girl." Greeff smiled.

Greef ended the call and stared out of his office window. The city spread out before him, unaware of the machinations that controlled it. He had built his empire on the bones of the desperate and the corrupt, and he wouldn't let it be torn down by a few loose ends. Just as he was about to turn away, his phone buzzed again. This time, the name on the screen made him pause for a few seconds. It was the Minister of Security, a man whose silence had been bought at a high price.

"Greef," the Minister's voice was strained. "The situation is getting out of hand. The press is digging too deep. I can only keep the cover and turn a blind eye for so long."

Greef clenched his jaw. "I understand. I'm dealing with it. You'll get your usual payment, plus a bonus for the inconvenience.

There was a pause on the other end. "It better be worth it, Greef. If this explodes, I won't go down with you. I can promise you that".

Greef forced a menacing smile into his voice. "Trust me, Minister. It will be worth your efforts."

The Man in the Shadows

In a dark, secluded room on the outskirts of the city, a figure sat hunched over a small wooden table. He is flicking a knife in his hand looking heavily disturbed as he turns over the newspaper The room was dimly lit by a single lamp, casting shadows that obscured the man's face. Newspapers were spread out before him covering the entire surface of the table, their headlines reflecting the latest developments in Jennifer O'Nelly's murder and the mysterious diamond found on her body.

He had been working on this case for a very long time, gathering information, piecing together the puzzle that connected a shadowy figure known only as "the Bear" to a web of corruption and crime. The article by Samantha Grey had accelerated his plans, cutting their time short. He knew for a fact that Barend Visagie, his key witness and ally, would be in immediate danger.

The man took a deep breath, put down his coffee cup and picked up his phone, dialing a number he had memorized long ago. It rang twice before a gruff voice answered.

"Inspector..."

"It's me," the man said, his voice low and steady. "We don't have much time."

But are you sure we need to move now?" the inspector asks.

"We don't have a choice," the man insisted. "If we wait any longer, the Bear will close off every avenue. Barend needs to be protected, and we need to take action against the Bear before he can cover his tracks."

We'll need all the evidence you've gathered."

"You'll have it," the man said, glancing at the files and documents stacked neatly on the table. "I'll come out of hiding and deliver it myself."

"Be careful. The Bear has eyes everywhere."

The man ended the call in a solemn, abrupt manner and stood up, gathering the papers and placing them in a secure briefcase. He had been in hiding, biding his time, but now the moment had come to take decisive action

The Meeting

W alking through the sprawling animal care center, Barend's mind raced with urgency. He observed the various primates and exotic animals in large enclosures, but his focus was on finding Katelyn. Approaching a worker, he asked with urgency, "I'm looking for Miss Katelyn."

"She's on lunch break, at the house," the worker replied, pointing towards a modest home nestled amidst the sanctuary.

"Thank you, ma'am" Barend nodded, his heart pounding as he made his way towards the house. He knocked softly, but receiving no answer, he heard the muffled sounds of a television inside. With a sense of urgency, Barend pushed open the door, entering cautiously. Children's toys scattered across the floor and photos of Katelyn's life adorned the walls, from her romantic wedding to the sweet portrait images of her child.

"Katelyn..." Barend called out softly, turning to find her seated at the kitchen table, engrossed in a newspaper.

Katelyn's eyes widened in a mix of shock, relief, and anger. "What? How did you..."

"Look ... We don't have much time," Barend interrupted urgently.

"Time for what? Are you here to take me on another one of your special missions?" With her arms folded she stared at him with disdain. Barend noticed how her voice was laced with bitterness. "Or perhaps you finally decided to tell me the truth? Is that it, eh?" She held up the newspaper, her voice trembling. "You want a happy ending for your story now?"

Her hand moved to the telephone, but Barend acted swiftly, pulling the cord from the wall. "You have no idea who you're dealing with. I came here to help."

A tear rolled down Katelyn's cheek, her emotions raw. "Yes, you're right. I have no idea..." Her voice faltered. "You need to get out of here. Save yourself..." she warned him sternly.

"You were my hero once, Dad," Katelyn continued, her voice cracking. "I believed in you. But there's no way I can go through this kind of ordeal again. I have my own family now!"

Barend glanced at the family photos, regret etched in his weary face. "All I cared about was myself and the gold..."

"That's not true," Katelyn interjected, her tone softer now, filled with pain and memories. "If you had time, you would've explained..."

Their fragile reunion was abruptly shattered by a chilling voice from the doorway. "So, we've come full circle, it seems," Greef's voice rang out, freezing both Barend and Katelyn in place.

Barend slowly turned to find Greef standing in the doorway, a gun pointed menacingly at them. "Thanks to your reporter friend, I've gathered all the evidence in one place."

"I have to thank you for that, Barend," Greef sneered. "You made it so easy for me. I'll have the last laugh after all."

Barend clenched his jaw, his mind racing with mixed thoughts of fear and rage as he calculated their options. "We're not going down without a fight, Greef."

Greef's smirk widened. "Oh, I don't doubt that. But who will they believe, Barend? An escaped convict, a murderer?"

As Greef's attention shifted between Barend and Katelyn, Barend seized a moment of distraction, lunging towards Greef with all his might. A shot rang out, echoing through the house, and Barend staggered back, wounded. Greef fell to the ground, scrambling for his gun.

Barend gritted his teeth through the pain, stepping on Greef's hand to prevent him from reaching the weapon. "It ends here, Greef. For once and for all."

Greef laughed in a delusional manner, breathing heavily through bloodied lips. "You never stood a chance against me, Barend."

Their struggle intensified, fists flying and bodies grappling in a fight fueled by years of animosity and betrayal. Greef managed to overpower Barend briefly, landing a vicious blow that sent him reeling across the floor. With a cruel grin, Greef turned towards Katelyn, his evil intention as clear as daylight.

Sensing the tension in the atmosphere, the animals start making loud noises, filling the space with their chants.

"You killed her, just like you killed the cops?" Greef taunted as he stroked the gun in his hand maliciously, advancing towards Katelyn with calculated steps.

"No!" Barend roared, summoning every ounce of strength left in him. Despite his painful injuries, he lunged at Greef once more, managing to tackle him to the ground.

But as Greef raised the gun towards Katelyn, a sudden commotion erupted around them. Rescue animals had made their way to the traumatic scene. There were monkeys, a stray dog Katelyn had nursed back to health, and even three African grey parrots. These all descended upon Greef, teeth bared and claws slashing. The chaos unfolded in a frenzy of fur and fury as the animals fiercely defended their caretaker.

Katelyn's heart raced as she watched in disbelief, tears streaming down her face. The animals' unexpected intervention gave her a moment of reprieve. With a surge of courage, she grabbed a heavy object nearby, striking Greef with all her might.

Greef stumbled back, dazed and bleeding from multiple wounds inflicted by the animals. Disoriented and outnumbered, he struggled to regain control. He managed to shoot off a shot with his gun, with his arm on the floor and the animals ran for hiding.

Barend managed to crawl towards Katelyn, reaching out to her desperately. "We have to go, Katelyn. Now!!"

As Greef lay on the ground, writhing in pain like a snake and clutching his wounded side, the wail of sirens grew louder, signaling the imminent arrival of law enforcement. Samantha emerged from one of the vehicles, her expression a mix of relief and determination as she hurried towards the scene, nearly jogging in her leather boots. The police, alerted by Samantha, converged swiftly, their movements precise and methodical.

Greef, initially disoriented by pain and disbelief, squinted through the flashing lights and the approaching figures. His heart sank as he recognized one of them emerging from the police lineup - a figure he thought he had killed and disposed of years ago.

"Lloyd," Greef gasped, his voice hoarse with shock and realization. "No... It can't be."

But there stood Lloyd, alive and resolute, his gaze cold and unyielding as he folded his arms and locked eyes with Greef. It was clear Lloyd had burnscars. Some were even covering his face. For years, Greef had believed that all traces to the past was cleared, buried beneath layers of lies and deceit. Now, in an ironic twist of fate, one of the very men whom he had underestimated and thought he had wiped out, had emerged from hiding, working alongside law enforcement to bring Greef to justice.

The lead detective, a seasoned woman with kempt hair and a steely resolve, approached Greef with a measured look of contempt. "You're under arrest," she declared, her voice cutting through the tense silence.

As Greef scrambled to escape, his mind a whirlwind of panic and desperation, he barely registered the swift movement of Lloyd's arm. In a split second, a knife flashed through the air like an arrow with deadly accuracy, embedding itself deep into Greef's fatigued calf muscle. A cry of pain and surprise tore from Greef's throat as he stumbled and fell, his escape thwarted by the precise strike.

Lloyd approached calmly, his expression unreadable yet tinged with a hint of grim satisfaction. He stood there towering over Greef, who writhed in agony, his hands clawing at the grass as if to escape the pain coursing through his leg.

"Still got it, what you think?" Lloyd remarked with a wry smile, his voice carrying a mix of irony and assurance.

Greef gritted his teeth, his face contorted with pain and fury. He glared up at Lloyd with venomous eyes, realizing with bitter resignation that his attempts to flee had been decisively halted.

After watching the scene for a few seconds and nodding at each in agreement, the police didn't waste any time. They closed in swiftly, their movements fast and efficient as they secured Greef, now subdued and defeated. Barend stood there out of breath with sweat droplets running down his face and neck. Exhausted from the aftermath of adrenaline, he watched the whole event from a distance, a mix of relief and disbelief washing over him at the turn of events. Beside him, Katelyn stood with a tissue in one hand, wiping the tears from her eyes, her other hand tightly gripping his, revealing the emotions roiling within her. After everything, she knew deep inside her heart that her father was a man of integrity, a man who would do anything to protect his daughter, no matter what the cost. This realization along with the abrupt turn of events made her heart break in a million pieces. Barend, noticing the flood of tears, pulled her closer and embraced her with the intense kind of love that only a relieved father could feel towards his daughter.

Samantha, clutching her emotions tightly, stepped closer to Barend, who was pale and weakened by his injuries. She spared a brief, proud glance towards Lloyd, silently acknowledging his role in bringing Greef to justice.

As Greef was handcuffed and read his rights, Samantha looked at Barend, who was clutching his side, blood staining his clothes. She rested her hand on his shoulder, gently offering her continued support and consolation without speaking a word.

The police, thorough in their procedure, cuffed Barend as well, despite his injuries. Katelyn, unable to hold back her emotions any longer, rushed forward. Tears streamed down her face as she kissed her father on the forehead, her love and gratitude pouring out in that simple gesture.

"I remember…" Katelyn whispered, her voice thick with emotion. "…when I went for the transplant, I thought it was a just a dream. Then I dimly saw you on a bed next to me. You brought me my pony toy and you …." she struggled to utter the words.

"You were the donor, weren't you?" she asked, looking at him with eyes laden with tears. Barend nodded tenderly. The large cut that scarred Barend from the rushed procedure marking his body, was a reminder for life. It was not a dream then, after all, she realised.

Barend smiled weakly, his heart swelling with pride and love for his daughter. "I would do it all over again," he murmured, his voice barely above a whisper. "For you."

The officers gently guided Barend towards the waiting police car, mindful of his injuries. Katelyn watched with a mixture of pride and concern, her hands pressed against her mouth to stifle a sob.

As Barend was loaded into the car, he turned to Samantha one last time. "I never thought you really would get to the ending of the story" he said, his voice filled with a strange awe.

Samantha nodded solemnly, managing a slightly suppressed smile. "Well, you must be one heck of a storyteller if you made me part of yours…" she responded, leaving Barend with no response except a fond expression.

With a final yearning glance back at Katelyn, who stood strong despite her tears, Barend was driven away, leaving behind a trail of uncertainty and hope. For him, the journey was far from over, but in that moment, as the police car disappeared into the distance, he knew that justice, though elusive and hard-won, was finally within reach.

Aftermath

A s the sun dipped low over the Mozambican coast, painting the sky with vibrant hues of amber and rose, Barend found himself sitting on the porch of a small white-washed wooden beachside cottage. Katelyn, now a mature woman with a child of her own, sat beside him on a rocking chair, gently petting the little dachshund that had become their new loyal companion. Barend sipped his Early Grey tea and smiled gently at her affection towards the puppy. It was a scene of serenity and contentment, a stark contrast to the tumultuous events that had recently shaped their lives.

The newspaper company's check, received for Barend's gripping life story, lay on the coffee table inside. It wasn't just a financial reward; it symbolized closure and recognition for the trials he had endured. Yet, amidst the peaceful outcome, thoughts and memories of the past still lingered, haunting him from time to time

After staring into the glorious sunset for a while, he takes a last swig of his favourite tea and picks up the newspaper on the little coffee table in front of him. "Have you ever chased after a rainbow?" Barend mused aloud, breaking the calm evening air as he reads from the newspaper story. His words carried the weight of experience and reflection. "Probably not, I presume. One must clearly be a fool to believe in such things..."

Katelyn looked at him with tenderness, her eyes reflecting both curiosity and understanding. "But what if the rainbow isn't really about the pot of gold at the end?" she ventured softly. Barend knew her very well as a creative and critical thinker, always challenging the norm. She must have received that trait from him, he thought to himself as he paused to consider his response.

Barend nodded slowly, exposing a slight smile, his gaze turning towards the horizon where the last remnants of daylight mingled with the ocean. "Riches have a way of blinding a person's sight, Katelyn" he admitted, thinking back to the allure of wealth that had once consumed him. "But what would you do if you could have more riches than you could ever imagine... would you take it?"

"Mmm, well...those people who are too scared to try..." Katelyn continued, her voice tinged with conviction, "They always mutter to themselves that those who pursue might never return, that it is all in vain... even worse, that it is only a myth."

Barend smiled gently and put down his cup on the table, proud of the wisdom his daughter had gained through her own journey. "But I have stood at the rainbow's end," he said with quiet certainty, "...and I will tell you without a shadow of a doubt that it surely is no myth."

"However," Barend added thoughtfully as he twiddled the newspaper's edges between his fingers before folding it, his tone turning more introspective, "May this be a brief warning to you, that you, like everyone else will have to face the question and therefore the consequences too, at some point or another."

Katelyn looked at him, her expression softening with empathy as her blue eyes pierced through him. "Some might say that subsequent events were foreshadowed," she murmured, "...that what is real treasure in life..."

Before she could finish her thought, the distant sound of ocean waves crashing against the shore filled the silence between them, a reminder of the timeless rhythm of life and the enduring bond they shared.

"And what is the real treasure in life?" Barend asked, glancing briefly at his granddaughter who ran playfully past them with a twinkle in his eye. Barend places the folded newspaper on the table in front of him and turns toward Katelyn, giving her his full attention.

Katelyn smiled warmly, almost blushing... her gaze flickering between the sunset and her daughter playing in the sand. "Love... grace... and forgiveness" she replied softly, "And the moments we get to share with those who matter the most in our lives."

Barend nodded in agreement and smiled warmly at her, this time failing to hide his beaming emotion, as was his habit of doing. At this very moment he felt a profound sense of gratitude for this second chance at life God had granted him. As the evening deepened into a peaceful autumn night stirring rustling leaves in the bushes nearby, he fell quiet as he made a silent promise to cherish each moment. He was determined to continue making up for lost time in the embrace of his family and to be content with the simple joys of everyday life.